Summary of Contents

D1216491

The CSS Anthology
101 Essential Tips, Tricks & Hacks

by Rachel Andrew

The CSS Anthology: 101 Essential Tips, Tricks & Hacks

by Rachel Andrew

Copyright © 2004 SitePoint Pty. Ltd.

Editor: Georgina Laidlaw   **Index Editor**: Bill Johncocks
Managing Editor: Simon Mackie   **Cover Designer**: Julian Carroll
Expert Reviewer: Simon Willison   **Cover Illustrator**: Lucas Licata
Technical Director: Kevin Yank
Printing History:
   First Edition: November 2004
Latest Update: May 2005

Notice of Rights

Notice of Liability

Trademark Notice

Published by SitePoint Pty. Ltd.

424 Smith Street Collingwood
VIC Australia 3066.
Web: www.sitepoint.com
Email: business@sitepoint.com

ISBN 0–9579218–8–8
Printed and bound in the United States of America

About The Author

Rachel Andrew is Web developer and director of Web solutions provider edgeofmyseat.com. When not writing code, she writes *about* writing code and is the coauthor of several books promoting the practical usage of Web standards alongside other everyday tools and technologies. Rachel takes a common sense, real world approach to Web standards, with her writing and teaching being based on the experiences she has in her own company every day.

Rachel lives in the UK with her partner Drew and daughter Bethany. When not working, they can often be found wandering around the English countryside hunting for geocaches and nice pubs that serve Sunday lunch and a good beer.

About SitePoint

SitePoint specializes in publishing fun, practical, and easy-to-understand content for Web professionals. Visit http://www.sitepoint.com/ to access our books, newsletters, articles and community forums.

For Bethany

Table of Contents

Preface

When I'm not writing books like this one, I'm writing code. I make my living by building Websites and applications, as, I'm sure, will many readers of this book. I use CSS to get jobs done every day. And I know what it's like to struggle to get something to work when the project needs to be finished the next morning.

When I talk to designers and developers who don't use CSS, or use CSS only for simple text styling, one thing that I hear over and over again is that they just don't have time to learn this whole new way of doing things. After all, tables and spacer GIFs work, they get the job done, and they pay the bills.

I was lucky. I picked up CSS very early in the piece, and started to play with it because it interested me. As a result of that early interest, my knowledge grew as the CSS techniques themselves were developed, and I can now draw on three years' experience building CSS layouts every time I tackle a project.

This book is my attempt to pass on the tricks and techniques that allow me to quickly and easily develop Websites and applications using CSS.

You won't find pages and pages of theory in this book. What you will find are solutions that will enable you to do the cool stuff today, but which should also act as a starting point for your own creativity. In my experience, it's far easier to learn by doing than by reading, so while you can use this book to find solutions that will help you get that client Website up and running by the deadline, please do experiment with these examples and use them as a way to learn new techniques.

The book was designed to let you quickly find the answer to the particular CSS problem with which you're struggling at any given point in time. You don't need to read it from cover to cover—just grab the technique that you need, or that interests you, and you're set to go. Along with each solution, I've provided an explanation to help you to understand why the technique works. This knowledge will allow you to expand on, and experiment with the technique in your own time.

I hope you enjoy this book! It has been great fun to write, and my hope is that it will be useful as a day-to-day reference, as well as a tool that helps give you the confidence to explore new CSS techniques.

Who Should Read This Book?

This book is aimed at people who need to work with CSS—Web designers and developers who have seen the cool CSS designs out there, but don't have the time to wade through masses of theory and debate in order to create a site. Each problem is solved with a working solution that can be implemented as-is or used as a starting point.

This book isn't a tutorial; while Chapter 1 covers the very basics of CSS, and the early chapters cover simpler techniques than those that follow, you will find the examples easier to grasp if you have a basic grounding in CSS.

What's Covered in This Book?

Chapter 1: *Getting Started with CSS*

This chapter does not follow the same format as the rest of the book—it's simply a quick CSS tutorial for anyone who needs to brush up on the basics of CSS. If you've been using CSS in your own projects, you might want to skip this chapter and refer back to it on a needs basis, if you find you want to look into basic concepts in more detail.

Chapter 2: *Text Styling and Other Basics*

This chapter covers techniques for styling and formatting text in your documents; font sizing, colors, and the removal of annoying extra white space around page elements are explained as the chapter progresses. Even if you're already using CSS for text styling, you will find some useful tips here.

Chapter 3: *CSS and Images*

Combining CSS and images can create powerful visual effects. This chapter looks at the ways in which you can do this, and covers background images (not just on the body), and positioning text with images, among other topics.

Chapter 4: *Navigation*

We all need navigation, and this chapter explains how to do it, CSS-style. The questions of CSS replacements for image-based navigation, CSS "tab" navigation, combining background images with CSS text to create attractive and accessible menus, and using lists to structure navigation in an accessible way are addressed in this chapter.

Chapter 5: *Tabular Data*

While the use of tables for layout is to be avoided wherever possible, tables should be used for their real purpose: the display of tabular data, such as that contained in a spreadsheet. This chapter will demonstrate techniques for the application of tables to create attractive and usable tabular data displays.

Chapter 6: *Forms and User Interfaces*

Whether you're a designer or a developer, it's likely that you'll spend a fair amount of time creating forms for data entry. CSS can help you to create forms that are attractive and more usable; this chapter shows how we can do that while bearing the key accessibility principles in mind.

Chapter 7: *Browser and Device Support*

How can we deal with older browsers, browsers with CSS bugs, and alternate devices? These questions form the main theme of this chapter. We'll also see how to troubleshoot CSS bugs—and where to go for help—and discuss the ways you can test your site in as many browsers as possible.

Chapter 8: *CSS Positioning and Layout*

In this chapter, we explore the use of CSS to create beautiful and accessible pages. We cover a range of different CSS layouts, and a variety of techniques, which can be combined and extended upon to create a range of different page layouts.

Chapter 9: *Experimentation, Browser Specific CSS, and Future Techniques*

Through the text so far, I've presented techniques that will work well cross-browser, and don't involve rafts of CSS "hacks" in order to work. But, in this chapter, we look at newer techniques that don't work so well cross-browser, or that need quite a lot of extra effort on your part, in order to do so.

The Book's Website

Located at http://www.sitepoint.com/books/cssant1/, the Website that supports this book will give you access to the following facilities:

The Code Archive

As you progress through this book, you'll note file names above most of the code listings. These refer to files in the code archive, a downloadable ZIP archive that contains all of the finished examples presented in this book. Simply click the Code Archive link on the book's Website to download it.

Updates and Errata

No book is error-free, and attentive readers will no doubt spot at least one or two mistakes in this one. The Errata page on the book's Website will provide the latest information about known typographical and code errors, and will offer necessary updates for new releases of browsers and related standards.

The SitePoint Forums

If you'd like to communicate with me or anyone else on the SitePoint publishing team about this book, you should join SitePoint's online community.[2] The CSS forum,[3] in particular, offers an abundance of information above and beyond the solutions in this book.

In fact, you should join that community even if you *don't* want to talk to us. There are a lot of fun and experienced Web designers and developers hanging out there. It's a good way to learn new stuff, get questions answered in a hurry, and just have a good time.

The SitePoint Newsletters

In addition to books like this one, SitePoint publishes free email newsletters including *The SitePoint Tribune*, *The SitePoint Tech Times*, and *The SitePoint Design View*. Reading them will keep you up to date on the latest news, product releases, trends, tips, and techniques for all aspects of Web development. If nothing else, you'll get useful CSS articles and tips. If you're interested in learning other technologies, you'll find them especially valuable. Sign up to one or more SitePoint newsletters at http://www.sitepoint.com/newsletter/.

Your Feedback

If you can't find your answer through the forums, or if you wish to contact us for any other reason, the best place to write is books@sitepoint.com. We have an email support system set up to track your inquiries. If our support staff members can't answer your question, they'll send it straight to me. Suggestions

---

[2] http://www.sitepointforums.com/
[3] http://www.sitepoint.com/forums/forumdisplay.php?f=53

for improvements as well as notices of any mistakes you may find are especially welcome.

Acknowledgements

Firstly, I'd like to thank the SitePoint team for making this book a reality, and for being easy to communicate with despite the fact that our respective time zones saw me going to bed as they started work each day. Particular thanks must go to Simon Mackie, whose encouragement throughout the writing process was a great support.

Thanks also to Technical Editor Simon Willison, who picked up on the slightest error or inconsistency, and whose attention to detail and well thought-out comments ensured that this book is accurate and clear.

To those people who are really breaking new ground in the world of CSS, those whose ideas are discussed throughout this book, and those who share their ideas and creativity with the wider community, thank you.

Thanks to Drew for his support and encouragement, for being willing to discuss CSS concepts as I worked out my examples for the book, for making me laugh when I was growing annoyed, and for putting up with our entire lack of a social life. Finally, thanks must go to my daughter Bethany, who is very understanding of the fact that her mother is constantly at a computer, and who reminds me of what is important every day. You both make so many things possible, thank you.

1

Getting Started with CSS

Cascading Style Sheets sound intimidating. The name alone conjures up images of cryptic code and syntax too difficult for the layperson to grasp. In reality, however, CSS is one of the simplest and most convenient tools available to Web developers. In this first chapter, which takes a different format than the rest of the book, I'll guide you through the basics of CSS and show you how it can be used to simplify the task of managing a consistently formatted Website. If you've used CSS to format text on your sites, you may want to skip this chapter and jump straight to the solutions that begin in Chapter 2.

The Problem with HTML

CSS is a language that's used to define the formatting applied to a Website, including colors, background images, typefaces (fonts), margins, and indentation. If you've never used CSS before, you could be forgiven for thinking, "Well, I do all that now with HTML tags. Why would I need CSS?" It's a valid question that's best answered with an illustration of the problems that can arise when we define styles using HTML.

At present, a popular design choice is to use a sans-serif font (such as Arial, Verdana, Tahoma, etc.) for the main body text of a site. Since most Web browsers default to a serif font like Times New Roman, creating a complex Web page layout using a sans-serif font will often involve a lot of `<font>` tags. In a complex layout, you might see ten or twenty `<font>` tags dedicated to applying the same font to all text on a page. Multiply this by five—the number of pages on a modest site—and we're in the neighborhood of one hundred tags. A beefier site might have fifty pages or more, in which case you're looking at one thousand `<font>` tags, all of them dedicated to applying that one basic, consistent style to your document's text.

Now here's the kicker: your client calls you late one Friday afternoon to say, "Verdana is nice, but everyone uses it. Let's use Tahoma instead." Fancy search-and-replace tools aside, you're now faced with the task of adjusting one hundred, one thousand, or even more `<font>` tags to make what, from your client's per-spective, seems like a very simple change. You can kiss that ski weekend you had planned goodbye. And, try not to groan aloud—it doesn't go over well with most customers.

If you know your HTML, you may be thinking that the `<basefont>` tag, which lets you set the default font to be used throughout a page, provides a nice solution to this problem. But even then, you'd have to adjust one tag for each page of your site. Add another font style to the equation (if, say, you wanted to use a different font for that fancy navigation bar of yours), and the problem returns in full.

Another reason why you shouldn't use HTML to format your site is that these presentational elements are deprecated (flagged to be removed in future specific-ations) and can't be used if you wish to follow a Strict DOCTYPE such as HTML 4.01 Strict or XHTML 1.0 Strict. While your page will still be valid if you use a transitional DOCTYPE, it's good practice to avoid using these deprecated elements where possible. As you'll discover through the examples in this book, CSS allows you to do lots of things that you can't do with HTML alone, so there are many reasons why you should use CSS—but let's stop talking and see some CSS in action!

Defining Styles with CSS

The basic purpose of CSS is to allow the designer to define a style (a list of formatting details such as fonts, sizes, and colors) and then, to apply it to one or more portions of one or more HTML pages using a selector. Let's look at a basic example to see how this is done.

Consider the following HTML document outline:

```
<!DOCTYPE html PUBLIC "-//W3C//DTD XHTML 1.0 Transitional//EN"
    "http://www.w3.org/TR/xhtml1/DTD/xhtml1-transitional.dtd">
<html xmlns="http://www.w3.org/1999/xhtml">
<head>
<title>A Simple Page</title>
<meta http-equiv="content-type"
    content="text/html; charset=iso-8859-1" />
</head>
<body>
<h1><font face="sans-serif" color="#3366CC">First Title</font>
</h1>
<p>...</p>

<h2><font face="sans-serif" color="#3366CC">Second Title</font>
</h2>
<p>...</p>

<h2><font face="sans-serif" color="#3366CC">Third Title</font>
</h2>
<p>...</p>
</body>
</html>
```

This document contains three headings, created using <h1> and <h2> tags. To make these headings stand out more, I used <font> tags to display them in a light blue, sans-serif font (Windows browsers will display them in Arial, for example). Notice the repetition involved, even at this basic level. I had to specify the details of the font I wanted three separate times. Wouldn't it make sense to define the font just once, then apply it to my headings? Here's the CSS version:

```
<!DOCTYPE html PUBLIC "-//W3C//DTD XHTML 1.0 Transitional//EN"
    "http://www.w3.org/TR/xhtml1/DTD/xhtml1-transitional.dtd">
<html xmlns="http://www.w3.org/1999/xhtml">
<head>
<title>A Simple Page</title>
<meta http-equiv="content-type"
    content="text/html; charset=iso-8859-1" />
<style type="text/css">
h1, h2 {
 font-family: sans-serif;
 color: #3366CC;
}
</style>
</head>
<body>
<h1>First Title</h1>
```

```
<p>…</p>

<h2>Second Title</h2>
<p>…</p>

<h2>Third Title</h2>
<p>…</p>
</body>
</html>
```

All the magic lies between the `<style>` tags in the `<head>` of the document, where we define our light blue, sans-serif font and apply it to all `<h1>` and `<h2>` tags in the document. Don't worry about the syntax; I'll explain it in detail in a moment. Meanwhile, the `<font>` tags have completely disappeared from the `<body>`, leaving our document looking a lot less cluttered. Changes to the style definition at the top of the page will affect all three headings, as well as any other headings that are added to the page.

Now that you have an idea of what CSS does, let me explain the different ways of using CSS styles in your HTML documents. The simplest way of putting CSS styles into your Web pages is to use the `<style>` tag, as I did in the example above. This lets you declare any number of CSS styles by placing them inside the `<style>` tag, as follows:

```
<style type="text/css">
CSS Styles here
</style>
```

The `type` attribute specifies the language that you're using to define your styles. CSS is the only language in wide use as of this writing, and is indicated with the value `text/css`.

While it's nice and simple, the `<style>` tag has one major disadvantage. Specifically, if you want to use a particular set of styles throughout your site, you'll have to repeat those style definitions in a `<style>` tag at the top of every one of your site's pages.

A more sensible alternative is to put those definitions in a plain text file (usually given a `.css` filename), then link your documents to that file. Any changes to the style definitions in that one file will affect all the pages that link to it. This achieves the objective of site-wide style definitions mentioned earlier.

To link a document to a CSS text file (say, `styles.css`), place a `<link>` tag in the document's header:

```
<link rel="stylesheet" type="text/css" href="styles.css" />
```

Let's return to the original example in which three headings shared a single style; that document would now look like this:

```
<!DOCTYPE html PUBLIC "-//W3C//DTD XHTML 1.0 Transitional//EN"
    "http://www.w3.org/TR/xhtml1/DTD/xhtml1-transitional.dtd">
<html xmlns="http://www.w3.org/1999/xhtml">
<head>
<title>A Simple Page</title>
<meta http-equiv="content-type"
    content="text/html; charset=iso-8859-1" />
<link rel="stylesheet" type="text/css" href="styles.css" />
</head>
<body>
<h1>First Title</h1>
<p>...</p>

<h2>Second Title</h2>
<p>...</p>

<h2>Third Title</h2>
<p>...</p>
</body>
</html>
```

The `styles.css` file would contain the style definition:

```
h1, h2 {
  font-family: sans-serif;
  color: #3366CC;
}
```

As with an image file, you can reuse this `styles.css` file across as many pages as you need. Not only will it save you typing, it also ensures a consistent look to the headings across your entire site.

CSS Selectors

Every CSS style definition has two components: the **selector**, which defines the tags to which the style will be applied, and the **properties**, which specify what the style actually does. In the previous example, the selector was h1, h2, specifying that the style should apply to all <h1> and <h2> tags. The remainder of the style definition comprised the attributes, specifying the font and color that should be applied by the style. In this section, I'll describe the basic CSS selector types and give examples of each.

Tag Selectors

The most basic form of selector is that which we have already seen. By naming a particular HTML tag, you can apply a style definition to every occurrence of that tag in the document. This is often used to set the basic styles that will appear throughout a Website. For example, the following might be used to set the default font for a Website:

```
body, p, td, th, div, blockquote, dl, ul, ol {
  font-family: Tahoma, Verdana, Arial, Helvetica, sans-serif;
  font-size: 1em;
  color: #000000;
}
```

This rather long selector is a list of tags, all of which will take on the style definition (font, size, and color). In theory, the <body> tag is all that's needed (as all the other tags appear inside the <body> tag, and would thus inherit its properties), but many browsers don't properly carry style properties into tables and other elements. Thus, I specified the other elements for the sake of completeness.

Pseudo-Class Selectors

The formatting of the <a> tag in HTML is more versatile than is the formatting of most other tags. By specifying link, vlink, and alink attributes in the <body> tag, you can set the colors for the various states of the links in your page (unvisited, visited, and being clicked on, respectively). CSS provides its own way of doing this, and adds a fourth state that's applied when the mouse hovers over the link. Consider the following example:

```
a:link { color: #0000FF; }
a:visited { color: #FF00FF; }
a:hover { color: #00CCFF; }
a:active { color: #FF0000; }
```

This code contains four CSS style definitions. Each of the selectors uses what is termed a **pseudo-class** of the <a> tag. The first, link, applies to unvisited links only, and specifies that they should be blue. The second, visited, applies to visited links, and makes them magenta. The third style definition, hover, overrides the first two by making links light blue when the mouse is moved over them, whether they've been visited or not. The final style definition makes links red when they're clicked on. Because `active` appears last, it overrides the first three, so it will take effect whether the links have been visited or not, and whether the mouse is over them or not.

Class Selectors

Assigning styles to tags is all well and good, but what happens if you want to assign different styles to identical tags occurring in different places within your document? This is where CSS **classes** come in. Consider the following style, which makes all paragraph text in the page blue:

```
p { color: #0000FF; }
```

Now, what if you had a sidebar on your page with a blue background? You wouldn't want text in the sidebar to be blue as well, because it would be invisible! What you need to do is define a class for your sidebar text, then assign a CSS style to that class:

```
p { color: #0000FF; }
.sidebar { color: #FFFFFF; }
```

This second rule uses a class selector that indicates that the style should be applied to any tag of the `sidebar` class. The period indicates that a class is being named, instead of a tag. To create a paragraph of text of the `sidebar` class, you add a `class` attribute to the tag:

```
<p class="sidebar">This text will be white, as specified by the
   CSS style definitions above.</p>
```

Now, what if there were links in your sidebar? By default, they'd be rendered just like any other links in your page; however, add a `class="sidebar"` attribute to the tag, and they'll turn white, too:

```
<p class="sidebar">This text will be white, <a class="sidebar"
     href="link.html">and so will this link</a>.</p>
```

That's pretty neat, but what if you wanted to make the links stand out a bit more by displaying them in bold text? Adding the `bold` text attribute to the `sidebar` class will make your whole sidebar bold. You need a CSS selector that selects links of the `sidebar` class only. By combining a tag selector with a class selector, you can do exactly that:

```
p { color: #0000FF; }
.sidebar { color: #FFFFFF; }
a.sidebar:link, a.sidebar:visited { font-weight: bold; }
```

Note that we've also used the :link and :visited pseudo-classes to specify <a> tags that are links (as opposed to <a name="…"> tags that are not).

Note also that our sidebar links are still white—both of the styles pertaining to the sidebar class apply to our sidebar links. If we specified a different color in the third style, however, links would adopt that new color, because the third selector is more specific, and CSS styles are applied in order of increasing selector specificity.

Incidentally, the process of applying multiple styles to a single page element is called **cascading**, and is where Cascading Style Sheets got their name.

Contextual Selectors

If your sidebar happens to contain a lot of links, it becomes tedious to assign the sidebar class to every single <a> tag. Wouldn't it be nice to use a selector to select any link that appeared inside a paragraph of the sidebar class? That's what contextual selectors are for: selecting a tag based on its **context**, that is, based on the tag(s) that contain it.

Here's the new CSS:

```
p { color: #0000FF; }
.sidebar { color: #FFFFFF; }
p.sidebar a:link, p.sidebar a:visited {
  font-weight: bold;
  color: #FFFFFF;
}
```

And here's the updated HTML:

```
<p class="sidebar">This text will be white,
  <a href="link.html">and so will this link</a>.</p>
```

As you can see, a contextual selector provides a list of selectors separated by spaces that must match tags "from the outside in." In this case, since the link (matched by the a:link or a:visited selector) occurs inside a sidebar paragraph (matched by the p.sidebar selector), the style applies to the link.

Note that, to keep the link white, we had to add that color to the CSS attributes for the links, as the style for the `sidebar` class no longer applies to the links.

ID Selectors

Similar to class selectors, ID selectors are used to select one particular tag, rather than a group of tags. The tag that you select is identified by an ID attribute as follows:

```
<p id="sidebar1">This paragraph is uniquely identified by the ID
  "sidebar1".</p>
```

An ID selector is simply the ID preceded by a hash (#). Thus, the following style will make the above paragraph white:

```
#sidebar1 { color: #FFFFFF; }
```

ID selectors can be used in combination with the other selector types. The following style, for example, applies to unvisited links appearing in the `sidebar1` paragraph:

```
#sidebar1 a:link {
  font-weight: bold;
  color: #FFFFFF;
}
```

Other selector types exist, but they're not widely used. Support for them in some browsers (especially Netscape 4) is buggy at best.

CSS Properties

In the examples used so far in this chapter, we've used several common CSS properties like `color`, `font-family`, `font-size`, and `font-weight`. In the rest of the book, we'll be using these properties—and a lot more.

Summary

This chapter has given you a taste of CSS and its usage at the most basic level. If you haven't used CSS before, but have a basic understanding of the concepts discussed in this chapter, you should be able to start using the examples in this book. The examples in the early chapters of this book are somewhat simpler than those found near the end, so, if you haven't worked with this technology before, you might want to begin with the earlier chapters. These will build on the knowledge you gained in this chapter to get you using and, I hope, enjoying CSS.

2

Text Styling and Other Basics

This chapter explores the applications of CSS for styling text, and covers a lot of CSS basics as well as answering some of the more frequently asked questions. If you're new to CSS, these examples will introduce you to a variety of properties and usages, and will give you a broad overview from which to start your own experiments with CSS. For those who are already familiar with CSS, this chapter will serve as a quick refresher for those moments when you can't quite remember how to achieve a certain effect.

The examples provided here are well supported across a variety of browsers and versions. As always, testing your code across different browsers is important; however, the text styling properties have good support. While there may be small inconsistencies or some lack of support in older browsers, nothing here should cause you any serious problems.

How do I replace font tags with CSS?

The styling of text with CSS is supported by version 4 browsers and above, so there is no compelling reason to continue to use `<font>` tags to style text. At its very simplest, you can use CSS to replace the font tags in your site.

Using font tags, you would need to set the style for each paragraph on your page.

```
<p><font color="#800080"
    face="Verdana,Geneva,Arial,Helvetica,sans-serif">These
stuffed peppers are lovely as a starter, or as a side dish
for a Chinese meal. They also go down well as part of a
buffet and even children seem to like them.</font></p>
```

Solution

Using CSS, you would simply define in the style sheet that the `color` property of the `<p>` tag is `#800080`, and that the `font-family` should be `Verdana,Geneva,Arial,Helvetica,sans-serif`:

```
p {
  color: #800080;
  font-family: Verdana,Geneva,Arial,Helvetica,sans-serif;
}
```

Now, every time you add to your document text enclosed in a `<p>` tag, it will take on this style, and save you from needing to add reams of extra markup to your document. It also makes life a lot easier if your client suddenly wants to change the font from Verdana to Times on 100 documents!

Should I use pixels, points, ems or something else for font sizes?

You can size text in CSS using the `font-size` property. For example:

```
font-size: 12px;
```

However, there are a variety of other ways to set the size of your fonts. Deciding which to use requires you to know a little about the relative merits of each.

Solution

The Units of Font Sizing

Table 2.1 describes the units that you can use to size fonts.

Table 2.1. Font Sizing Units

Unit identifier	Corresponding Units
pt	Points
pc	Picas
px	Pixels
em	Ems
ex	Exes
%	Percentages

Points and Picas

```
p {
  font-size: 10pt;
}
```

You should avoid using points and picas to style text for display on screen. These units are an excellent way to set sizes for print design, as their measurements were designed for that purpose. A point has a fixed size of one seventy-second of an inch, while a pica is one sixth of an inch. A printed document specified using these units will come out exactly as you intended. However, computers cannot accurately predict the actual size at which elements will appear on the monitor, so they guess—and guess badly—at the size of a point or pica, with varying results across platforms. If you're creating a print style sheet, or a document that's intended for print, not on-screen, viewing, these are the units to use. However, a general rule of thumb is to avoid them when designing for the Web.

Pixels

```
p {
  font-size: 12px;
}
```

Many designers like to measure font sizes in pixels, as this unit of measurement makes it easy to achieve consistent displays across various browsers and platforms. However, pixels ignore any preferences users may have set in their own browsers and, in most browsers, font sizes that the designer has dictated in pixels cannot be resized by users. This is a serious accessibility problem for those who need to make text larger in order to read it clearly. Therefore, while pixels may seem like the easiest option, pixel measurements should be avoided if another method can be used, particularly for large blocks of content. If you're creating a document for print, or using a print style sheet, you should avoid pixels entirely. Pixels have no meaning in the world of print and, similar to the application of points to the on-screen environment, print applications provided with a pixel measurement will simply try to guess the size at which the font should appear on paper, with erratic results.

Ems

The em is a relative font measurement, where one em is equal to the height of the letter "M" in the default font size. Where CSS is concerned, 1em is seen to be equal to the user's default font size, or the font size of the parent element when it differs. If you use ems (or any other relative unit) for all your font sizing, users will be able to resize the text, which will comply with the text size preferences they have set in their browsers. For example, imagine I create a declaration that sets text within the <p> tag to 1em, as is shown in the following CSS:

```css
p {
    font-size: 1em;
}
```

A user with an Internet Explorer 6 browser in which text size is set to Medium will see the paragraph shown in Figure 2.1.

Figure 2.1. The `font-size` is set to 1em and text size is Medium.

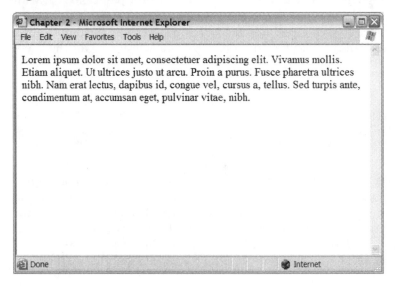

If the users have their text set to Largest, the 1em text will display as shown in Figure 2.2.

Figure 2.2. The `font-size` is set to 1em and text size is set to Largest.

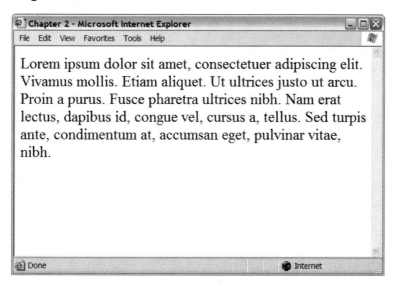

As a designer, this gives you less control over the way users view the document. However, it means that users who need a very large font size, for instance, can read your content.

Ems values can be set using decimal numbers. For example, to display text at a size 10% smaller than the user's default (or the font size of its parent element) you could use:

```
p {
  font-size: 0.9em;
}
```

To display the text 10% larger than the default or inherited size:

```
p {
  font-size: 1.1em;
}
```

Exes

The ex is a relative unit measurement that corresponds to the height of the lowercase letter "x" in the default font size. In theory, if you set the `font-size` of a paragraph to `1ex`, the uppercase letters of the text should be the same height as the letter "x" would have been if the font size had not been specified.

Unfortunately, modern browsers don't yet support the typographical features needed to determine the size of an ex precisely. They usually make a rough guess for this measurement. For this reason, exes are rarely used at this time.

Percentages

```
p {
  font-size: 100%;
}
```

As with ems and exes, font sizes that are set in percentages will honor users' text size settings and are resizable by the user. Setting the `<p>` tag to `100%` would display your text at users' default settings for font size (as would setting the font size to `1em`). Decreasing the percentage will make the text smaller:

```
p {
  font-size: 90%;
}
```

Increasing the percentage will make the text larger:

```
p {
  font-size: 150%;
}
```

Keywords

You can also size text using absolute and relative keywords.

Absolute Keywords

There are seven absolute keyword sizes for use in CSS, as follows:

- ❏ `xx-small`

- ❏ `x-small`

- ❏ `small`

- ❏ `medium`

- ❏ `large`

- ❏ `x-large`

- ❏ `xx-large`

These keywords are defined relative to each other, and browsers implement them in different ways. Most browsers display `medium` at the same size as unstyled text, with the other keywords resizing text to varying degrees. Internet Explorer 5 (and version 6, depending on the document type), however, treats `small` as being the same size as unstyled text.

These keyword measurements are considered absolute in that they don't inherit from any parent element. Yet, unlike the absolute values provided for height, such as pixels and points, they do allow the text to be resized in the browser, and will honor the user's browser settings. The main problem with using these keywords is the fact that, for example, `x-small`-sized text may be perfectly readable in one browser, and miniscule in another.

Relative Keywords

Relative keywords—`larger` and `smaller`—take their size from the parent element, in the same way that `em` and `%` do. Therefore, if you set your `<p>` tag to `small` using absolute keywords, and you simply want emphasized text to display comparatively larger, you'd add the following to the style sheet:

File: **relative.css**

```
p {
  font-size: small;
}
em {
  font-size: larger;
}
```

The following markup would display as shown in Figure 2.3, because the text wrapped in the `<em>` tag will display larger than its parent—the `<p>` tag.

File: **relative.html (excerpt)**

```
<p>These <em>stuffed peppers</em> are lovely as a starter, or as a
   side dish for a Chinese meal. They also go down well as part of
   a buffet and even children seem to like them.</p>
```

Figure 2.3. The emphasized text displays larger than its containing paragraph.

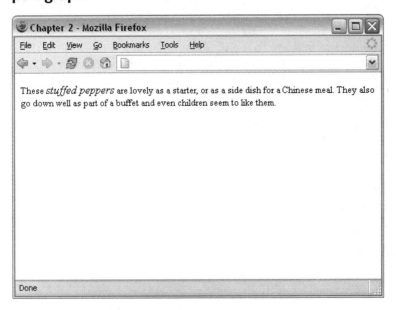

Relative Sizing and Inheritance

When you use any kind of relative sizing, remember that the element inherits its starting size from its parent element, then adjusts its size accordingly. This is fairly easy to understand in layouts in which elements are not nested in a complex manner; however, this inheritance pattern can become problematic in nested table layouts in which the parent element is not always obvious—things can seem to inherit very strangely indeed! The following example demonstrates this.

My style sheet contains the following code, which sets td to display text at 80%. This is slightly smaller than the user's default font size, but they will be able to resize it:

File: **nesting.css**

```
td {
  font-size: 80%;
}
```

On a page in which there are no nested table cells, the text will display consistently at that slightly smaller size. However, in a nested table layout, the text within each nested table will display at 80% of the font size of its containing table.

File: **nesting.html (excerpt)**

```
<table>
  <tr>
    <td>This is a table
      <table>
        <tr>
          <td>This is the second table
            <table>
              <tr>
                <td>This is the third table</td>
              </tr>
            </table>
          </td>
        </tr>
      </table>
    </td>
  </tr>
</table>
```

The example markup above will display as in Figure 2.4. As you can see, the text becomes progressively smaller in each nested table.

Figure 2.4. The display demonstrates the use of relative font sizing within nested tables.

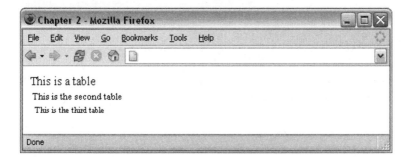

Discussion

When choosing which method of sizing text to use, it's best to select one that allows all users to resize the text, and that ensure that the text complies with the settings users have chosen in their browsers. Relative font sizing tends to work well with CSS layouts and simple table-based layouts, but it can be tricky to implement in a complex nested table layout because of the way the elements inherit sizing. If you decide that your only option is to size fonts using an absolute unit of measurement, consider developing a style sheet switcher to allow users to change the font size from within the interface of your site.

How do I specify that my text is shown in a certain font?

Solution

Specify the typeface that your text will adopt using the `font-family` property like so:

```
p {
    font-family: Verdana;
}
```

Discussion

As well as specific fonts, such as Verdana or Times, CSS allows the specification of some more generic font families, which are:

- ❑ serif
- ❑ sans-serif
- ❑ monospace
- ❑ cursive
- ❑ fantasy

When you specify fonts, it's important to remember that users probably don't have the same fonts you have on your computer. If you define a font that they don't have, your text will display in their Web browser's default font, regardless of what you'd have preferred, or your site design.

You can simply use generic font names and let users' systems decide which font to apply. For instance, if you want your document to appear in a sans-serif font such as Arial, you could simply use the following code:

```
p {
    font-family: sans-serif;
}
```

However, you'll probably want to have a little more control over the way your site displays—and you can. It's possible to specify font names as well as generic fonts. Take, for example, the following CSS declaration for the <p> tag. Here, we've specified that if Verdana is installed on the system, it should be used; if it's not installed, the computer is directed to see if the user has Geneva installed; failing that, the computer will look for Arial, then Helvetica. If none of these fonts is available, the computer is instructed to use that system's default sans-serif font.

```
p {
    font-family: Verdana, Geneva, Arial, Helvetica, sans-serif;
}
```

How do I remove underlines from my links?

The default indication that text on a Web page is a link to another document is that it's underlined and is a different color from the rest of the text. There may be instances in which you want to remove that underline.

Solution

We use the `text-decoration` property to remove the underlines. By default, the browser will set the `text-decoration` of an `<a>` tag to `underline`. To remove the underline, simply set the following property for the link:

```
text-decoration: none;
```

The CSS used to create the effect shown in Figure 2.5 is as follows:

File: **textdecoration.css**

```
a:link, a:visited {
  text-decoration: none;
}
```

Figure 2.5. Use `text-decoration` to create links that aren't underlined.

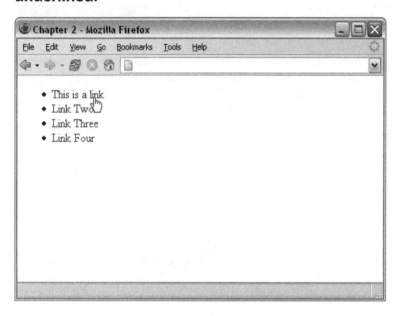

Discussion

In addition to `underline` and `none`, there are other values for `text-decoration` that you can try out:

❏ `overline`

❏ `line-through`

❏ `blink`

You can also combine these values. For instance, should you wish to have an underline and overline on a particular link, as shown in Figure 2.6, you'd use the following code:

File: **textdecoration2.css**

```
a:link, a:visited {
  text-decoration: underline overline;
}
```

Figure 2.6. Combine `text-decoration` values to create links with underlines and overlines.

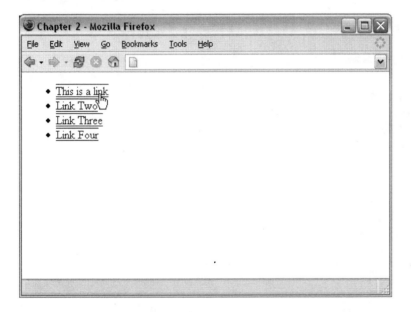

Misleading Lines

Tip

You can use the `text-decoration` property on text that's not a link, however, be wary of this. The underlining of links is such a widely-accepted convention that users tend to think that any underlined text is a link to another document.

When is Removing Underlines a Bad Idea?

Underlining links is a standard convention followed by all Web browsers and, consequently, users expect to see links underlined. Removing the underline from links that are within text can make it very difficult for people to realize that these words are in fact links—not just highlighted text. I'd advise against removing the underlines from links within text. There are other ways in which you can style links so they look attractive and removal of the underline is rarely, if ever, necessary.

Links that are used as part of a menu, or in some other situation in which the text is quite obviously a link—for instance, where the text is styled with CSS to resemble a graphical button—are a different story. If you wish, you can remove the underline from these kinds of links because it's obvious from their context that they're links.

How do I create a link that changes color on mouseover?

An attractive link effect changes the color or otherwise alters the appearance of links when the cursor moves across them. This effect can be applied to great advantage when CSS is used to replace navigation buttons; however, it can also be used on links within your document.

Solution

To create this effect, we style the `:hover` and `:active` pseudo-classes differently than the other pseudo-classes of the anchor tag.

Our links are styled with the following declaration in the style sheet:

File: **textdecoration3.css**

```
a:link, a:visited, a:hover, a:active {
  text-decoration: underline;
  color: #6A5ACD;
  background-color: transparent;
}
```

When this style sheet is applied, our links will display in the blue color #6A5ACD with an underline, as shown in Figure 2.7.

Figure 2.7. The same declaration is used for all pseudo-classes of these links.

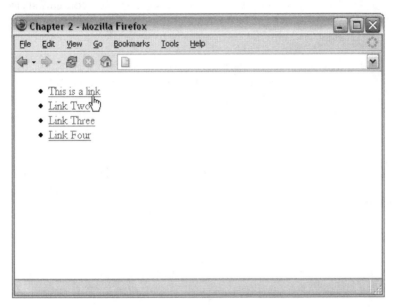

To make our :hover and :active pseudo-classes different, we need to remove them from the declaration with the other pseudo-classes and give them their own declaration. I decided to apply an overline in addition to the underline, a background color, and make the text a darker color. The resulting CSS is below (see also Figure 2.8):

File: **textdecoration4.css**

```css
a:link, a:visited {
  text-decoration: underline;
  color: #6A5ACD;
  background-color: transparent;
}
a:hover, a:active {
  text-decoration: underline overline;
  color: #191970;
  background-color: #C9C3ED;
}
```

Figure 2.8. The effect of our CSS is evident when we roll over a link with a hover style.

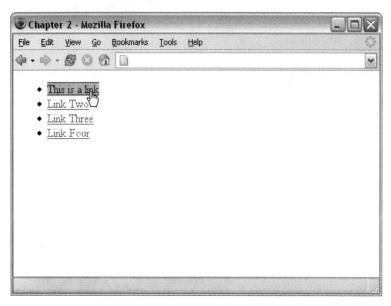

As you've probably realized, you can style the other pseudo-classes separately, too. In particular, you might like to style differently links that the user has visited. To do this, you'd simply style the `:visited` pseudo-class separately.

When styling pseudo-classes, take care that you don't change either the size or weight (boldness) of the text. If you do, you'll find that your page appears to "jiggle," as the content has to move to make way for the larger text to appear on hover.

Tip

Pseudo Order

The link pseudo-classes should be declared in the following order: `link`, `visited`, `hover`, `active`. If they aren't, you may find that they don't work as you intended. One way to remember this order is the mnemonic: LoVe-HAte.

How do I display two different styles of link on one page?

The previous tip explained how to style the different selectors of the anchor tag, but what if you want to use different link styles within the same document? Perhaps you want to display links without underlines in your navigation menu, yet make sure that links within the body content are easily identifiable. Maybe part of your document has a dark background color, so you need to use a light-colored link style there.

Solution

To demonstrate how to create multiple styles for links, let's take an example in which we've already styled the links.

File: **linktypes.css** (excerpt)

```css
a:link, a:visited {
  text-decoration: underline;
  color: #6A5ACD;
  background-color: transparent;
}

a:hover, a:active {
  text-decoration: underline overline;
  color: #191970;
  background-color: #C9C3ED;
}
```

These should be taken as the default style—this is how links will normally be styled within your documents. This link style makes the link blue, so, if you have an area with a blue background on your page, the links will be unreadable. You need to create a second set of styles for any link within that area.

First, you need to give a class or an ID to the area that will contain the differently colored links. If the area is already styled with CSS, it will already have a class or ID that you can use. Imagine your document contains the following markup:

File: **linktypes.html** (excerpt)

```html
<div class="boxout">
  <p>Visit our <a href="store.html">online store</a>, for all your
```

```
      widget needs.</p>
</div>
```

You will need to create a CSS rule to affect any link appearing within an area for which the parent element has the class boxout applied:

File: **linktypes.css (excerpt)**

```
.boxout {
  color: #FFFFFF;
  background-color: #6A5ACD;
}
.boxout a:link, .boxout a:visited {
  text-decoration: underline;
  color: #E4E2F6;
  background-color: transparent;
}

.boxout a:hover, .boxout a:active {
  background-color: #C9C3ED;
  color: #191970;
}
```

Figure 2.9. Two different styles of links can be used in one document.

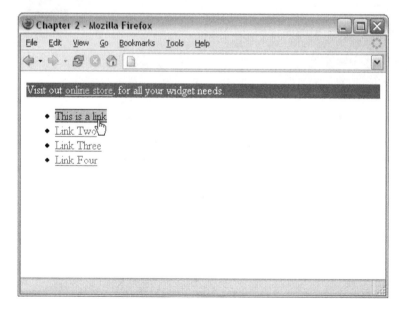

As shown in Figure 2.9, this will display all links in the document as per the first style except those that appear in the `boxout`—these links will be displayed in the lighter color.

How do I add a background color to a heading?

You can add a background color to any element, including a heading.

Solution

Below, we've created a CSS rule for all level one headings in a document. The result is shown in Figure 2.10.

File: **headingcolor.css (excerpt)**

```css
h1 {
  background-color: #ADD8E6;
  color: #256579;
  font: 18px Verdana, Geneva, Arial, Helvetica, sans-serif;
  padding: 2px;
}
```

Figure 2.10. Headings can display with a background color.

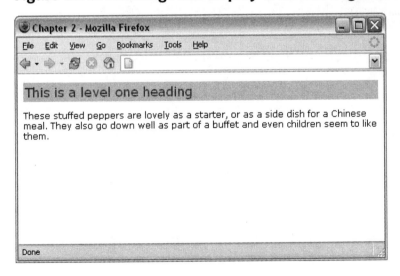

Make Way for Color

Tip When adding a background to a heading, you may also want to adjust the padding so that there's space between the heading text and the edge of the colored area, as we did in the above example.

How do I style headings with underlines?

Solution

There are two ways in which you can add an underline to your text. The simplest way is to use the `text-decoration` property that we encountered when styling links above. This method will allow you to underline the text in the same color as the text itself, as shown in Figure 2.11.

File: **headingunderline.css** (excerpt)

```
h1 {
    font: 18px Verdana, Geneva, Arial, Helvetica, sans-serif;
    text-decoration: underline;
}
```

Figure 2.11. Add an underline to a heading using `text-decoration`.

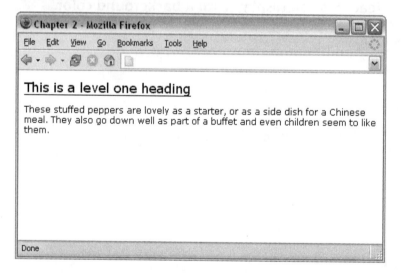

You can also create an underline effect by adding a bottom border to the heading. This solution is more flexible, in that you can separate the underline and the heading with the use of padding, and you can change the color of the underline to be different than the text. However, the effect may display slightly differently in different browsers, so you'll need to test it to make sure the effect looks reasonable on the browsers your visitors may use (see Figure 2.12).

File: **headingunderline2.css**

```
h1 {
    font: 18px Verdana, Geneva, Arial, Helvetica, sans-serif;
    padding: 2px;
    border-bottom: 1px solid #aaaaaa;
}
```

Figure 2.12. Add an underline effect using a bottom border.

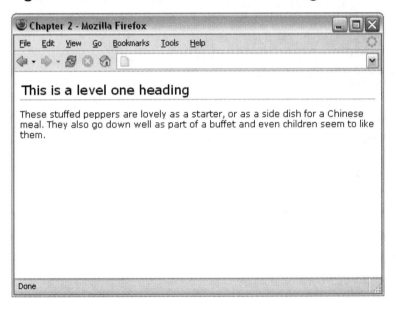

How do I get rid of the large gap between an <h1> tag and the following paragraph?

Solution

By default, browsers render a gap between heading and paragraph tags. This is produced by a default top and bottom margin that browsers apply to these tags.

To remove all space between a heading and the paragraph that follows it, you must not only remove the bottom margin from the heading, but also the top margin from the paragraph. But since it can be inconvenient to target the first paragraph following a heading with a CSS selector, it's easier to simply assign a negative bottom margin to the heading. Margins can be set to negative values, though padding cannot.

The margin of the heading shown in Figure 2.13 has not been changed.

Figure 2.13. This heading and paragraph show the default spacing.

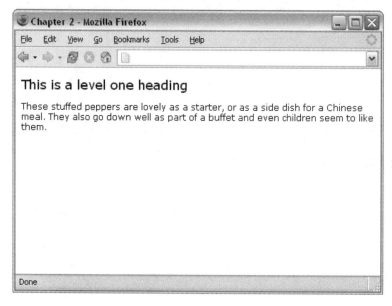

Figure 2.14 shows the same heading after the CSS below has been applied to the <h1> tag.

```
h1 {
  font: 18px Verdana, Geneva, Arial, Helvetica, sans-serif;
  margin-bottom: -12px;
}
```

Figure 2.14. The heading display changes when the `margin-bottom` is set to `-12px`.

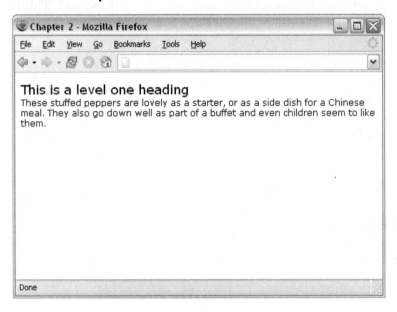

How do I highlight text on the page without using font tags?

Before CSS, we might have used font tags to highlight an important term on the page, or to identify the search terms visitors had used to locate the document through a search engine.

Solution

CSS allows you to create a class for the highlighting style and apply it by wrapping the highlighted text with <span> tags that apply the class. For example, in the following paragraph, we've wrapped a phrase in span tags that apply the class, hilite.

File: **hilite.html (excerpt)**

```
<p>These <span class="hilite">stuffed peppers</span> are lovely as
  a starter, or as a side dish for a Chinese meal. They also go
  down well as part of a buffet and even children seem to like
  them.</p>
```

The hilite class is shown below; the section will display as in Figure 2.15:

File: **hilite.css (excerpt)**

```
.hilite {
  background-color: #FFFFCC;
  color: #B22222;
}
```

Figure 2.15. Highlight text with CSS.

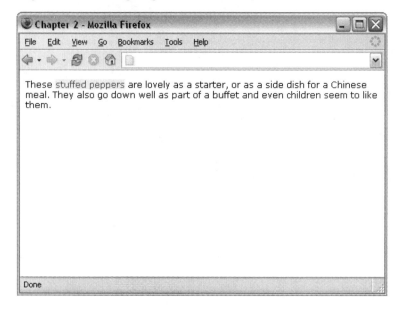

How do I alter the line-height (leading) on my text?

One of the great advantages of using CSS instead of font tags is that you have far more control over the look of the text on the page. In this solution, we'll see how to alter the leading of text in your document.

Solution

If the default spacing between lines of text looks a little narrow, change it with the `line-height` property.

File: **leading.css**

```
p {
  font: 11px Verdana, Geneva, Arial, Helvetica, sans-serif;
  line-height: 2.0;
}
```

The result is shown in Figure 2.16.

Figure 2.16. Alter the leading using the `line-height` property.

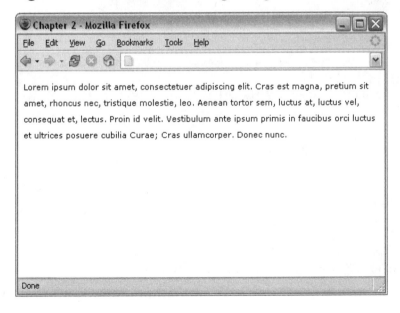

Be careful not to space the text out so much that it becomes difficult to read.

No Units?

You can also specify the **line-height** using standard CSS units of measurement, such as ems or even pixels. But doing so breaks the link between the line height and font size for child elements.

For example, if the example above contained a **<span>** that set a large **font-size**, then the line height would scale up proportionally to maintain the same ratio because **line-height** of the paragraph was set to the numerical value **2.0**. If, however, **line-height** was set to **2em** or **200%**, the **<span>** would inherit the actual line height, not the ratio, and the large font size would not affect the line height of the span. Depending on the effect you're going for, this may actually be desirable.

How do I justify text?

When you justify text, you alter the spacing between the words so that both the right and left margins are straight, as with the text in this book. You can create this effect using CSS.

Solution

You can justify paragraph text with the help of the **text-align** property.

File: **justify.css**

```
p {
    text-align: justify;
    font: 11px Verdana, Geneva, Arial, Helvetica, sans-serif;
    line-height: 2.0;
}
```

Figure 2.17 shows the effect of this code.

Figure 2.17. Justify text using `text-align`.

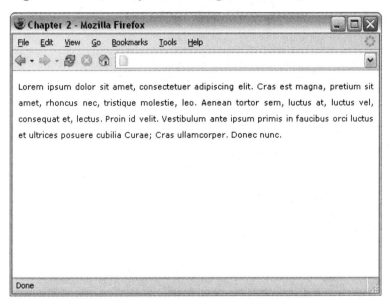

Discussion

Other values for `text-align` are:

right   aligns the text to the right of the container

left   aligns the text to the left of the container

center   aligns the text center

How do I style a horizontal rule?

Solution

You can change the color, height and width of a horizontal rule. Note that, in the CSS below, I've used the same values for `color` and `background-color` because Mozilla-based browsers color the rule using `background-color`, while IE uses `color`.

File: **hrstyle.css (excerpt)**

```
hr {
  border: none;
  background-color: #ADD8E6;
  color: #ADD8E6;
  height: 1px;
  width: 80%;
}
```

The result can be seen in Figure 2.18.

Figure 2.18. Change the color, height and width of a horizontal rule.

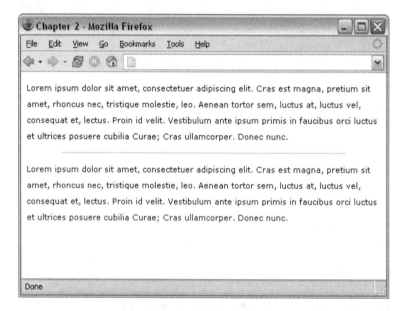

How do I indent text?

Solution

You can indent text by applying a rule to the container that sets a `padding-left` value.

File: **indent.html** (excerpt)

```
<p class="indent">Lorem ipsum dolor sit amet, consectetuer
  adipiscing elit. Vivamus mollis. Etiam aliquet. Ut ultrices
  justo ut arcu. Proin a purus. Fusce pharetra ultrices nibh.
  Nam erat lectus, dapibus id, congue vel, cursus a, tellus.
  Sed turpis ante, condimentum at, accumsan eget, pulvinar
  vitae, nibh.</p>
```

File: **indent.css** (excerpt)

```
.indent {
  padding-left: 30px;
}
```

You can see the indented paragraph in Figure 2.19.

Figure 2.19. Indent text using CSS.

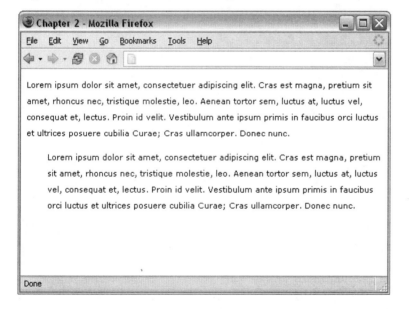

Discussion

You should not use the HTML tag `<blockquote>` to indent text, unless the text is actually a quote. Although visual editing environments such as Macromedia Dreamweaver frequently refer to `<blockquote>` as "indent text," resist the temptation to use it for this purpose; instead, set up a CSS rule to indent the appropriate blocks. `<blockquote>` is designed to mark up a quote, and devices such a screen readers for the visually impaired will read this text in a way that helps users understand that what they're hearing is a piece of quoted text. If you use `<blockquote>` to indent regular paragraphs, it will be very confusing for users to whom the content is read as a quote.

Tip

A One-Liner

A related technique enables the indentation of just the first line of each paragraph. To do this, use the CSS property `text-indent` applied either to the paragraph, or to a class that's applied to paragraphs you wish to display in this way.

```
p {
    text-indent: 20px;
}
```

How do I center text?

Solution

You can center text, or any other element, using the `text-align` property with a value of `center`.

File: **center.html (excerpt)**

```
<p class="centered">Lorem ipsum dolor sit amet, consectetuer
    adipiscing elit. Vivamus mollis. Etiam aliquet. Ut ultrices
    justo ut arcu. Proin a purus. Fusce pharetra ultrices nibh. Nam
    erat lectus, dapibus id, congue vel, cursus a, tellus. Sed
    turpis ante, condimentum at, accumsan eget, pulvinar vitae,
    nibh.</p>
```

File: **center.css (excerpt)**

```
.centered {
    text-align: center;
}
```

The result can be seen in Figure 2.20.

Figure 2.20. Center text using `text-align`.

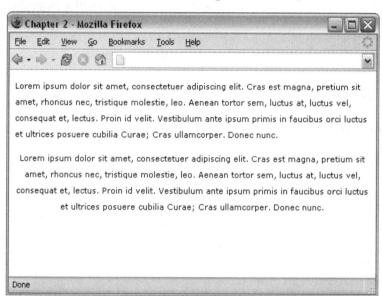

How do I change text to all-capitals using CSS?

Solution

You can change text to all-capitals and perform other transformations using the `text-transform` property.

File: **uppercase.html** (excerpt)

```
<p class="transform">Lorem ipsum dolor sit amet, consectetuer
   adipiscing elit. Vivamus mollis. Etiam aliquet. Ut ultrices
   justo ut arcu. Proin a purus. Fusce pharetra ultrices nibh. Nam
   erat lectus, dapibus id, congue vel, cursus a, tellus. Sed
   turpis ante, condimentum at, accumsan eget, pulvinar vitae,
   nibh.</p>
```

File: **uppercase.css (excerpt)**

```
.transform {
  text-transform: uppercase;
}
```

Note the uppercase text in Figure 2.21.

Figure 2.21. This `text-transform` makes all the letters uppercase.

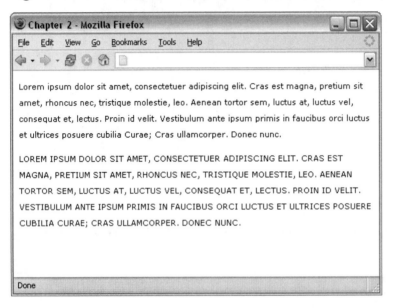

Discussion

There are other useful values for the `text-transform` property. The value `capitalize` will capitalize the first letter of each word, as shown in Figure 2.22:

File: **capitalize.css (excerpt)**

```
.transform {
  text-transform: capitalize;
}
```

Figure 2.22. The application of `text-transform` changes the appearance of the words.

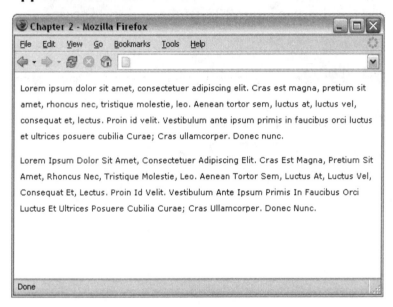

Other values of the `text-transform` property are:

☐ `lowercase`

☐ `none` (the default)

How do I change or remove the bullets on list items?

Solution

You can change the style of bullets used in your lists by altering the `list-style-type` property.

File: **`listtype.html`** (excerpt)

```
<ul>
  <li>list item one</li>
  <li>list item two</li>
```

```
   <li>list item three</li>
</ul>
```

To use square bullets, as shown in Figure 2.23, set the property to `square`:

File: **listtype.css**

```
ul {
   list-style-type: square;
}
```

Figure 2.23. This list uses square bullets.

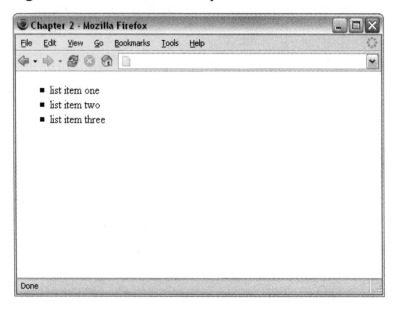

Discussion

Other values for the `list-style-type` property are:

☐ `disc`

☐ `circle`

☐ `decimal-leading-zero`

☐ `decimal`

- ❏ lower-roman

- ❏ upper-roman

- ❏ lower-greek

- ❏ lower-alpha

- ❏ lower-latin

- ❏ upper-alpha

- ❏ upper-latin

- ❏ Hebrew

- ❏ Armenian

- ❏ Georgian

- ❏ none

Not all of these values are supported by all browsers; those that don't provide support for a particular type will display the default bullet type instead. You can see the different types and check your browser's support for them at the CSS Test Suite for list style type.[1] Setting list-style-type to none will result in no bullets being displayed, although the list will still be indented as if the bullets were there. You can see this in Figure 2.24.

File: **listtype2.css**

```
ul {
  list-style-type: none;
}
```

[1] http://www.meyerweb.com/eric/css/tests/css2/sec12-06-02a.htm

Figure 2.24. This list displays without bullets.

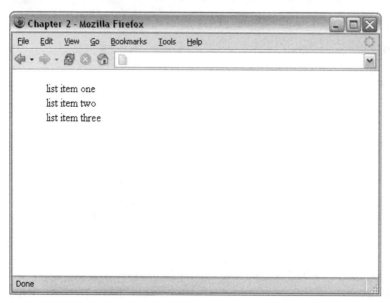

How do I use an image for a list item bullet?

Solution

To use an image for a bullet, create your image, then use the `list-style-image` property, instead of `list-style-type`, for your bullets. This property accepts a URL, which incorporates the path to your image file as a value.

File: **listimage.css**

```
ul {
  list-style-image: url(bullet.gif);
}
```

You can see an example of an image used as a bullet in Figure 2.25.

Figure 2.25. Use an image as a list bullet.

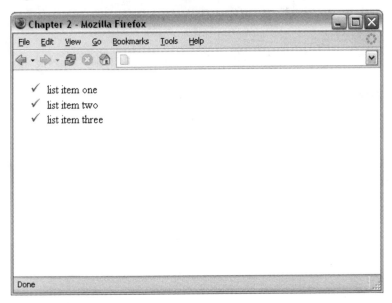

Per Item Bullets

Tip

The `list-style-image` property actually applies to the list item (`<li>`) tags in the list, but by applying it to the list as a whole the individual items will inherit it. You do, however, have the option of setting the property on individual list items, giving individual items their own bullet images.

How do I remove the indented left margin from a list?

If you have set `list-style-type` to `none`, you may also wish to remove or decrease the default left margin that the browser sets on a list.

Solution

To remove the indentation entirely so that the list will align left with any other content, as shown in Figure 2.26, use the following code:

File: **listnomargin.css**

```
ul {
  list-style-type: none;
  padding-left: 0;
  margin-left: 0;
}
```

Figure 2.26. The list has no indentation or bullets.

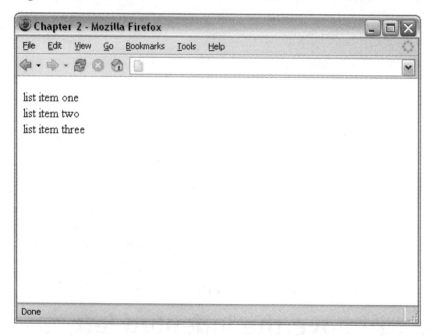

Discussion

You can tweak the indentation after doing this. To indent the content by a few pixels, try this:

```
ul {
  list-style-type: none;
  padding-left: 5px;
  margin-left: 0;
}
```

How do I display a list horizontally?

By default, list items display as block elements; therefore, each new item will display on a new line. However, there may be times when some content on your page is, structurally speaking, a list, even though you mightn't want to display it as such. What happens if, for instance, you want to display the "list items" horizontally?

Solution

You can make a list display horizontally by altering the `display` property of the `<li>` tag to `inline`.

File: **`listinline.html` (excerpt)**

```
<ul class="horiz">
  <li>list item one</li>
  <li>list item two</li>
  <li>list item three</li>
</ul>
```

File: **`listinline.css`**

```
ul.horiz li {
  display: inline;
}
```

The result of the above code can be seen in Figure 2.27.

How do I add comments to my CSS file?

You can, and should, add comments to your CSS file. CSS files that are very simple, with just a few rules for text styling, for instance, may not require commenting. However, once you start to use large CSS files and multiple style sheets for a site, comments come in very handy! Without them, you can spend a lot of time hunting around for the right classes, pondering which class does what and in which style sheet it lives.

Figure 2.27. A list can be displayed horizontally.

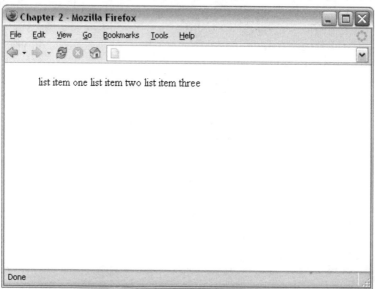

Solution

CSS supports multiline C-style comments, just like JavaScript. So, to comment out an area, use the following:

```
/*
  ...
*/
```

At the very least, you should add a comment at the top of each style sheet to explain what's in that style sheet.

```
/* This is the default style sheet for all text on the site */
```

How do I get rid of the page margins without adding attributes to the body tag?

Before CSS support, we would remove the default gutter between the document and the browser window by adding attributes to the `<body>` tag:

```
<body topmargin="0" leftmargin="0" marginheight="0"
    marginwidth="0">
```

Solution

The above attributes of the body tag are now deprecated. They should be replaced by CSS defined for the `<body>` tag.

```
body {
  margin: 0;
  padding: 0;
}
```

Tip

Opera Sings its Own Tune

Some versions of Opera apply `margin` and `padding` to the `<html>` element instead of the `<body>` tag. Therefore, to support Opera, you'll need to use this code:

```
html, body {
  margin: 0;
  padding: 0;
}
```

Summary

In this chapter, we've covered some of the more common questions asked by those who are relatively new to CSS: questions that relate to styling and manipulating text on the page. By combining these techniques, you can create attractive effects that will degrade appropriately for those who aren't using a browser that supports CSS.

3

CSS and Images

Given many of the designs favored by the CSS purists, you'd be forgiven for thinking that the image is soon to be a thing of the past, eschewed in favor of clean, standards-compliant, CSS-formatted, text-based design. However, while sites that rely entirely on sliced-up images are beginning to look a little dated in comparison with the clean simplicity of the CSS layout "style," well-placed images can bring an otherwise commonplace design to life. And, as designers begin to push the boundaries of what can be achieved with standards-compliant semantic markup, sites that have managed to combine semantics and beauty are becoming much more commonplace.

Working with images in CSS requires a few simple skills, which can then be combined to create interesting effects. The solutions in this chapter demonstrate the basic concepts of working with images while answering some common questions. However, as with most of the solutions in this book, don't be afraid to experiment and see what unique effects you can create.

How do I add a border to images?

Photographic images, perhaps used to illustrate an article, or as a display in a photo album, look neat when bordered with a thin line. However, opening each shot in a graphics program to add the border is a time consuming process and, if you ever need to change that border's color or thickness, you'll need to go through the same arduous process all over again to create the desired images.

Solution

Adding a border to an image is a simple procedure using CSS. There are two images in the document displayed in Figure 3.1.

Figure 3.1. Images are displayed in a Web browser.

```
img {
  border-width: 1px;
  border-style: solid;
  border-color: #000000;
}
```

This code could also be written as follows:

```
img {
  border: 1px solid #000000;
}
```

In Figure 3.2, you can see the effect this has on the images.

Figure 3.2. The images look neater once the CSS border is applied.

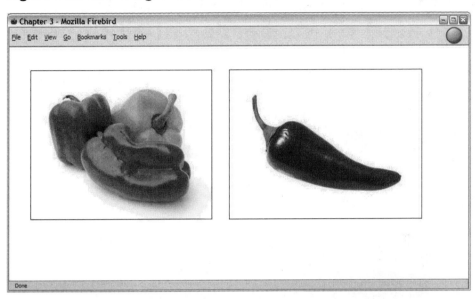

Your layout probably contains images to which you don't really want to apply a permanent black border. You can create a CSS class for the border and apply it to selected images as required.

```css
.imgborder {
  border: 1px solid #000000;
}
```

```html
<img src="myfish.jpg" alt="My Fish" class="imgborder" />
```

If you have a whole selection of images—such as a photograph album—on the page, you could set borders on all the images within a container.

File: **imageborders.css** (excerpt)

```css
#album img {
  border: 1px solid #000000;
}
```

This approach will save you having to add the class to each individual image within the container.

How do I use CSS to replace the deprecated HTML border attribute on images?

If you're anything like me, adding `border="0"` to images that are links to other documents is probably something you do almost automatically. Using the `border` attribute of the `<img>` tag is the way in which we all learned to ensure that an ugly blue border didn't appear around our navigation buttons and so on. However, `border` has been deprecated in the current versions of HTML and XHTML.

Solution

Just as you can create a border, so you can remove one. Setting an image's `border` property to `none` will remove those ugly borders.

```css
img {
  border: none;
}
```

How do I set a background image for my page with CSS?

Before CSS, backgrounds were added using the `background` attribute of the `<body>` tag. This attribute is now deprecated and replaced by CSS properties.

Solution

File: **backgrounds.css**

```css
body {
  background-color: #ffffff;
  background-image: url(peppers_bg.jpg);
  background-repeat: no-repeat;
}
```

The above rules add the image `peppers_bg.jpg` as a background to any page to which this style sheet is attached, as shown in Figure 3.3.

Figure 3.3. A standard image is displayed as a background image.

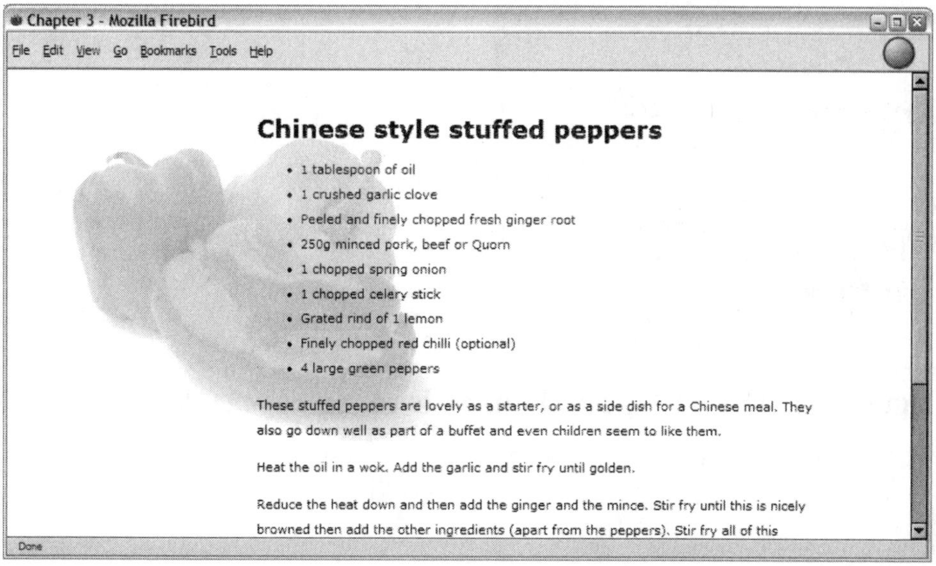

Discussion

The CSS property background-image enables you to specify as a URL the location of a background image. By default, the background will tile as shown in Figure 3.4.

As we don't want multiple peppers in this example, we need to prevent this image from tiling. To do so, we set the property background-repeat to no-repeat. Other values for background-repeat are:

repeat   This default value causes the image to tile across and down the page, as shown in Figure 3.4.

repeat-x   The image tiles across the page in a single row of images, as shown in Figure 3.5.

repeat-y   The image tiles down the page in a single column, as shown in Figure 3.6.

Figure 3.4. A background image is set to repeat by default.

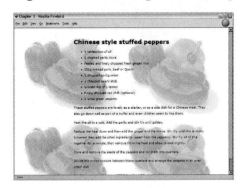

Figure 3.5. The background image is set to repeat-x.

Figure 3.6. The background image is set to repeat-y.

How do I position my background image?

By default, if you add a single, non-repeating background image to the page, it will appear in the top left corner of the viewport. If you have set the background to tile in any direction, the first image will appear at that location, and will tile from that point. However, it is also possible for the image to be displayed any-where else on the page.

Solution

To position the image, we need to use the CSS property background-position.

File: **backgroundposition.css** (excerpt)

```
body {
  background-color: #FFFFFF;
  background-image: url(peppers_bg.jpg);
  background-repeat: no-repeat;
  background-position: center center;
}
```

The above CSS will center the image on the page as shown in Figure 3.7.

Figure 3.7. The background-position property can be used to center the image.

Discussion

The `background-position` property can take as values keywords, percentage values, or values in units, such as pixels.

Keywords

In the example above, we used keywords to specify that the background image should be displayed in the center of the page.

File: **backgroundposition.css (excerpt)**

```
background-position: center center;
```

Keyword combinations that you can use are:

- ☐ `top left`

- ☐ `top center`

- ☐ `top right`

- ☐ `center left`

- ☐ `center center`

- ☐ `center right`

- ☐ `bottom left`

- ☐ `bottom center`

- ☐ `bottom right`

If you only specify one of the values, the other will default to center.

```
background-position: top;
```

The above code is the same as the following:

```
background-position: top center;
```

Percentage Values

To ensure more accurate image placement, you can specify the values as percentages. This is particularly useful in a liquid layout where other page elements are specified in percentages so that they resize in accordance with the user's screen resolution and size.

```
background-position: 30% 80%;
```

The first of the two percentages included here refers to the horizontal position; the second is the vertical position. Percentages are taken from the top left corner, with 0% 0% placing the top left corner of the image against the top left corner of the browser window, and 100% 100% placing the bottom right corner of the image against the bottom right corner of the window.

As with keywords, a default value comes into play if you only specify one value. That default is 50%.

```
background-position: 30%;
```

The above code is, therefore, the same as that shown below:

```
background-position: 30% 50%;
```

Unit Values

You can set the values using any CSS units, such as pixels or ems.

```
background-position: 20px 20px;
```

Just as with percentages, the first value dictates the horizontal position, while the second dictates the vertical. But unlike percentages, the measurements directly control the position of the top left corner of the background image.

You can mix units with percentages and, if you only specify one value, the second will default to 50%.

How do I make a background image that stays still while the text moves when the page is scrolled?

You may have seen sites where the background image remains static while the content scrolls over it. This effect is achieved using CSS.

Solution

File: **backgroundfixed.html** (excerpt)

```
body {
  background-color: #FFFFFF;
  background-image: url(peppers_bg.jpg);
  background-repeat: no-repeat;
  background-position: 20px 20px;
  background-attachment: fixed;
}
```

Figure 3.8. The background image is fixed and doesn't scroll off the page with the content.

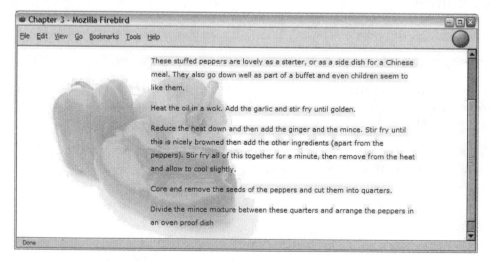

We can use the property background-attachment with a value of fixed to fix the background so that it doesn't move with the content, as shown in Figure 3.8.

Discussion

In this solution, we're using several CSS properties to add our image to the background, position it, and detail how it behaves when the document is scrolled. It is also possible to use a shorthand method to write out this information, applying the CSS property, background. This property allows you to declare background-color, background-image, background-repeat, background-attachment and background-position in a single property declaration.

Take, for example, the CSS declarations shown below:

File: **backgroundfixed.css (excerpt)**

```
body {
  background-color: #FFFFFF;
  background-image: url(peppers_bg.jpg);
  background-repeat: no-repeat;
  background-attachment: fixed;
  background-position: 20px 20px;
}
```

These could also be written as follows:

```
body {
  background: #ffffff url(peppers_bg.jpg) no-repeat fixed 20px
    20px;
}
```

How do I set background images for other elements?

In this chapter, we've already looked at setting background images for the document. However, background images can be used on other elements, too.

Solution

File: **backgrounds2.css (excerpt)**

```
#smallbox {
  background-image: url(mini_chilli.jpg);
```

```
    background-repeat: repeat-y;
    float: left;
    padding-left: 60px;
    margin-right: 20px;
    width: 220px;
    border: 1px solid #F5C9C9;
}
```

The red chillies appearing down the left-hand side of the box in Figure 3.9 comprise a background that's created by tiling the background image on the y-axis. The background image shown here is applied to a <div>, along with other rules, to create the box.

Figure 3.9. The chilli image is a tiled background image.

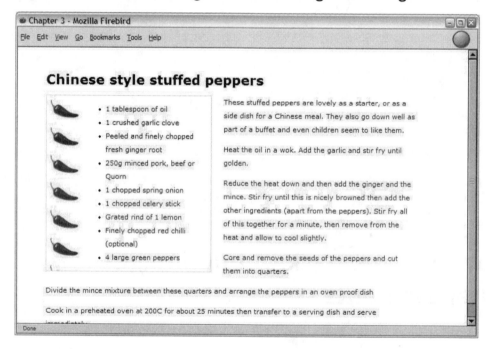

Discussion

Background images can be used on any page element. You can apply a background to a heading, as shown in Figure 3.10:

File: **backgrounds2.html** (excerpt)

```
<h1 class="header">Chinese style stuffed peppers</h1>
```

File: **backgrounds2.css** (excerpt)

```
.header {
  background-image: url(dotty.gif);
  width: 400px;
  height: 30px;
  padding: 6px 6px 4px 8px;
  color: #B22222;
  background-color: transparent;
}
```

Figure 3.10. The heading has a background image.

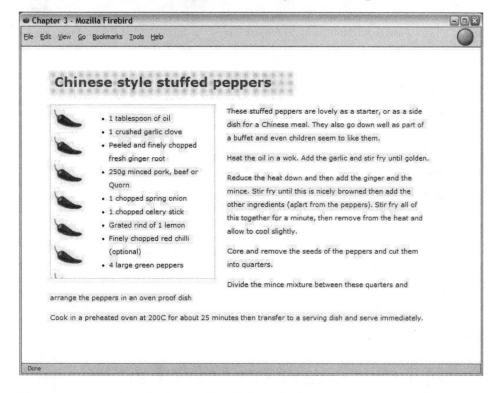

You can even apply a background to links, which can assist you in making some interesting effects, as in Figure 3.11.

File: **backgrounds2.css (excerpt)**

```
a:link, a:visited {
  color: #B22222;
  background-color: transparent;
  font-weight: bold;
}
a:hover {
  background-image: url(dotty.gif);
  text-decoration: none;
}
```

Figure 3.11. A background image is applied to the link on hover.

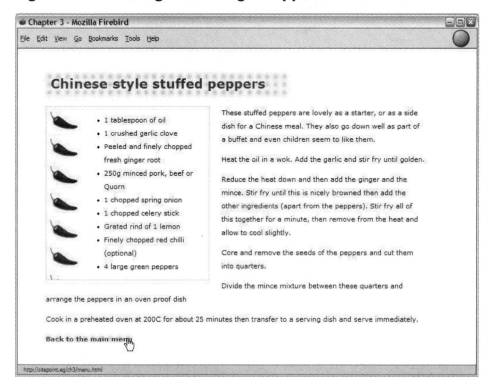

How do I place text on top of an image?

In the bad old pre-CSS days, the only way to add text to an image was to add the text in your graphics program! CSS provides far better means to achieve this effect.

Solution

The easiest way to layer text on top of an image is to make the image a background image. The chilli image beneath the list of ingredients shown in Figure 3.12 is added using the following properties:

File: **backgrounds3.css** (excerpt)

```
background-image: url(chilli2.jpg);
background-repeat: no-repeat;
```

Figure 3.12. The chilli image is a background image.

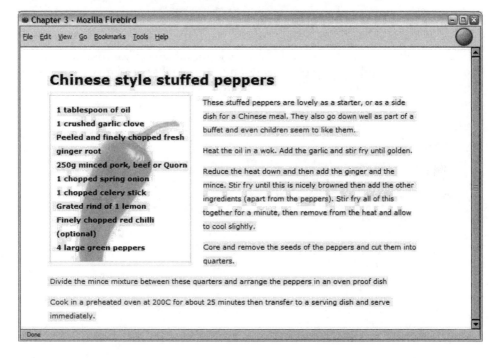

Discussion

Using CSS to lay text over images has many advantages over the process of simply adding the text to the image in a graphics program.

First, it's more difficult to change text that is part of a graphic. To do so, you need to find the original graphic, edit it in a graphics program, and upload it every time you need to change the text.

Second, text is far more accessible as text content than as part of an image. Browsers that don't support images will still be able to read text that has been added as CSS. This also benefits your search engine ranking—search engines can't index text that's part of an image, but will see text laid over an image as regular text, and index it accordingly.

How do I add more than one background image to my document?

It isn't possible to add more than one background image to your document. However, it is possible to give the effect of multiple background images by applying a background to elements that are nested, such as the <html> tag and the <body> tag.

File: **backgrounds4.css (excerpt)**

```css
html {
  background-image: url(mini_chilli.jpg);
  background-repeat: repeat-y;
  background-position: 2px 2px;
  background-attachment: fixed;
}
body {
  background-image: url(peppers_bg.jpg);
  background-repeat: no-repeat;
  background-position: 80px 20px;
}
```

This effect can be seen in Figure 3.13.

Figure 3.13. Background images are applied to the `<html>` and `<body>` elements.

Discussion

This simple example can form the basis of more complex effects using multiple background images. As you've seen through the examples in this chapter, a background image can be applied to any element on the page. The careful and creative use of images in this way can create many interesting visual effects while maintaining the accessibility of the document (as the background images will not interfere with the document's structure).

Many of the entries in the CSS Zen garden[1] rely on such careful use of background images to achieve their layouts.

Summary

This chapter has explained the answers to some common image-related questions. There are, of course, going to be image-related questions all through this book.

---

[1] http://www.csszengarden.com/

In particular, the chapters that deal with positioning will explore the positioning of images along with other elements on the page.

4

Navigation

Unless you limit yourself to one-page Web sites, you will need to design navigation. In fact, navigation is among the most important parts of any Web design, and requires a great deal of thought if visitors are to get around your site easily.

Making site navigation easy is one area in which CSS really comes into its own. Older methods of creating navigation tended to rely on lots of images, nested tables and JavaScript—all of which can seriously affect the usability and accessibility of a site. If your site cannot be navigated using a device that doesn't support JavaScript, for example, not only are you blocking users who have turned JavaScript off, you're also locking out text-only devices such as screen readers, and search engine robots—they'll never get past your home page to index the content of your site. If your design clients don't care about accessibility, tell them their clunky menu is stopping them from achieving a decent search engine ranking!

CSS allows you to create attractive navigation that is, in reality, no more than text—text that can be marked up in such a way as to ensure that it's both accessible and understandable by all those who can't physically see your design, but still want to get to your content. In this chapter, we'll look at a variety of solutions. Some are suited to implementation on an existing site, to make it load more quickly, and boost its accessibility by replacing an old-fashioned, image-based navigation. Others are more suited to being incorporated within a pure CSS layout.

How do I replace image-based navigation with CSS?

Creating an image as a navigation "button" is still a common way to design the navigation for a site. The images usually contain text to show where each navigation item leads. There are a variety of problems associated with using images for navigation buttons:

- ❑ To add a new item, a new image must be created. If, at this point, you discover that you've lost the original Photoshop file, you must recreate the whole navigation from scratch!

- ❑ Imagine your navigation is created dynamically, perhaps using database content. While it's possible to create new images on the fly, someone will have to write a whole lot more code to integrate them onto every page!

- ❑ Users who have turned images off, or use devices such as screen readers, will be unable to read the text within the button.

- ❑ Additional images slow page load times.

Solution

Using CSS, you can replace much image-based navigation with text styled using CSS. The following CSS and HTML creates a simple navigation menu by styling the cells of a table and the links within them.

File: **replaceimages.html**

```
<!DOCTYPE html PUBLIC "-//W3C//DTD XHTML 1.0 Transitional//EN"
    "http://www.w3.org/TR/xhtml1/DTD/xhtml1-transitional.dtd">
<html xmlns="http://www.w3.org/1999/xhtml">
<head>
<title>Replace images</title>
<meta http-equiv="content-type"
    content="text/html; charset=iso-8859-1" />
<link rel="stylesheet" type="text/css" href="replaceimages.css" />
</head>
<body>
<table id="navigation">
  <tr>
    <td>
```

```
      <a href="#">Recipes</a>
    </td>
  </tr>
  <tr>
    <td>
      <a href="#">Contact Us</a>
    </td>
  </tr>
  <tr>
    <td>
      <a href="#">Articles</a>
    </td>
  </tr>
  <tr>
    <td>
      <a href="#">Buy Online</a>
    </td>
  </tr>
</table>
</body>
</html>
```

File: **replaceimages.css**

```
#navigation {
  width: 180px;
  padding: 0;
  margin: 0;
  border-collapse: collapse;
}
#navigation td {
  height: 26px;
  border-bottom: 2px solid #460016;
  background-color: #FFDFEA;
  color: #460016;
}
#navigation a:link, #navigation a:visited {
  margin-left: 12px;
  color: #460016;
  background-color: transparent;
  font-size: 12px;
  font-family: Arial, Helvetica, sans-serif;
  text-decoration: none;
  font-weight: bold;
}
```

This technique could be used to ease the maintenance of an existing site by allowing the addition of new menu items without the need to create new images, and by reducing load times.

Discussion

CSS can be used to create attractive navigation systems through the simple styling of plain text. Figure 4.1 shows a menu created by inserting images into table cells—a common way to create a site menu.

Figure 4.1. Images are commonly used to create navigation.

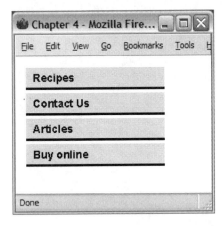

The markup for this table is as follows.

```
<table width="180" cellpadding="0" cellspacing="0">
  <tr>
    <td>
      <a href="#"><img src="images/nav1.gif" width="180"
          height="28" alt="Recipes" border="0" /></a>
    </td>
  </tr>
  <tr>
    <td>
      <a href="#"><img src="images/nav2.gif" width="180"
          height="28" alt="Contact Us" border="0" /></a>
    </td>
  </tr>
  <tr>
    <td>
```

```
     <a href="#"><img src="images/nav3.gif" width="180"
          height="28" alt="Articles" border="0" /></a>
   </td>
  </tr>
  <tr>
    <td>
      <a href="#"><img src="images/nav4.gif" width="180"
          height="28" alt="Buy Online" border="0" /></a>
    </td>
  </tr>
</table>
```

By removing the images and replacing them with text for each navigation item, we immediately make our code smaller and the page more accessible. However, simply using plain text doesn't do much for the appearance of the page, as you can see in Figure 4.2.

Figure 4.2. The navigation system looks bland when images are removed.

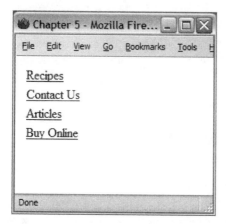

We can use CSS to recreate the look of this menu without the images. First, let's give the navigation table an ID. This will enable us to identify it within the document, and create CSS selectors for the elements within that table.

We can create CSS for the ID navigation, which means that we can also lose the attributes from the <table> tag.

File: **replaceimages.html (excerpt)**

```
<table id="navigation">
```

Here's the CSS that controls how the table as a whole looks:

File: **replaceimages.css (excerpt)**

```
#navigation {
  width: 180px;
  padding: 0;
  margin: 0;
  border-collapse: collapse;
}
```

Setting the `border-collapse` property to `collapse` causes the cells of the table to stick together, with only a single border between cells. The default behavior of table cells is for each cell to have its own border, with additional margins between cells.

We now need to style the `<td>` tags in the table. We want to give the cells the desired background color, and to add a bottom border to each:

File: **replaceimages.css (excerpt)**

```
#navigation td {
  height: 26px;
  border-bottom: 2px solid #460016;
  background-color: #FFDFEA;
  color: #460016;
}
```

It's already looking pretty good, as you can see in Figure 4.3.

Figure 4.3. The new styles are applied to the navigation.

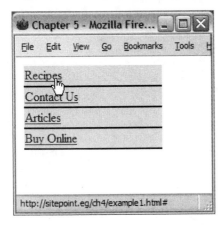

Now we must create CSS for the links within the table cells. We need to set a left margin to move the text away from the edge of the cell; to define a color, size, font family and weight; and to remove the underline from the link.

File: **replaceimages.css** (excerpt)

```
#navigation a:link, #navigation a:visited {
  margin-left: 12px;
  color: #460016;
  background-color: transparent;
  font-size: 12px;
  font-family: Arial, Helvetica, sans-serif;
  text-decoration: none;
  font-weight: bold;
}
```

Figure 4.4 shows the finished effect.

Figure 4.4. The navigation is created using CSS instead of images.

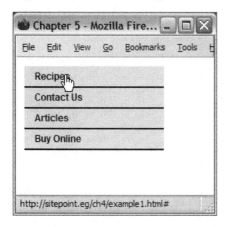

How do I style a structural list as a navigation menu?

The previous example illustrated the use of CSS to create navigation elements within a table. That method proves very useful where you are retrofitting an existing site to improve its accessibility and load time but, for new sites, you're likely to be trying to avoid using tables for layout, or using them only where it's absolutely necessary. Therefore, a navigation solution that doesn't require the use of tables is useful; by eradicating the table tags, you'll find that your page contains far less markup as well.

Solution

Navigation is simply a list of places that users can visit on the site. Therefore, a list is the ideal way to mark up your navigation. The navigation in Figure 4.5 is created using CSS to style a list.

Figure 4.5. Navigation can be created by styling a list.

File: **listnav1.html**

```
<!DOCTYPE html PUBLIC "-//W3C//DTD XHTML 1.0 Transitional//EN"
    "http://www.w3.org/TR/xhtml1/DTD/xhtml1-transitional.dtd">
<html xmlns="http://www.w3.org/1999/xhtml">
<head>
<title>Lists as navigation</title>
<meta http-equiv="content-type"
    content="text/html; charset=iso-8859-1" />
<link rel="stylesheet" type="text/css" href="listnav1.css" />
</head>
<body>
<div id="navigation">
  <ul>
    <li><a href="#">Recipes</a></li>
    <li><a href="#">Contact Us</a></li>
    <li><a href="#">Articles</a></li>
    <li><a href="#">Buy Online</a></li>
  </ul>
```

```
    </div>
  </body>
</html>
```

File: **listnav1.css**

```
#navigation {
  width: 200px;
  font-family: Arial, Helvetica, sans-serif;
}
#navigation ul {
  list-style: none;
  margin: 0;
  padding: 0;
}
#navigation li {
  border-bottom: 1px solid #ED9F9F;
}
#navigation li a {
  display: block;
  padding: 5px 5px 5px 0.5em;
  border-left: 12px solid #711515;
  border-right: 1px solid #711515;
  background-color: #B51032;
  color: #FFFFFF;
  text-decoration: none;
}
```

Discussion

To create navigation based on a list, first create your list, placing each navigation link inside an <li> tag.

File: **listnav1.html (excerpt)**

```
<ul>
  <li><a href="#">Recipes</a></li>
  <li><a href="#">Contact Us</a></li>
  <li><a href="#">Articles</a></li>
  <li><a href="#">Buy Online</a></li>
</ul>
```

Wrap this list in a <div> with an appropriate ID.

File: **listnav1.html (excerpt)**

```
<div id="navigation">
  <ul>
```

```
    <li><a href="#">Recipes</a></li>
    <li><a href="#">Contact Us</a></li>
    <li><a href="#">Articles</a></li>
    <li><a href="#">Buy Online</a></li>
  </ul>
</div>
```

As Figure 4.6 shows, this looks pretty ordinary with the browser's default styles applied.

Figure 4.6. An unstyled list is very basic.

The first thing we need to do is style the container in which the navigation sits, in this case, #navigation:

File: **listnav1.css (excerpt)**

```
#navigation {
  width: 200px;
  font-family: Arial, Helvetica, sans-serif;
}
```

I have given #navigation a width and a font family. If this were part of a CSS page layout, I'd probably add some positioning information to this ID as well.

Next, we style the list:

File: **listnav1.css (excerpt)**

```
#navigation ul {
  list-style: none;
  margin: 0;
```

```
    padding: 0;
}
```

As Figure 4.7 illustrates, the above rule removes list bullets and the indented margin that browsers apply, by default, when displaying a list.

Figure 4.7. The list's indentation and bullets have been removed.

The next step is to style the `<li>` tags within `#navigation`, to give them a bottom border:

File: **listnav1.css (excerpt)**

```
#navigation li {
  border-bottom: 1px solid #ED9F9F;
}
```

Finally, we style the link itself:

File: **listnav1.css (excerpt)**

```
#navigation li a:link, #navigation li a:visited  {
  display: block;
  padding: 5px 5px 5px 0.5em;
  border-left: 12px solid #711515;
  border-right: 1px solid #711515;
  background-color: #B51032;
  color: #FFFFFF;
  text-decoration: none;
}
```

Most of the work is done here, creating CSS rules to add left and right borders, removing the underline, and so on. The first property declaration in this rule sets the `display` property to `block`. This causes the link to display as a block element, meaning that the whole area of the navigation "button" is active when you hold your cursor over it—the same effect you'd see if you used an image for the navigation.

How do I use CSS to create rollover navigation without images or JavaScript?

Site navigation often features a rollover effect—when a user holds the cursor over a button, it displays a new image, creating a "highlight" effect. To achieve this effect using image-based navigation, you'd need to use two images and JavaScript.

Solution

Using CSS for your navigation makes the creation of attractive rollover effects far simpler than it would be if you used images. The CSS rollover is created using the `:hover` pseudo-class selector, just as you'd use to style a hover state for your links.

Using the above list navigation example, we could add the following markup to create a rollover effect:

File: **listnav2.css (excerpt)**

```
#navigation li a:hover {
  background-color: #711515;
  color: #FFFFFF;
}
```

Figure 4.8 shows what the menu looks like with the mouse cursor over the first menu item.

Figure 4.8. The CSS navigation shows a rollover effect.

Discussion

The CSS we used to create this effect is very simple. You can create hover states for heavily-styled links just as you can for standard links. In this example, I simply changed the background color to make it the same as the left hand border; however, you could alter the background, text and border color to create interesting effects for the navigation.

Hover Here? Hover There!

In Mozilla, you can apply the :hover pseudo-selector to any element you like, but in Internet Explorer it can only be applied to links.

Can I use CSS and lists to create a navigation system with sub-navigation?

The previous examples in this chapter have assumed that you only have one level of navigation to display. Sometimes more than one level is necessary—but is it possible using CSS styled lists?

Solution

A list with a sub-list is the perfect way to display navigation with sub-navigation. The two levels will be easy to understand when marked up in this way, even in browsers that don't support CSS.

To produce multilevel navigation, we can edit the above example single-level navigation to add a nested list and some more CSS:

File: **listnav_sub.html**

```
<!DOCTYPE html PUBLIC "-//W3C//DTD XHTML 1.0 Transitional//EN"
    "http://www.w3.org/TR/xhtml1/DTD/xhtml1-transitional.dtd">
<html xmlns="http://www.w3.org/1999/xhtml">
<head>
<title>Lists as navigation</title>
<meta http-equiv="content-type"
    content="text/html; charset=iso-8859-1" />
<link rel="stylesheet" type="text/css" href="listnav_sub.css" />
</head>
<body>
<div id="navigation">
  <ul>
    <li><a href="#">Recipes</a>
      <ul>
        <li><a href="#">Starters</a></li>
        <li><a href="#">Main Courses</a></li>
        <li><a href="#">Desserts</a></li>
      </ul>
    </li>
    <li><a href="#">Contact Us</a></li>
    <li><a href="#">Articles</a></li>
    <li><a href="#">Buy Online</a></li>
  </ul>
</div>
</body>
</html>
```

File: **listnav_sub.css**

```
#navigation {
  width: 200px;
  font-family: Arial, Helvetica, sans-serif;
}
#navigation ul {
  list-style: none;
```

```
  margin: 0;
  padding: 0;
}
#navigation li {
  border-bottom: 1px solid #ED9F9F;
}
#navigation li a:link, #navigation li a:visited  {
  display: block;
  padding: 5px 5px 5px 0.5em;
  border-left: 12px solid #711515;
  border-right: 1px solid #711515;
  background-color: #B51032;
  color: #FFFFFF;
  text-decoration: none;
}
#navigation li a:hover {
  background-color: #711515;
  color: #FFFFFF;
}
#navigation ul ul {
  margin-left: 12px;
}
#navigation ul ul li {
  border-bottom: 1px solid #711515;
  margin:0;
}
#navigation ul ul a:link, #navigation ul ul a:visited {
  background-color: #ED9F9F;
  color: #711515;
}
#navigation ul ul a:hover {
  background-color: #711515;
  color: #FFFFFF;
}
```

The result is shown in Figure 4.9.

Discussion

Nested lists are a perfect way to describe the navigation that we're using here. The first list contains the main sections of the site; the sub-list under "Recipes" shows the sub-sections within the Recipes category. Even without CSS, the structure of this list is still apparent and comprehensible, as you can see in Figure 4.10.

Figure 4.9. This CSS list navigation contains sub-navigation.

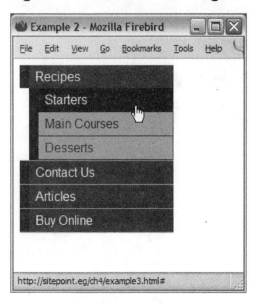

Figure 4.10. The navigation makes sense without the CSS.

The HTML that marks up this list simply nests the sub-list inside the `<li>` tag of the appropriate main item.

```
<ul>
  <li><a href="#">Recipes</a>
    <ul>
      <li><a href="#">Starters</a></li>
      <li><a href="#">Main Courses</a></li>
      <li><a href="#">Desserts</a></li>
    </ul>
  </li>
  <li><a href="#">Contact Us</a></li>
  <li><a href="#">Articles</a></li>
  <li><a href="#">Buy Online</a></li>
</ul>
```

Without any changes to the CSS, the menu will now display as shown in Figure 4.11, where the `<li>` tags inherit the styles of the main menu.

Figure 4.11. The sub-list has taken on the styles of the main navigation.

Let's add CSS for the nested list to show visually that it is a submenu, and not part of the main navigation.

File: **listnav_sub.css** (excerpt)

```
#navigation ul ul {
  margin-left: 12px;
}
```

The above will indent the `subnav` so that it's in line with the end of the border on the main menu, as you can see in Figure 4.12.

Figure 4.12. Indent the sub-navigation.

Add some simple styles to the `<li>` and `<a>` tags within the nested list to complete the effect:

File: **listnav_sub.css** (excerpt)

```css
#navigation ul ul li {
  border-bottom: 1px solid #711515;
  margin:0;
}
#navigation ul ul a:link, #navigation ul ul a:visited {
  background-color: #ED9F9F;
  color: #711515;
}
#navigation ul ul a:hover {
  background-color: #711515;
  color: #FFFFFF;
}
```

How do I make a horizontal menu using CSS and lists?

All the examples we've seen in this chapter have dealt with vertical navigation—the kind of navigation that will most likely be found in a column to the left or right of a site's main content area. However, site navigation is also commonly found as a horizontal menu close to the top of the document.

Solution

As shown in Figure 4.13, this type of menu can be created using CSS-styled lists. The `<li>` tags must be set to display inline so that each list item does not move onto the next line.

Figure 4.13. Use CSS to create horizontal list navigation.

File: **listnav_horiz.html**

```
<!DOCTYPE html PUBLIC "-//W3C//DTD XHTML 1.0 Transitional//EN"
    "http://www.w3.org/TR/xhtml1/DTD/xhtml1-transitional.dtd">
<html xmlns="http://www.w3.org/1999/xhtml">
<head>
<title>Lists as navigation</title>
<meta http-equiv="content-type"
    content="text/html; charset=iso-8859-1" />
<link rel="stylesheet" type="text/css" href="listnav_horiz.css" />
</head>
<body>
<div id="navigation">
  <ul>
    <li><a href="#">Recipes</a></li>
    <li><a href="#">Contact Us</a></li>
```

```
    <li><a href="#">Articles</a></li>
    <li><a href="#">Buy Online</a></li>
  </ul>
</div>
</body>
</html>
```

File: **listnav_horiz.css**

```css
#navigation {
  font-family: Arial, Helvetica, sans-serif;
  font-size: .9em;
}
#navigation ul {
  list-style: none;
  margin: 0;
  padding: 0;
  padding-top: 4px;
}
#navigation li {
  display: inline;
}
#navigation a:link, #navigation a:visited {
  padding: 3px 10px 2px 10px;
  color: #FFFFFF;
  background-color: #B51032;
  text-decoration: none;
  border: 1px solid #711515;
}
#navigation a:hover {
  color: #FFFFFF;
  background-color: #711515;
}
```

Discussion

To create the horizontal navigation, we start with a list that's identical to the one we created for our vertical list menu.

File: **listnav_horiz.html** (excerpt)

```html
<div id="navigation">
  <ul>
    <li><a href="#">Recipes</a></li>
    <li><a href="#">Contact Us</a></li>
    <li><a href="#">Articles</a></li>
    <li><a href="#">Buy Online</a></li>
```

```
    </ul>
  </div>
```

We style the ID navigation to give some basic font information, as we did with the vertical navigation. In a CSS layout, this ID would probably also contain some properties to determine the navigation's position on the page.

File: **listnav_horiz.css** (excerpt)
```
#navigation {
  font-family: Arial, Helvetica, sans-serif;
  font-size: .9em;
}
```

In styling the <ul>, we remove the list bullets and default indentation applied to the list by the browser.

File: **listnav_horiz.css** (excerpt)
```
#navigation ul {
  list-style: none;
  margin: 0;
  padding: 0;
  padding-top: 4px;
}
```

The property that transforms our list from vertical to horizontal is applied to the <li> tag. After setting the display property to inline, the list looks like Figure 4.14.

File: **listnav_horiz.css** (excerpt)
```
#navigation li {
  display: inline;
}
```

Figure 4.14. The list menu displays horizontally.

All that's left for us to do is to style the links for our navigation.

File: **listnav_horiz.css (excerpt)**

```css
#navigation a:link, #navigation a:visited {
  padding: 3px 10px 2px 10px;
  color: #FFFFFF;
  background-color: #B51032;
  text-decoration: none;
  border: 1px solid #711515;
}
#navigation a:hover {
  color: #FFFFFF;
  background-color: #711515;
}
```

If you're creating boxes around each link, as I have here, remember that, in order to make more space between the text and the edge of its container, you'll need to add more left and right padding. To create more space between the navigation items, add left and right margins.

How do I create button-like navigation using CSS?

Navigation that looks to be composed of clickable buttons is a feature of many Websites. This kind of navigation is often created using images, with effects applied to make the edges look beveled and button-like. Often, an image swap JavaScript will be used so the button appears to depress when the cursor is held over it or the image is clicked.

Is it possible to create such button-like navigation systems using straight CSS? Absolutely!

Solution

Creating a button effect like that shown in Figure 4.15 is possible, and fairly straightforward, using CSS. The effect hinges on your use of the CSS border properties.

Figure 4.15. Button-style navigation can be built with CSS.

File: **listnav_button.html**

```
<!DOCTYPE html PUBLIC "-//W3C//DTD XHTML 1.0 Transitional//EN"
    "http://www.w3.org/TR/xhtml1/DTD/xhtml1-transitional.dtd">
<html xmlns="http://www.w3.org/1999/xhtml">
<head>
<title>Lists as navigation</title>
<meta http-equiv="content-type"
    content="text/html; charset=iso-8859-1" />
<link rel="stylesheet" type="text/css" href="listnav_button.css"
    />
</head>
<body>
<div id="navigation">
  <ul>
    <li><a href="#">Recipes</a></li>
    <li><a href="#">Contact Us</a></li>
    <li><a href="#">Articles</a></li>
    <li><a href="#">Buy Online</a></li>
  </ul>
</div>
</body>
</html>
```

File: **listnav_button.css**

```
#navigation {
  font-family: Arial, Helvetica, sans-serif;
  font-size: .9em;
}
#navigation ul {
  list-style: none;
  margin: 0;
  padding: 0;
  padding-top: 4px;
```

```
}
#navigation li {
  display: inline;
}
#navigation a:link, #navigation a:visited {
  margin-right: 2px;
  padding: 3px 10px 2px 10px;
  color: #A62020;
  background-color: #FCE6EA;
  text-decoration: none;
  border-top: 1px solid #FFFFFF;
  border-left: 1px solid #FFFFFF;
  border-bottom: 1px solid #717171;
  border-right: 1px solid #717171;
}
#navigation a:hover {
  border-top: 1px solid #717171;
  border-left: 1px solid #717171;
  border-bottom: 1px solid #FFFFFF;
  border-right: 1px solid #FFFFFF;
}
```

Discussion

To create this effect, we'll use the horizontal list navigation described in the previous example. However, to create the button look, we'll use different colored borders at the top and left than we do for the bottom and right sides of each button. By giving the top and left edges of the button a lighter colored border than we assign the button's bottom and right edges, we create a slightly beveled effect.

File: **listnav_button.css** (excerpt)

```
#navigation a:link, #navigation a:visited {
  margin-right: 2px;
  padding: 3px 10px 2px 10px;
  color: #A62020;
  background-color: #FCE6EA;
  text-decoration: none;
  border-top: 1px solid #FFFFFF;
  border-left: 1px solid #FFFFFF;
  border-bottom: 1px solid #717171;
  border-right: 1px solid #717171;
}
```

We reverse the border colors for the hover state, which gives the effect of the button being pressed.

File: **listnav_button.css** (excerpt)

```css
#navigation a:hover {
  border-top: 1px solid #717171;
  border-left: 1px solid #717171;
  border-bottom: 1px solid #FFFFFF;
  border-right: 1px solid #FFFFFF;
}
```

Try using heavier borders, and changing the background images on the links, to create effects that fit in with your design.

How do I create tabbed navigation with CSS?

Navigation that appears as tabs across the top of the page is becoming increasingly popular. Commonly, this effect is built with images, but it's also possible to achieve using only CSS!

Solution

The tabbed navigation shown in Figure 4.16 can be created with an advanced version of the horizontal list.

File: **tabs.html**

```html
<!DOCTYPE html PUBLIC "-//W3C//DTD XHTML 1.0 Transitional//EN"
    "http://www.w3.org/TR/xhtml1/DTD/xhtml1-transitional.dtd">
<html xmlns="http://www.w3.org/1999/xhtml">
<head>
<title>Lists as navigation</title>
<meta http-equiv="content-type"
    content="text/html; charset=iso-8859-1" />
<link rel="stylesheet" type="text/css" href="tabs.css" />
</head>
<body id="recipes">
<ul id="tabnav">
 <li class="recipes"><a href="#">Recipes</a></li>
 <li class="contact"><a href="#">Contact Us</a></li>
 <li class="articles"><a href="#">Articles</a></li>
 <li class="buy"><a href="#">Buy Online</a></li>
```

```
</ul>
<div id="content">
<h1>Recipes</h1>
<p>Lorem ipsum dolor sit amet, …</p>
</div>
</body>
</html>
```

Figure 4.16. CSS can be used to create tabbed navigation.

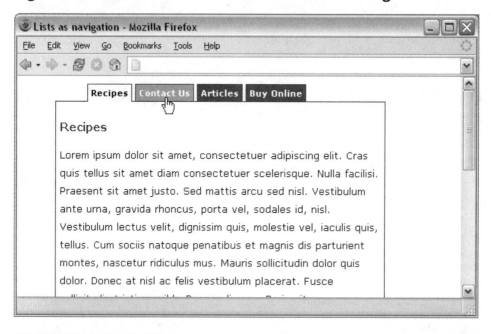

File: **tabs.css**

```
body {
    font: .8em/1.8em verdana, arial, sans-serif;
    background-color: #FFFFFF;
    margin-left: 50px;
    margin-right: 100px;
}
#content {
    border-left: 1px solid #711515;
    border-right: 1px solid #711515;
    border-bottom: 1px solid #711515;
    padding: 10px 5px 6px 5px;
}
```

```
#content h1 {
  font-size: 1.2em;
  color: #711515;
  background-color: transparent;
}
ul#tabnav {
  list-style-type: none;
  margin: 0;
  padding-left: 40px;
  padding-bottom: 24px;
  border-bottom: 1px solid #711515;
  font: bold 11px verdana, arial, sans-serif;
}
ul#tabnav li {
  float: left;
  height: 21px;
  background-color: #B51032;
  color: #FFFFFF;
  margin: 2px 2px 0 2px;
  border: 1px solid #711515;
}
ul#tabnav a:link, ul#tabnav a:visited {
  display: block;
  color: #FFFFFF;
  background-color: transparent;
  text-decoration: none;
  padding: 4px;
}
ul#tabnav a:hover {
  background-color: #F4869C;
  color: #FFFFFF;
}
body#recipes li.recipes, body#contact li.contact,
body#articles li.articles, body#buy li.buy {
  border-bottom: 1px solid #fff;
  color: #000000;
  background-color: #FFFFFF;
}
body#recipes li.recipes a:link, body#recipes li.recipes a:visited,
body#contact li.contact a:link, body#contact li.contact a:visited,
body#articles li.articles a:link,
body#articles li.articles a:visited, body#buy li.buy a:link,
body#buy li.buy a:visited {
  color: #000000;
  background-color: #FFFFFF;
}
```

Discussion

The tabbed navigation I've used here is adapted from a CSS Tabs example by Joshua Kaufman[1]. The basis for this example is the kind of simple ordered list we've seen throughout this chapter, except that each list item is assigned a **class** attribute that describes the link it contains:

File: **tabs.html** (excerpt)

```
<ul id="tabnav">
  <li class="recipes"><a href="#">Recipes</a></li>
  <li class="contact"><a href="#">Contact Us</a></li>
  <li class="articles"><a href="#">Articles</a></li>
  <li class="buy"><a href="#">Buy Online</a></li>
</ul>
```

To build the tabbed effect, first create the CSS for the <ul> with an ID of **tabnav**.

File: **tabs.css** (excerpt)

```
ul#tabnav {
  list-style-type: none;
  margin: 0;
  padding-left: 40px;
  padding-bottom: 24px;
  border-bottom: 1px solid #711515;
  font: bold 11px verdana, arial, sans-serif;
}
```

This CSS removes the bullets, controls the margin and padding, adds a bottom border to the list, and sets the desired font. Figure 4.17 shows the result so far.

[1] http://unraveled.com/projects/css_tabs/

Figure 4.17. The navigation displays after the `<ul>` is styled.

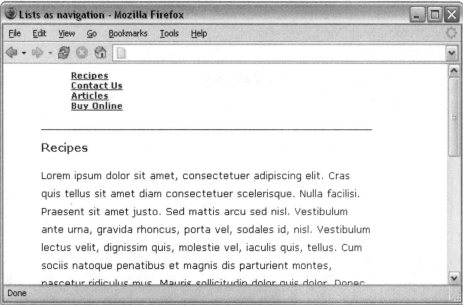

We now need to style the list items:

File: **tabs.css (excerpt)**

```
ul#tabnav li {
  float: left;
  height: 21px;
  background-color: #B51032;
  color: #FFFFFF;
  margin: 2px 2px 0 2px;
  border: 1px solid #711515;
}
```

This rule uses the `float` property to move each list item up onto the same line while maintaining its block-level status.

We also set `color` and `background-color`, and add a border, creating a visual style for the tabs. See what we have so far in Figure 4.18.

Figure 4.18. The navigation tabs reflect the new styles.

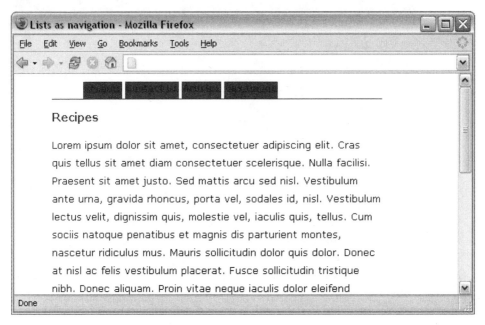

Next, we style the links, finishing the look of the tabs in their unselected state. The results are shown in Figure 4.19.

File: tabs.css (excerpt)

```css
ul#tabnav a:link, ul#tabnav a:visited {
  display: block;
  color: #FFFFFF;
  background-color: transparent;
  text-decoration: none;
  padding: 4px;
}
ul#tabnav a:hover {
  background-color: #F4869C;
  color: #FFFFFF;
}
```

Figure 4.19. Style the navigation links.

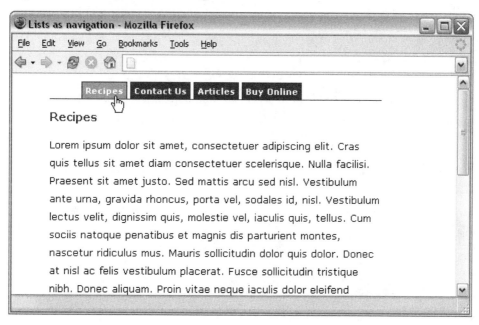

Now, to complete the tab navigation we must highlight the tab which corresponds to the page currently displayed. You'll recall that each list item has been assigned a unique class name. If we assign an ID to the `<body>` tag that matches the tab class that we wish to highlight for that page, the CSS code can do the rest of the work:

File: **tabs.html** (excerpt)

```
<body id="recipes">
```

Though bulky in the selector department (since it targets both unvisited and visited links), the CSS code that styles the tab matching the `<body>` ID is relatively straightforward:

File: **tabs.css** (excerpt)

```
body#recipes li.recipes, body#contact li.contact,
body#articles li.articles, body#buy li.buy {
  border-bottom: 1px solid #fff;
  color: #000000;
  background-color: #FFFFFF;
}
body#recipes li.recipes a:link, body#recipes li.recipes a:visited,
```

```
body#contact li.contact a:link, body#contact li.contact a:visited,
body#articles li.articles a:link,
body#articles li.articles a:visited, body#buy li.buy a:link,
body#buy li.buy a:visited {
  color: #000000;
  background-color: #FFFFFF;
}
```

With this code in place, the <body> ID recipes will cause the Recipes tab to be highlighted, contact will cause the Contact Us tab to be highlighted, and so on. The results are shown in Figure 4.20.

Figure 4.20. Highlight Contact Us by adding contact as the ID of the <body> tag.

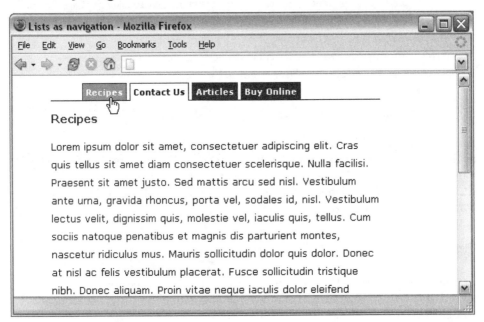

Identifying a Useful Technique

Tip

This technique of adding an ID to the <body> tag can be very useful. For example, you may have different color schemes for different sections of your site, to help the user identify which section they're in. You can simply add the section name to the <body> tag and pick it up exactly as we did in this example, within the style sheet.

To complete the tabbed navigation, we simply add a border to the content area, neatly blending with the navigation along its top.

File: **tabs.css** (excerpt)

```
#content {
  border: 1px solid #711515;
  border-top: none;
  padding: 10px 5px 6px 5px;
}
```

How do I change the cursor type?

It is usual for the browser to change the cursor to a hand icon when users move the mouse over a link on any part of the page. Occasionally—perhaps to fit in with a particular interface—you might want to change the cursor to represent something else.

Solution

Changing the cursor is achieved with the CSS property, cursor. Figure 4.21 shows this property in action.

Figure 4.21. cursor: wait causes an hourglass to display as the cursor.

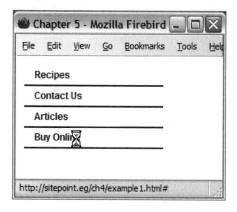

103

Table 4.1. CSS2 Standard Cursors

cursor value	Appearance (as in IE6)	IE (Win)	IE (Mac)	NS/Moz
auto	n/a	4	4	6/1
crosshair	+	4	4	6/1
default	▷	4	4	6/1
e-resize	↔	4	4	6/1
help	▷?	4	4	6/1
move	✛	4	4	6/1
n-resize	↕	4	4	6/1
ne-resize	↗	4	4	6/1
nw-resize	↖	4	4	6/1
pointer	↑	4	4	6/1
s-resize	↕	4	4	6/1
se-resize	↖	4	4	6/1
sw-resize	↗	4	4	6/1
text	I	4	4	6/1
url(*url*)	n/a	6	–	–
w-resize	↔	4	4	6/1
wait	⧗	4	4	6/1

Discussion

The cursor property can take a range of values, which create cursors commonly seen in graphical user interfaces. Changing the cursor can be a useful way to provide user feedback in a Web application that tries to create a friendly interface. For example, you might decide to use a question mark cursor to indicate help text. However, you should use this effect with care, and keep in mind the fact that people are generally used to standard browser behavior where, for instance, the cursor represents a hand icon when it's hovered over a link.

Table 4.1 lists the various properties that are available in the CSS standard, and the common browser versions that support them. Table 4.2 lists additional values that are only supported by Internet Explorer browsers.

Table 4.2. Internet Explorer-only Cursors

cursor value	Appearance (as in IE6)	IE (Win)	IE (Mac)
all-scroll		6	–
col-resize		6	–
hand		4	4
no-drop		6	–
not-allowed		6	–
progress		6	–
row-resize		6	–
vertical-text		6	–

How do I create rollovers in CSS without JavaScript?

CSS-based navigation can provide some really interesting effects, but there are still some things that require images. Is it possible to enjoy the advantages of text-based navigation, and still use images?

Solution

It is possible to combine images and CSS to create JavaScript-free rollovers. This solution is based on a technique described at wellstyled.com.[2]

---

[2] http://wellstyled.com/css-nopreload-rollovers.html

File: **images.html**

```
<!DOCTYPE html PUBLIC "-//W3C//DTD XHTML 1.0 Transitional//EN"
    "http://www.w3.org/TR/xhtml1/DTD/xhtml1-transitional.dtd">
<html xmlns="http://www.w3.org/1999/xhtml">
<head>
<title>Lists as navigation</title>
<meta http-equiv="content-type"
    content="text/html; charset=iso-8859-1" />
<link rel="stylesheet" type="text/css" href="images.css" />
</head>
<body>
<ul id="nav">
  <li><a href="#">Recipes</a></li>
  <li><a href="#">Contact Us</a></li>
  <li><a href="#">Articles</a></li>
  <li><a href="#">Buy Online</a></li>
</ul>
</body>
</html>
```

File: **images.css**

```
ul#nav {
  list-style-type: none;
  padding: 0;
  margin: 0;
}
#nav a:link, #nav a:visited {
  display: block;
  width: 150px;
  padding: 10px 0 16px 32px;
  font: bold 80% Arial, Helvetica, sans-serif;
  color: #FF9900;
  background: url("peppers.gif") top left no-repeat;
  text-decoration: none;
}
#nav a:hover {
  background-position: 0 -69px;
  color: #B51032;
}
#nav a:active {
  background-position: 0 -138px;
  color: #006E01;
}
```

The results can be seen in Figure 4.22, but since the effect is color-based I suggest you try it for yourself. Don't forget to click on a link or two!

Figure 4.22. The completed menu uses images to advantage.

Discussion

This solution offers a means of using images in your navigation without having to resort to preloading lots of separate files.

The navigation has three states. These three states are not depicted using three separate images; rather, they use one large image that contains all three images, as seen in Figure 4.23.

Figure 4.23. The pepper image contains all three states.

The navigation is marked up as a simple list.

File: **images.html (excerpt)**

```
<ul id="nav">
  <li><a href="#">Recipes</a></li>
  <li><a href="#">Contact Us</a></li>
  <li><a href="#">Articles</a></li>
  <li><a href="#">Buy Online</a></li>
</ul>
```

In the CSS, the rule for the links displays the background image. Because the image is far bigger than the area required for this element, however, we only see the first, yellow, pepper at first:

File: **images.css (excerpt)**

```
#nav a:link, #nav a:visited {
  display: block;
  width: 150px;
  padding: 10px 0 16px 32px;
  font: bold 80% Arial, Helvetica, sans-serif;
  color: #FF9900;
  background: url("peppers.gif") top left no-repeat;
  text-decoration: none;
}
```

The :hover state simply shifts the background image up a number of pixels sufficient to reveal the red pepper. I had to move it 69 pixels, but the distance you'll need to move your image will depend on the graphic itself. You could probably work it out mathematically, or you could do as I do and simply increment the image a few pixels at a time, until it appears in the right location on hover.

File: **images.css (excerpt)**

```
#nav a:hover {
  background-position: 0 -69px;
  color: #B51032;
}
```

The active state again shifts the background image, this time to display the green pepper when the link is clicked.

File: **images.css (excerpt)**

```
#nav a:active {
  background-position: 0 -138px;
  color: #006E01;
}
```

That's all there is to it! The effect can fall apart if the text is resized to a larger font, allowing the edges of the hidden images to display. You can get around that issue, to some degree, by leaving quite large spaces between the images, but this is a point to be aware of.

The site on which I found the technique we've discussed here also offers a technique that counters a flickering effect you can unwittingly achieve in Internet Explorer. In my tests, that effect tends only to be a problem when the image is larger than the ones we've used here; however, if your navigation items flicker, check out the link given above.

Summary

This chapter has discussed a range of different ways in which we can create navigation using structurally sound markup. These examples can be used as starting points for your own experiments and ideas. On existing sites, where a full redesign is not possible, switching to a CSS-based navigation system can be a good way to improve the accessibility and load speed of the site without affecting its look and feel in a big way.

5

Tabular Data

Tables have had bad press of late. Originally designed to display tabular data correctly in HTML documents, they were soon misappropriated as a way to lay out Web pages. Understanding how to create complex layouts using nested tables has become part of the standard skillset of the Web designer. However, using tables in this way requires large amounts of markup and can cause real problems for users who are trying to access your content using screen readers or other text-only devices. Thus, the Web Standards movement has pushed for the replacement of tables with CSS layout, which is designed for the job and is, ultimately, far more flexible, as we'll discover in Chapter 8.

But, what of the poor table? Is it to be relegated to out-of-date Websites gathering dust in the far corners of the 'net? Not quite! Tables are becoming less popular as a layout tool, as designers take on the newer CSS techniques for which browser support is becoming widespread. However, tables can (and should) be used for their real purpose—that of displaying tabular data.

If you have ever created tables for large amounts of data, and have styled them using font tags, you'll know how quickly they can double the length of your document markup. Whenever I come across tables that have been styled in this way (and I think I can get away with it), I'll whip out the `<font>` tags and stick them into a style sheet. Dynamically writing out data in which I have to include all these additional tags is a real nuisance—it just creates extra work. Also, CSS provides far more flexibility for styling tables than simply replicating what you used to do with `<font>` tags and the `border` and `bgcolor` attributes of `<table>` tags.

The solutions in this chapter demonstrate some of the popular ways in which we can use CSS to style tables, and address common questions that relate to this area of Web design.

How do I lay out spreadsheet data using CSS?

Solution

The quick answer is, you don't! Spreadsheet data is tabular by nature and, therefore, should be displayed in an HTML table. However, we should still be concerned about the accessibility of our tables, even when we're using them for the right kind of content.

Discussion

Tabular data is information displayed in a table, and which may be logically arranged into columns and rows.

Your accounts, stored in spreadsheet format, are a good example of tabular data. If you needed to mark up the annual accounts of an organization for which you were building a site, you might be given a spreadsheet that looked like Figure 5.1.

Figure 5.1. The accounts information displays as tabular data in Excel.

	A	B	C	D	E	F
1		1999	2000	2001	2002	
2	Grants	11,980	12,650	9,700	10,600	
3	Donations	4,780	4,989	6,700	6,590	
4	Investments	8,000	8,100	8,760	8,490	
5	Fundraising	3,200	3,120	3,700	4,210	
6	Sales	28,400	27,100	27,950	29,050	
7	Miscellaneous	2,100	1,900	1,300	1,760	
8	Total	58,460	57,859	58,110	60,700	

This is obviously tabular data. We see column and row headings, and the data in each cell relates to these headings. Ideally, we'd display this data in a table, as shown in Figure 5.2, complete with table headings to ensure that the data is structured logically.

Figure 5.2. The accounts data is formatted as an HTML table.

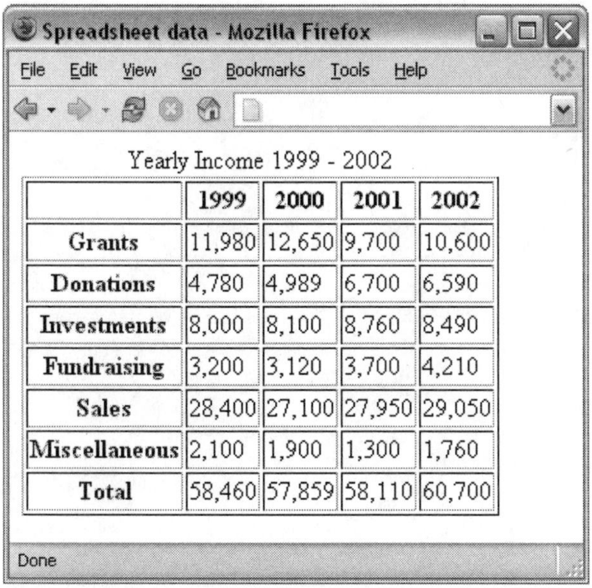

How do I ensure that my tabular data is accessible as well as attractive?

Solution

The(X)HTML table specification includes tags and attributes that go beyond the basics required to achieve a certain look. These tags can be used to ensure that the content of the table is clear when it's read out to users who can't see the layout.

File: **table.html** (excerpt)

```
<table summary="This table shows the yearly income for years 1999
    through 2002">
```

```
<caption>Yearly Income 1999 - 2002</caption>
<tr>
  <th></th>
  <th scope="col">1999</th>
  <th scope="col">2000</th>
  <th scope="col">2001</th>
  <th scope="col">2002</th>
</tr>
<tr>
  <th scope="row">Grants</th>
  <td>11,980</td>
  <td>12,650</td>
  <td>9,700</td>
  <td>10,600</td>
</tr>
<tr>
  <th scope="row">Donations</th>
  <td>4,780</td>
  <td>4,989</td>
  <td>6,700</td>
  <td>6,590</td>
</tr>
<tr>
  <th scope="row">Investments</th>
  <td>8,000</td>
  <td>8,100</td>
  <td>8,760</td>
  <td>8,490</td>
</tr>
<tr>
  <th scope="row">Fundraising</th>
  <td>3,200</td>
  <td>3,120</td>
  <td>3,700</td>
  <td>4,210</td>
</tr>
<tr>
  <th scope="row">Sales</th>
  <td>28,400</td>
  <td>27,100</td>
  <td>27,950</td>
  <td>29,050</td>
</tr>
<tr>
  <th scope="row">Miscellaneous</th>
  <td>2,100</td>
```

```
    <td>1,900</td>
    <td>1,300</td>
    <td>1,760</td>
  </tr>
  <tr>
    <th scope="row">Total</th>
    <td>58,460</td>
    <td>57,859</td>
    <td>58,110</td>
    <td>60,700</td>
  </tr>
</table>
```

Discussion

The above code creates a table that uses tags and attributes to explain clearly the content of each cell.

The summary Attribute of the <table> Tag

File: **table.html (excerpt)**

```
<table summary="This table shows the yearly income for years 1999
    through 2003">
```

The summary will not be visible on-screen for regular browsers, but will be read out to users of screen readers. The summary can be used to explain the context of the table—information that, while apparent to the sighted user with a standard browser, might be less apparent when the text is being read in a linear manner by the screen reader. Use the summary attribute to make sure that users with screen readers understand the purpose of the table.

The <caption> Tag

File: **table.html (excerpt)**

```
<caption>Yearly Income 1999 - 2002</caption>
```

The <caption> tag adds a caption to the table. By default, the browsers will generally display the caption above the table, however, you can manually set the position of the caption in relation to the table using the caption-side CSS property.

```
table {
  caption-side: bottom;
}
```

Why might you want to use a caption, instead of just adding a heading or paragraph text for display with the table? Using a caption ensures that the text is tied to the table and that it's recognized as the table's caption—there's no chance that the screen reader could interpret it as a separate element. If you want your table captions to display as paragraph text or level three headings in a graphical browser, no problem! You can create CSS rules for captions in the same way you would for any other tag.

The `<th>` Tag

```
<th scope="col">2000</th>
```

The `<th>` tag identifies data that is a row or column heading. The example code contains both row and column headings and, to ensure that this is clear, we use the `scope` attribute of the `<th>` tag. The `scope` attribute shows whether a given heading is applied to the column (`col`) or row (`row`).

Before you begin to style your tables to complement the look and feel of the site, it's good practice to ensure that those tables are accessible to users of devices such as screen readers. Accessibility is one of those things that many developers brush off, saying, "I'll check it when I'm finished." However, leave accessibility checks until the end of development and you may never get around to them; if you do, the problems they identify may well require time-consuming fixes, particularly in complex applications with many tables. Once you get into the habit of keeping accessibility in mind as you design, you'll find that it becomes second nature and adds nothing to development time.

Additionally, CSS attributes make the styling of tables used for data simple and quick. For instance, when I begin a new site on which I know I'll have to create a lot of data tables, I create a class called `.datatable`. This contains the basic styles I want to affect all data tables, and can be applied to the `table` tag of each. I then create rules for `.datatable th`, the heading cells, `.datatable td`, the regular cells, and `.datatable caption`, the table captions.

From that point, adding a new table is easy. All the styles are there—I just need to apply the class `.datatable`. And, if I decide to change the styles after I've created all the tables in my site, I simply edit my style sheet.

How do I add a border to a table without using the HTML border attribute?

Solution

The HTML border attribute doesn't create the prettiest of borders for tables, and it's deprecated in current versions of (X)HTML. You can replace this border with a CSS border, which will give you far more flexibility in terms of design.

File: **table.css (excerpt)**

```
.datatable {
  border: 1px solid #338BA6;
}
```

The above code example will display a one-pixel light blue border around your table, as in Figure 5.3.

Figure 5.3. A CSS border is applied to the table itself.

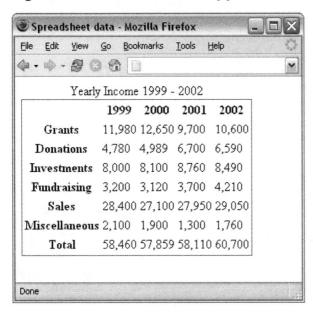

You can add borders to individual cells, as well:

File: **table.css (excerpt)**

```
.datatable td, .datatable th {
  border: 1px solid #73C0D4;
}
```

The code above renders a slightly lighter border around table cells created by `<td>` and `<th>` tags that have a class of `.datatable`, as in Figure 5.4.

Figure 5.4. A CSS border can also be applied to individual table cells.

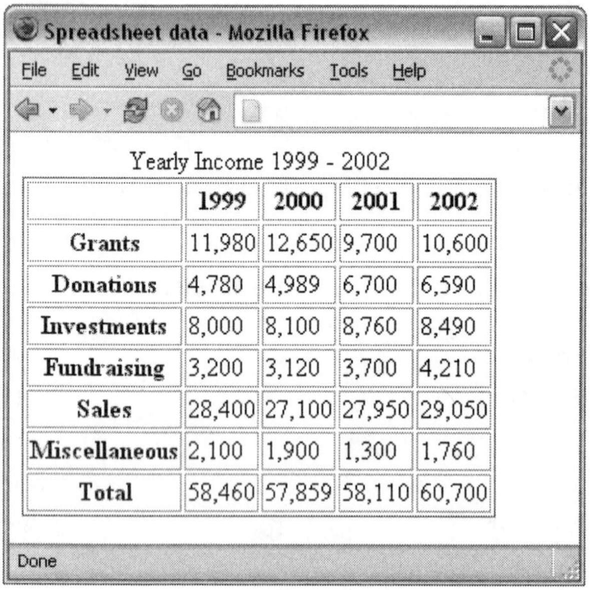

Yearly Income 1999 - 2002

	1999	2000	2001	2002
Grants	11,980	12,650	9,700	10,600
Donations	4,780	4,989	6,700	6,590
Investments	8,000	8,100	8,760	8,490
Fundraising	3,200	3,120	3,700	4,210
Sales	28,400	27,100	27,950	29,050
Miscellaneous	2,100	1,900	1,300	1,760
Total	58,460	57,859	58,110	60,700

Discussion

By experimenting with CSS borders on your tables you can create attractive effects—even if the data they contain is thoroughly dull! You can use differently colored borders for table headings and table cells, and apply various thicknesses and styles of border. You might even try out such tricks as using one shade for top and left borders, and another for bottom and right borders, creating an indented effect.

Border Styles

There is a range of different values that you can apply to the CSS `border-style` property. We've already met `solid`, which displays a solid line as the border. All of the options are shown in Table 5.1.

Table 5.1. CSS Border Style Constants

Constant	Supporting Browsers	Sample
double	All CSS browsers	double
groove		groove
inset		inset
none		none
outset		outset
ridge		ridge
solid		solid
dashed	Netscape 6, Mozilla, IE 5.5/Win, IE 4/Mac	dashed
dotted		dotted
hidden	Netscape 6, Mozilla, IE 5.5/Win, IE 4/Mac	hidden

How do I stop spaces appearing between the cells of my table when I've added borders using CSS?

If you've tried to get rid of the spaces between table cells using CSS, you might simply have set `cellspacing="0"`. This leaves you with a 2-pixel border, though, because borders touch, but don't overlap. The following solution explains how to create a neat, 1-pixel border around all cells.

Solution

You can get rid of the spaces that appear between cells applying the CSS property `border-collapse` to the table.

File: **table.css**

```
.datatable {
  border: 1px solid #338BA6;
  border-collapse: collapse;
}

.datatable td, .datatable th {
  border: 1px solid #73C0D4;
}
```

Figure 5.4 above shows a table before the `border-collapse` property is applied; Figure 5.5 shows the effect of adding this property.

Figure 5.5. The table's borders collapse.

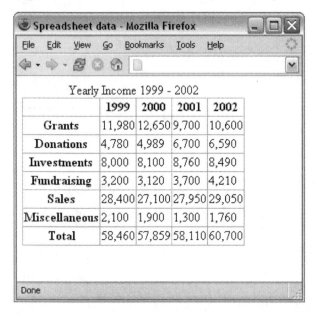

How do I display spreadsheet data in an attractive and usable way?

Solution

The (X)HTML table is the best way to display spreadsheet data; however, we can style the table using CSS, which keeps markup to a minimum and allows us to control our data table's appearance from the style sheet.

The data displayed as an HTML table earlier in this chapter is an example of spreadsheet data. That markup, shown unstyled in Figure 5.6, is the basis for the following example.

Figure 5.6. Unformatted tables are not attractive.

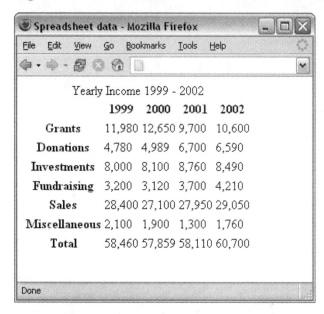

Let's apply the following style sheet to the page:

File: **spreadsheet.css**

```
p, td, th {
    font: 0.8em Verdana, Geneva, Arial, Helvetica, sans-serif;
```

```
}
.datatable {
  border: 1px solid #D6DDE6;
  border-collapse: collapse;
}
.datatable td {
  border: 1px solid #D6DDE6;
  text-align: right;
  padding: 4px;
}
.datatable th {
  border: 1px solid #828282;
  background-color: #BCBCBC;
  font-weight: bold;
  text-align: left;
  padding: 4px;
}
.datatable caption {
  font: bold 0.9em "Times New Roman", Times, serif;
  background-color: #B0C4DE;
  color: #33517A;
  padding-top: 3px;
  padding-bottom: 2px;
  border: 1px solid #789AC6;
}
```

Figure 5.7 shows the result, which is quite attractive, if I do say so myself.

Discussion

In the above solution, I aimed to display the table in a way that's similar to the appearance of a desktop spreadsheet. First, I provided a basic rule for <p>, <td> and <th> tags. This is the kind of rule that would be likely to appear in the style sheet of any CSS-styled site.

File: **spreadsheet.css** (excerpt)

```
p, td, th {
  font: 0.8em Verdana, Geneva, Arial, Helvetica, sans-serif;
}
```

Figure 5.7. The table is more attractive once it's formatted with CSS.

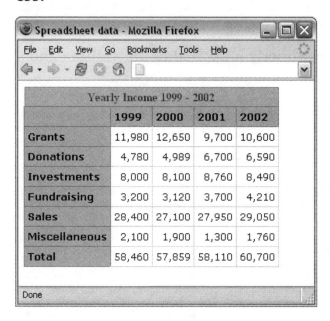

Next, I styled the table as a whole:

File: **spreadsheet.css (excerpt)**

```css
.datatable {
  border: 1px solid #D6DDE6;
  border-collapse: collapse;
}
```

As we have already seen, `border` displays a border around the outside of the table, while `border-collapse` will remove spaces between that table's cells.

Next, we turn our attention to the table cells:

File: **spreadsheet.css (excerpt)**

```css
.datatable td {
  border: 1px solid #D6DDE6;
  text-align: right;
  padding: 4px;
}
```

Here, I've added a border to the table cells and used `text-align` to right-align their contents for that nice, clean "spreadsheet look." If you preview the document at this point, you'll see a border around each cell in the table, except the header cells, as shown in Figure 5.8.

Figure 5.8. The `border` property is applied to the `<table>` and `<td>` tags.

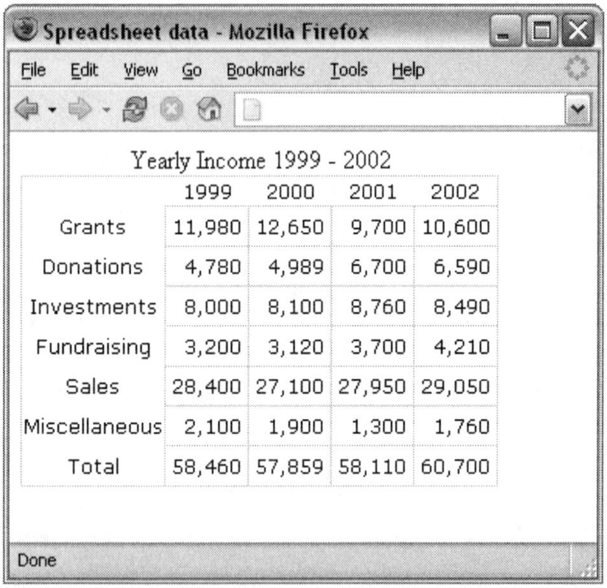

Yearly Income 1999 - 2002

	1999	2000	2001	2002
Grants	11,980	12,650	9,700	10,600
Donations	4,780	4,989	6,700	6,590
Investments	8,000	8,100	8,760	8,490
Fundraising	3,200	3,120	3,700	4,210
Sales	28,400	27,100	27,950	29,050
Miscellaneous	2,100	1,900	1,300	1,760
Total	58,460	57,859	58,110	60,700

Now, I add a border to the `<th>` (heading) cells. I use a darker color for this border, because I'm also adding a background color to these cells to highlight the fact that they're headings, not regular cells.

File: **spreadsheet.css (excerpt)**

```
.datatable th {
  border: 1px solid #828282;
  background-color: #BCBCBC;
  font-weight: bold;
  text-align: left;
  padding: 4px;
}
```

To complete my table, I style the caption to make it look like part of the table:

File: **spreadsheet.css** (excerpt)

```css
.datatable caption {
  font: bold 0.9em "Times New Roman", Times, serif;
  background-color: #B0C4DE;
  color: #33517A;
  padding-top: 3px;
  padding-bottom: 2px;
  border: 1px solid #789AC6;
}
```

How do I display table rows in alternating colors?

Solution

It can be difficult to ensure that you remain on a particular row as your eyes work across a large data table. Displaying table rows in alternating colors is a common way to help users identify which row they're focused on. Whether you're adding rows by hand, or you're displaying the data from a database, you can use CSS classes to create this effect.

Here's the table markup:

File: **alternate.html** (excerpt)

```html
<table summary="List of new students 2003" class="datatable">
  <caption>Student List</caption>
  <tr>
    <th scope="col">Student Name</th>
    <th scope="col">Date of Birth</th>
    <th scope="col">Class</th>
    <th scope="col">ID</th>
  </tr>
  <tr>
    <td>Joe Bloggs</td>
    <td>27/08/1997</td>
    <td>Mrs Jones</td>
    <td>12009</td>
  </tr>
  <tr class="altrow">
    <td>William Smith</td>
    <td>20/07/1997</td>
    <td>Mrs Jones</td>
```

```
      <td>12010</td>
    </tr>
    <tr>
      <td>Jane Toad</td>
      <td>21/07/1997</td>
      <td>Mrs Jones</td>
      <td>12030</td>
    </tr>
    <tr class="altrow">
      <td>Amanda Williams</td>
      <td>19/03/1997</td>
      <td>Mrs Edwards</td>
      <td>12021</td>
    </tr>
    <tr>
      <td>Kylie Jameson</td>
      <td>18/05/1997</td>
      <td>Mrs Jones</td>
      <td>12022</td>
    </tr>
    <tr class="altrow">
      <td>Louise Smith</td>
      <td>17/07/1997</td>
      <td>Mrs Edwards</td>
      <td>12019</td>
    </tr>
    <tr>
      <td>James Jones</td>
      <td>04/04/1997</td>
      <td>Mrs Edwards</td>
      <td>12007</td>
    </tr>
</table>
```

And the CSS to style it:

File: **alternate.css (excerpt)**

```
p, td, th {
  font: 0.8em Arial, Helvetica, sans-serif;
}
.datatable {
  border: 1px solid #D6DDE6;
  border-collapse: collapse;
  width: 80%;
}
.datatable td {
```

```
  border: 1px solid #D6DDE6;
  padding: 4px;
}
.datatable th {
  border: 1px solid #828282;
  background-color: #BCBCBC;
  font-weight: bold;
  text-align: left;
  padding-left: 4px;
}
.datatable caption {
  font: bold 0.9em Arial, Helvetica, sans-serif;
  color: #33517A;
  text-align: left;
  padding-top: 3px;
  padding-bottom: 8px;
}
.datatable tr.altrow {
  background-color: #DFE7F2;
  color: #000000;
}
```

The result can be seen in Figure 5.9.

Figure 5.9. Alternating row colors helps people use large tables of data.

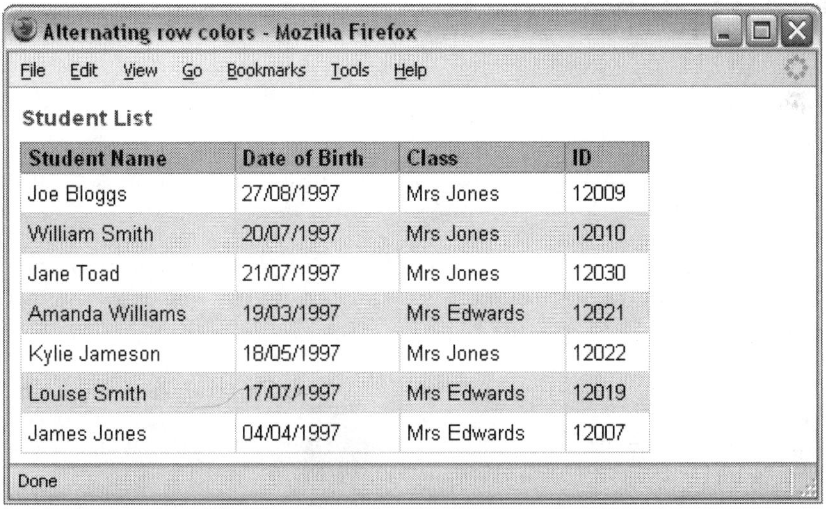

Discussion

In the HTML table above, I applied the `altrow` class to every second row:

File: **alternate.html (excerpt)**

```
<tr class="altrow">
```

In the CSS, I styled the table using properties that will be familiar if you've looked at the other solutions in this chapter. I also added the following:

File: **alternate.css (excerpt)**

```
.datatable tr.altrow {
  background-color: #DFE7F2;
  color: #000000;
}
```

This class will be applied to all `<tr>` tags with a class of `altrow` appearing within a table that has a class of `datatable`.

If you are creating your table dynamically—for instance, using ASP, PHP or a similar technology to pull data from a database—then, to create the alternating row effect, you must write this class out for every second row that you display.

How do I change a table row's background color on hover?

Solution

One way to assist readability is to change the color of a row when users mouse over it, to highlight the row they're reading (as shown in Figure 5.10).

This can be a very simple solution. In Mozilla-based browsers—Netscape 7, Firefox, etc.—all you need to do to create this effect is add the following to your CSS:

File: **alternate.css (excerpt)**

```
.datatable tr:hover {
  background-color: #DFE7F2;
  color: #000000;
}
```

Figure 5.10. A row highlights on mouseover.

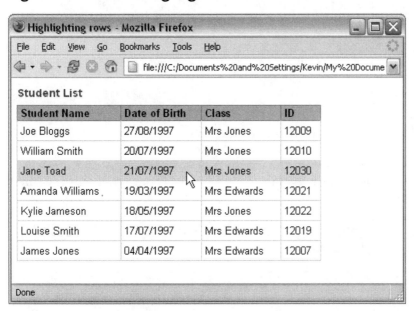

Job done! Unfortunately, `:hover` doesn't work on any element other than links in Internet Explorer (up to version 6), so, unless you're working on an intranet accessed only by Mozilla-based browsers, you'll need a way to achieve a similar effect in other browsers, too.

Using JavaScript to Change Classes

To change a row's background color on mouseover in Internet Explorer, you must first also apply the desired style properties to a CSS class, in this case `hilite`:

File: **hiliterow.css** (excerpt)

```css
.datatable tr:hover, .datatable tr.hilite {
  background-color: #DFE7F2;
  color: #000000;
}
```

Then, add the following JavaScript code to your page following the table:

File: **hiliterow.html** (excerpt)

```html
<script type="text/javascript">
var rows = document.getElementsByTagName('tr');
```

```
for (var i = 0; i < rows.length; i++) {
  rows[i].onmouseover = function() {
    this.className += ' hilite';
  }
  rows[i].onmouseout = function() {
    this.className = this.className.replace('hilite', '');
  }
}
</script>
```

This code locates all the `<tr>` tags in the document and assigns a "mouse over" and "mouse out" event handler to each. These event handlers apply the CSS `hilite` class to the rows when the mouse is placed over them, and removes it again when the mouse leaves. As shown in Figure 5.11, this produces the desired effect.

Figure 5.11. Highlighting a row in Internet Explorer is possible with the help of JavaScript.

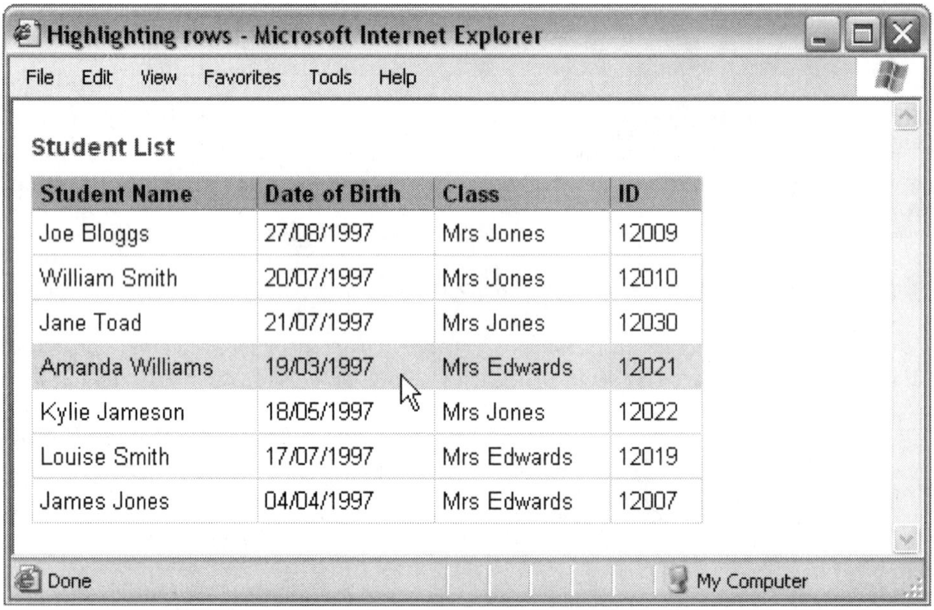

Discussion

This solution highlights (if you'll excuse the pun) one of the many areas in which Mozilla-based browsers have implemented a part of the CSS specification that Internet Explorer hasn't. In order to reproduce the effect across all browsers, we've had to use JavaScript. However, as long as your tables are clear without highlighting, this effect can be seen as "nice to have," rather than a necessary tool without which the site will be unusable (if, say, the user doesn't have JavaScript installed, or has turned off JavaScript support).

The JavaScript code works by setting the CSS class of a tag dynamically. In this case, we add the `hilite` class to a `<tr>` tag on mouseover:

File: **hiliterow.html (excerpt)**
```
rows[i].onmouseover = function() {
   this.className += ' hilite';
}
```

We then remove the class on mouseout:

File: **hiliterow.html (excerpt)**
```
rows[i].onmouseout = function() {
   this.className = this.className.replace('hilite', '');
}
```

You can create very attractive, subtle effects by changing the class of elements in response to user actions using JavaScript. Another way you could use this technique would be to highlight a box by changing the class applied to a `<div>`.

How do I display a calendar using CSS?

Calendars, such as the example from a desktop application shown in Figure 5.12, also involve tabular data. The days of the week along the top represent the headings of the columns below. Therefore, a calendar's display constitutes the legitimate use of a table, but you can keep markup to a minimum by using CSS to control the look and feel.

Figure 5.12. A calendar from a desktop application can be replicated using CSS.

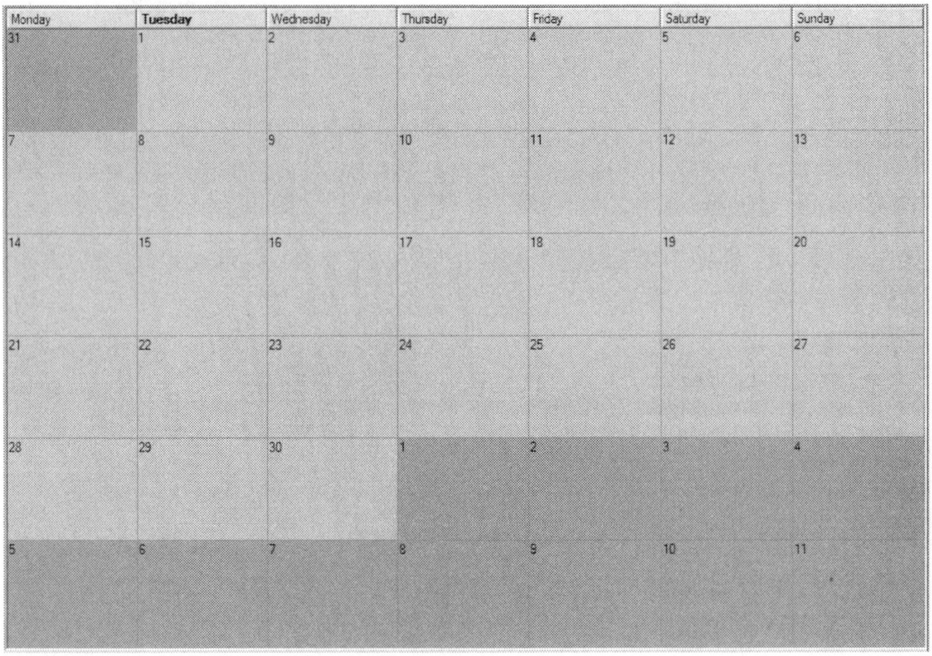

Solution

Our solution uses an accessible, simple table that leverages CSS styles to create the attractive calendar shown in Figure 5.13. Because of its simple structure, it's ideal for use in a database-driven application in which the table is created via server-side code.

File: **cal.html (excerpt)**

```
<table class="clmonth" summary="Calendar for June 2004">
<caption>June 2004</caption>
<tr>
  <th scope="col">Monday</th>
  <th scope="col">Tuesday</th>
  <th scope="col">Wednesday</th>
  <th scope="col">Thursday</th>
  <th scope="col">Friday</th>
  <th scope="col">Saturday</th>
  <th scope="col">Sunday</th>
```

```
</tr>
<tr>
  <td class="previous">31</td>
  <td class="active">1
    <ul>
      <li>New pupils open day</li>
      <li>Year 8 theatre trip</li>
    </ul>
  </td>
  <td>2</td>
  <td>3</td>
  <td>4</td>
  <td>5</td>
  <td>6</td>
</tr>
<tr>
  <td class="active">7
    <ul>
      <li>Year 7 English exam</li>
    </ul>
  </td>
  <td>8</td>
  <td>9</td>
  <td>10</td>
  <td>11</td>
  <td>12</td>
  <td>13</td>
</tr>
<tr>
  <td>14</td>
  <td>15</td>
  <td>16</td>
  <td class="active">17
    <ul>
      <li>Sports Day</li>
    </ul>
  </td>
  <td class="active">18
    <ul>
      <li>Year 7 Parents' evening</li>
      <li>Prizegiving</li>
    </ul>
  </td>
  <td>19</td>
  <td>20</td>
</tr>
```

```
<tr>
  <td>21</td>
  <td>22</td>
  <td>23</td>
  <td class="active">24
    <ul>
      <li>Year 8 parents' evening</li>
    </ul>
  </td>
  <td>25</td>
  <td>26</td>
  <td>27</td>
</tr>
<tr>
  <td>28</td>
  <td>29</td>
  <td class="active">30
    <ul>
      <li>First Night of school play</li>
    </ul>
  </td>
  <td class="next">1</td>
  <td class="next">2</td>
  <td class="next">3</td>
  <td class="next">4</td>
</tr>
</table>
```

File: **cal.css**

```
body {
  background-color: #ffffff;
  color: #000000;
  font-size: 90%;
}
.clmonth {
  border-collapse: collapse;
  width: 780px;
}
.clmonth caption {
  text-align: left;
  font: bold 110% Georgia, "Times New Roman", Times, serif;
  padding-bottom: 6px;
}
.clmonth th {
  border: 1px solid #AAAAAA;
  border-bottom: none;
```

```
  padding: 2px 8px 2px 8px;
  background-color: #CCCCCC;
  color: #3F3F3F;
  font: 80% Verdana, Geneva, Arial, Helvetica, sans-serif;
  width: 110px;
}
.clmonth td {
  border: 1px solid #EAEAEA;
  font: 80% Verdana, Geneva, Arial, Helvetica, sans-serif;
  padding: 2px 4px 2px 4px;
  vertical-align: top;
}
.clmonth td.previous, .clmonth td.next {
  background-color: #F6F6F6;
  color: #C6C6C6;
}
.clmonth td.active {
  background-color: #B1CBE1;
  color: #2B5070;
  border: 2px solid #4682B4;
}
.clmonth ul {
  list-style-type: none;
  margin: 0;
  padding-left: 12px;
  padding-right: 6px;
}
.clmonth li {
  margin-bottom: 8px;
}
```

Figure 5.13. The completed calendar is styled with CSS.

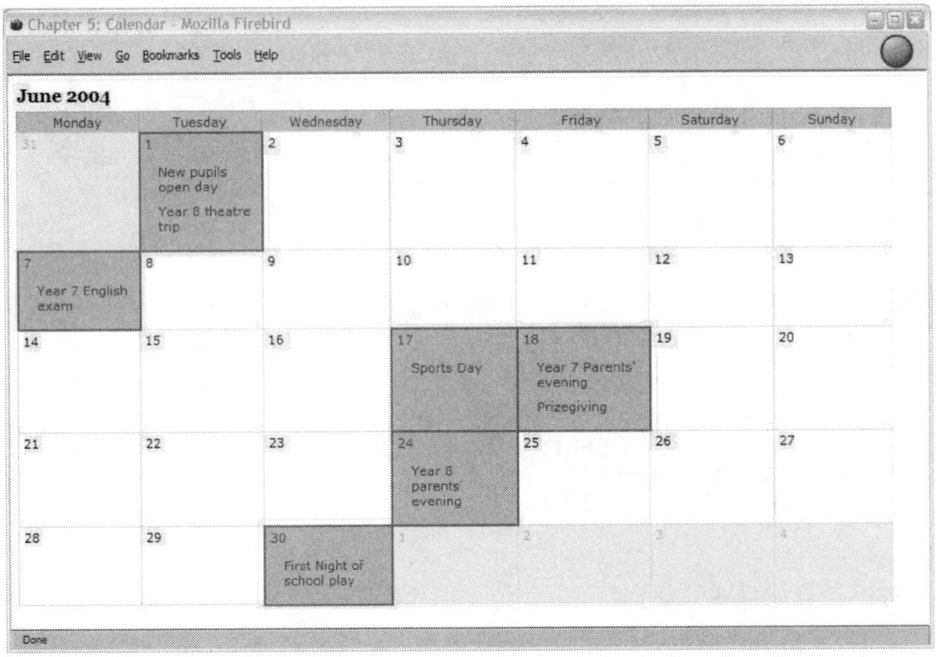

Discussion

This example starts out as a very simple table. It has a caption, which is the month we're working with, and the days of the week are marked up as table headers using the <th> tag.

File: **cal.html** (excerpt)

```
<table class="clmonth" summary="Calendar for June 2004">
  <caption>June 2004</caption>
  <tr>
    <th scope="col">Monday</th>
    <th scope="col">Tuesday</th>
    <th scope="col">Wednesday</th>
    <th scope="col">Thursday</th>
    <th scope="col">Friday</th>
    <th scope="col">Saturday</th>
    <th scope="col">Sunday</th>
  </tr>
```

The table has a class of clmonth. I've used a class rather than an ID because, in some situations, you might want to display more than one month on the page. If you then found you needed to give the table an ID—perhaps to allow you to show and hide the table using JavaScript—you could just add an ID as well as the class.

The days are held within individual table cells, and the events for each day are marked up as a list within the appropriate table cell.

In the markup below, you can see that classes have been added to two of the table cells. Class previous is applied to cells containing days that fall within the preceding month (next is used later for days in the following month); class active is applied to cells that contain event information, in order that we may highlight them.

File: **cal.html (excerpt)**

```
<tr>
  <td class="previous">31</td>
  <td class="active">1
    <ul>
      <li>New pupils open day</li>
      <li>Year 8 theatre trip</li>
    </ul>
  </td>
  <td>2</td>
  <td>3</td>
  <td>4</td>
  <td>5</td>
  <td>6</td>
</tr>
```

The table, without CSS, displays as in Figure 5.14.

Figure 5.14. The calendar is displayed without CSS.

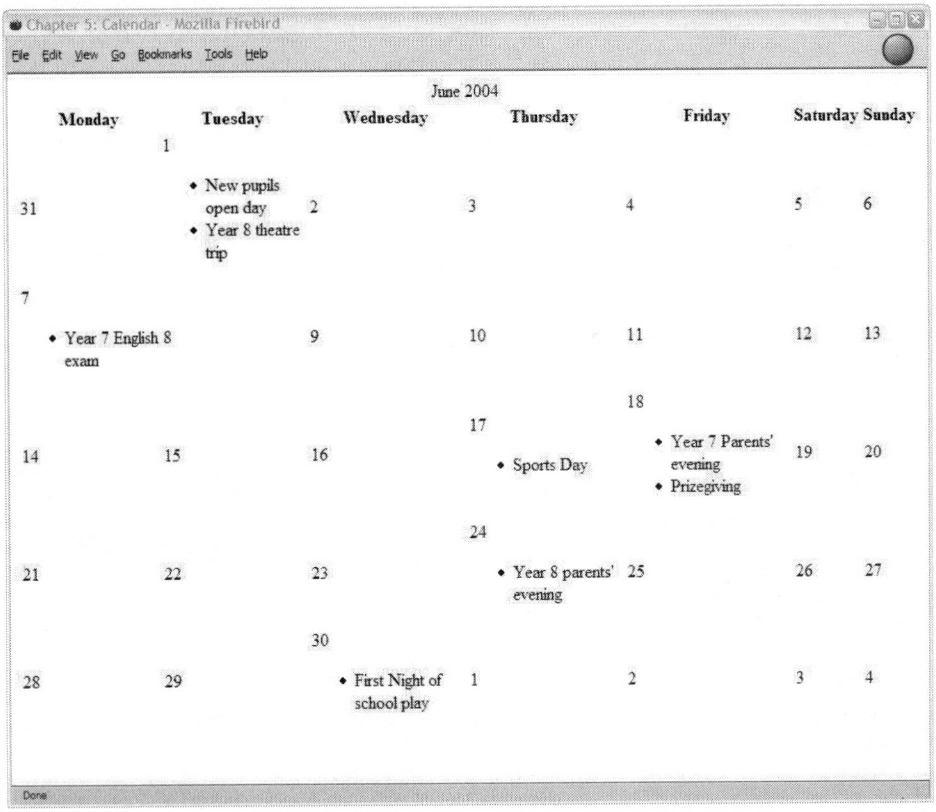

With the structural markup in place, we can style the calendar. I set a basic styles for the body, including a base font size. I then set a styles for the class `clmonth` in order for the borders to collapse, leaving no space between cells, and set a width for the table.

File: **cal.css (excerpt)**

```
body {
  background-color: #ffffff;
  color: #000000;
  font-size: 90%;
}
.clmonth {
  border-collapse: collapse;
```

```
  width: 780px;
}
```

I styled the <caption> within the class clmonth, then created styles for the table headers (<th>) and table cells (<td>).

File: **cal.css (excerpt)**

```
.clmonth caption {
  text-align: left;
  font: bold 110% Georgia, "Times New Roman", Times, serif;
  padding-bottom: 6px;
}
.clmonth th {
  border: 1px solid #AAAAAA;
  border-bottom: none;
  padding: 2px 8px 2px 8px;
  background-color: #CCCCCC;
  color: #3F3F3F;
  font: 80% Verdana, Geneva, Arial, Helvetica, sans-serif;
  width: 110px;
}
.clmonth td {
  border: 1px solid #EAEAEA;
  font: 80% Verdana, Geneva, Arial, Helvetica, sans-serif;
  padding: 2px 4px 2px 4px;
  vertical-align: top;
}
```

As can be seen in Figure 5.15, our calendar is beginning to take shape.

We can now style the lists of events within each table cell, removing the bullet, and adding space between list items.

File: **cal.css (excerpt)**

```
.clmonth ul {
  list-style-type: none;
  margin: 0;
  padding-left: 12px;
  padding-right: 6px;
}
.clmonth li {
  margin-bottom: 8px;
}
```

Figure 5.15. The calendar is more user-friendly once the `caption`, `th`, and `td` tags are styled.

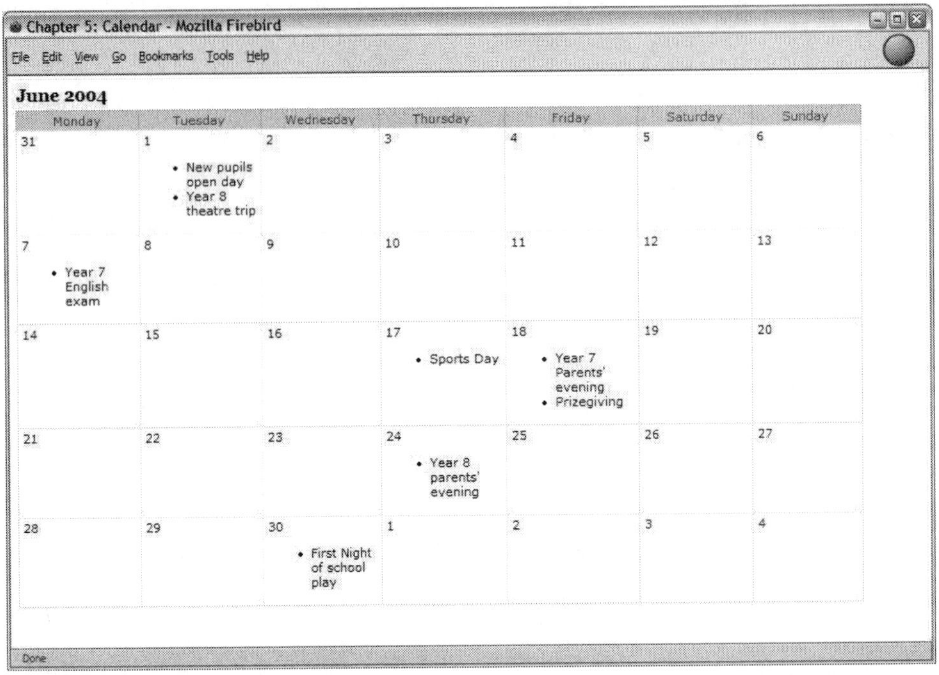

Finally, we add styles for the `previous` and `next` classes, which give the effect of graying out those days that are not part of the current month, and the `active` class, which highlights those days on which events will take place.

File: **cal.css (excerpt)**

```
.clmonth td.previous, .clmonth td.next {
  background-color: #F6F6F6;
  color: #C6C6C6;
}
.clmonth td.active {
  background-color: #B1CBE1;
  color: #2B5070;
  border: 2px solid #4682B4;
}
```

This is one of many ways to create a calendar. A common use of an online calendar is within a blog, where the calendar has clickable days that visitors can use to view entries made that month. By removing the events from our HTML markup, turning the days into single letters—M for Monday, etc.—and making a few simple changes to our CSS, we can create a simple mini-calendar suitable for this purpose, as shown in Figure 5.16.

Figure 5.16. With just a few changes, we create a mini-calendar.

File: **cal_mini.html (excerpt)**

```
<table class="clmonth" summary="Calendar for June 2004">
  <caption>June 2004</caption>
  <tr>
    <th scope="col">M</th>
    <th scope="col">T</th>
    <th scope="col">W</th>
    <th scope="col">T</th>
    <th scope="col">F</th>
    <th scope="col">S</th>
    <th scope="col">S</th>
  </tr>
  <tr>
    <td class="previous">31</td>
    <td class="active">1</td>
    <td>2</td>
    <td>3</td>
    <td>4</td>
    <td>5</td>
    <td>6</td>
  </tr>
  <tr>
    <td class="active">7</td>
    <td>8</td>
```

```
      <td>9</td>
      <td>10</td>
      <td>11</td>
      <td>12</td>
      <td>13</td>
    </tr>
    <tr>
      <td>14</td>
      <td>15</td>
      <td>16</td>
      <td class="active">17</td>
      <td class="active">18</td>
      <td>19</td>
      <td>20</td>
    </tr>
    <tr>
      <td>21</td>
      <td>22</td>
      <td>23</td>
      <td class="active">24</td>
      <td>25</td>
      <td>26</td>
      <td>27</td>
    </tr>
    <tr>
      <td>28</td>
      <td>29</td>
      <td class="active">30</td>
      <td class="next">1</td>
      <td class="next">2</td>
      <td class="next">3</td>
      <td class="next">4</td>
    </tr>
</table>
```

File: **cal_mini.css**

```
body {
  background-color: #ffffff;
  color: #000000;
  font-size: 90%;
}
.clmonth {
  border-collapse: collapse;
}
.clmonth caption {
  text-align: left;
```

```
   font: bold 110% Georgia, "Times New Roman", Times, serif;
   padding-bottom: 6px;
}
.clmonth th {
   border: 1px solid #AAAAAA;
   border-bottom: none;
   padding: 2px 8px 2px 8px;
   background-color: #CCCCCC;
   color: #3F3F3F;
   font: 80% Verdana, Geneva, Arial, Helvetica, sans-serif;
}
.clmonth td {
   border: 1px solid #EAEAEA;
   font: 80% Verdana, Geneva, Arial, Helvetica, sans-serif;
   padding: 2px 4px 2px 4px;
   vertical-align: top;
}
.clmonth td.previous, .clmonth td.next {
   background-color: #F6F6F6;
   color: #C6C6C6;
}
.clmonth td.active {
   background-color: #B1CBE1;
   color: #2B5070;
   border: 2px solid #4682B4;
}
```

Summary

In this chapter, we've discovered that tables are alive and well—when used for their original purpose of displaying tabular data, that is! CSS gives you the ability to create really attractive interface items from data tables, without affecting their accessibility at all. A well-thought out table is often the best way to display this kind of data to your users.

6

Forms and User Interfaces

Forms are an inescapable part of Web design and development. We use them to capture personal data from our users, to post information to message boards, to add items to shopping carts, and to update our blogs—among many other things!

Despite the necessity of forms on the Web, HTML makes virtually no styling options available to allow us to make forms more attractive. HTML attributes that are now deprecated, such as borders and background colors, did not give us an alternative to the gray boxes and buttons displayed by browser defaults. CSS, however, enables us to create attractive user interfaces for HTML forms, to integrate them fully with our sites, and, hopefully, to make them easier for our visitors to use and understand.

While this is a CSS book, in this chapter I will also cover some of the lesser-used HTML form tags and attributes. Their application can boost the accessibility and usability of forms, as well as providing additional elements to which we can apply CSS. I will be looking at forms laid out using CSS positioning as well as their table-based counterparts. Debate rages as to whether it is appropriate to lay out a form using a table; my take is that, if a form is tabular in nature—for instance, in the spreadsheet example below—a table is the most logical way to structure the fields. Otherwise, your form is likely to be more accessible if it's laid out using CSS. Therefore, you should try to do so wherever possible.

How do I style form elements using CSS?

Unstyled form elements will display according to browser and operating system defaults. However, using CSS, you can create forms that fit into your site design well.

Solution

Styles can be created for form elements just as they can for any other HTML element. The form shown in Figure 6.1 is unstyled; it's displayed according to Mozilla Firefox's default styles on the Windows XP operating system using the Silver theme.

Figure 6.1. An unstyled form assumes a basic appearance according to Mozilla's default styles.

File: **elements.html** (excerpt)

```
<form method="post" action="example1.html">
<p>What is your name?
<br /><input type="text" name="name" id="name" /></p>

<p>Select your favorite color:
<br /><select name="color" id="color">
<option value="blue">blue</option>
<option value="red">red</option>
<option value="green">green</option>
<option value="yellow">yellow</option>
</select></p>

<p>Are you male or female?<br />
  <input type="radio" name="sex" id="male" value="male" /> Male
  <br />
  <input type="radio" name="sex" id="female" value="female" />
  Female
</p>

<p>Comments:<br />
  <textarea name="comments" id="comments" cols="30" rows="4">
</textarea></p>

<p><input type="submit" name="btnSubmit" id="btnSubmit"
      value="Submit" /></p>
</form>
```

By creating CSS rules for the <form>, <input>, <textarea>, and <select> tags, we can change the look of this form.

File: **elements.css**

```
form {
  border: 1px dotted #aaaaaa;
  padding: 3px 6px 3px 6px;
}
input {
  color: #00008B;
  background-color: #ADD8E6;
  border: 1px solid #00008B;
}
select {
  width: 100px;
  color: #00008B;
  background-color: #ADD8E6;
  border: 1px solid #00008B;
```

```
}
textarea {
  width: 200px;
  height: 40px;
  color: #00008B;
  background-color: #ADD8E6;
  border: 1px solid #00008B;
}
```

The new look can be seen in Figure 6.2.

Figure 6.2. The form has a more attractive appearance, thanks to the application of CSS.

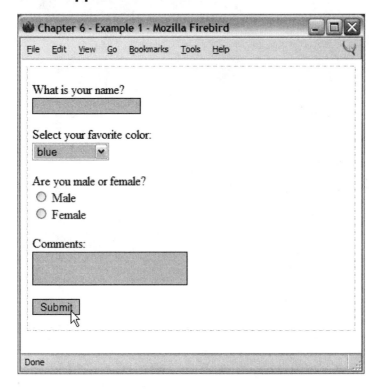

Discussion

Defining rules for the HTML elements `<form>`, `<input>`, `<textarea>`, and `<select>` will, as you would expect, affect any instance of these elements in a page to which a style sheet is attached. You can use a variety of CSS properties to change the appearance of a form's fields. For example, when styling an `<input type="text">` field, you can change almost every aspect of the field.

```
<input type="text" name="name" id="name" />
```

```
input {
  color: #00008B;
  background-color: #ADD8E6;
  border: 1px solid #00008B;
  font: 0.9em Arial, Helvetica, sans-serif;
  padding: 2px 4px 2px 4px;
  width: 200px;
}
```

color	Changes the color of the text that is typed inside the field.
background-color	Defines the field's background.
border	Affects the border around the field; you can use any of the other border styles here.
font	Changes the font size and typeface of the text within the field.
padding	Moves the text typed within a field away from the edges of the box.
width	Allows you to create form fields of the right width for the data you expect the user to enter—you don't need a long field for a user's first initial!

IMPORTANT

Safari and background colors

Unfortunately, as of this writing, Safari does not support setting background colors for form fields at all.

For this reason, you should never rely on field background colors for the usability of your site (e.g. "the yellow fields are required" would be a big no-no).

How do I apply different styles to fields in a single form?

The <input> tag has many different types, and the styles that you need for a text field are unlikely to be the same as those you want to use for your buttons or checkboxes. So, how can you create specific styles for different form fields?

Solution

You can use CSS classes to specify the exact styles individual fields will use. The form in the following example has two <input> tags, which display a text field and a submit button respectively. Different classes are applied to each.

File: **fields.html (excerpt)**

```
<form method="post" action="fields.html">
<p>What is your name?<br />
  <input type="text" name="name" id="name" class="txt" /></p>
<p><input type="submit" name="btnSubmit" id="btnSubmit"
      value="Submit" class="btn" /></p>
</form>
```

File: **fields.css**

```
form {
  border: 1px dotted #aaaaaa;
  padding: 3px 6px 3px 6px;
}
input.txt{
  color: #00008B;
  background-color: #ADD8E6;
  border: 1px inset #00008B;
  width: 200px;
}
input.btn {
  color: #00008B;
  background-color: #ADD8E6;
  border: 1px outset #00008B;
  padding: 2px 4px 2px 4px;
}
```

Figure 6.3 shows the result.

Figure 6.3. Different classes are applied to each of the input fields.

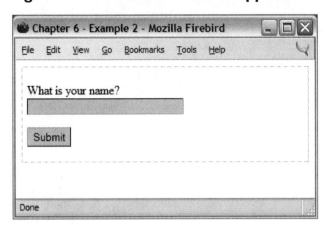

Discussion

As we've seen, the `<input>` tag can have several different types, and these types may require different styles in order to display appropriately. In the example above, we used classes to differentiate between an `<input>` tag with a type of `text` and an `<input>` tag with a type of `submit`. Had we simply created one set of styles for `<input>`, we might have ended up with the following (having set a width and used an inset border on the text field):

```
input {
  color: #00008B;
  background-color: #ADD8E6;
  border: 1px inset #00008B;
  width: 200px;
}
```

Applied to the form above, these styles would have displayed as shown in Figure 6.4.

Figure 6.4. Both input fields use the same styles.

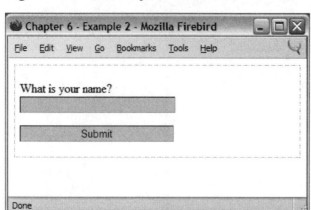

The submit button now looks rather like a text field; it certainly doesn't look like a button!

Using different classes allows us to define each element exactly as we want it to display. The forms in any application will likely need to cater for a variety of different types of data. Some text fields may only require the user to enter two characters; others may need to accept a name or other short word; others must take an entire sentence. By creating CSS classes for small, medium, and large text fields, you can choose the field that's appropriate to the data you expect the user to enter. This, in turn, helps users feel confident that they're entering the correct information.

 Tip

Style Early, Style Often

When I begin work on a site that has a lot of forms, one of my first steps is to create within the style sheet classes for standard forms. It doesn't matter if the style needs to change at a later date—that just involves tweaking the style sheet values. The important thing is that classes are applied from the outset, so that any changes affect all the forms on the site.

How do I stop my form creating additional white space and line breaks?

A form is a block-level element and, like a paragraph, will display on a new line by default. This is usually the behavior you'd want, however, there are occasions on which you may wish to add a small form within the flow of a document.

Solution

You can use the `display` property with a value of `inline` to display the form as an inline element.

File: **inline.html (excerpt)**

```
Your email address:
<form method="post" action="inline.html">
  <input type="text" name="name" id="name" class="txt" />
  <input type="submit" name="btnSubmit" id="btnSubmit"
      value="Submit" class="btn" />
</form>
```

File: **inline.css**

```
form {
  display: inline;
}
input.txt {
  color: #00008B;
  background-color: #E3F2F7;
  border: 1px inset #00008B;
  width: 200px;
}
input.btn {
  color: #00008B;
  background-color: #ADD8E6;
  border: 1px outset #00008B;
}
```

As you can see in Figure 6.5, the form now flows with the text around it.

Figure 6.5. The form is displayed inline.

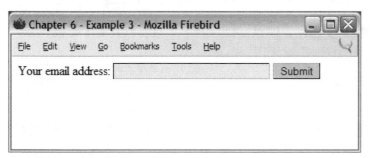

How do I make a submit button look like text?

It's generally a good idea to make buttons look like buttons if you expect people to click on them. However, occasionally, you might want to have your form submit button look more like plain text.

Solution

File: **textbutton.css** (excerpt)

```
.btn {
  background-color: transparent;
  border: 0;
  padding: 0;
}
```

Figure 6.6. A button can look like text.

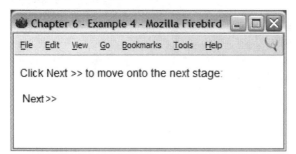

The text Next >> that appears on the second line in Figure 6.6 is actually a button!

IMPORTANT

Safari Protects its Buttons

Continuing the theme of limited form styling support, Safari doesn't let you alter the look of buttons the way other browsers do. This solution, therefore, does not apply to that browser.

How do I ensure that users with text-only devices understand how to complete my form?

It's good to create an attractive and usable form for visitors who have standard Web browsers, but bear in mind that there are many users who will have a text-only view of your site. Before you use CSS to style your form, ensure that it's structured in a way that makes the form's completion easy for text-only users.

Solution

One of the most important ways to make your form more accessible is to ensure that all users understand which label belongs with each form field. Using a text-only device—in particular, a screen reader, which typically reads the form aloud to a visually impaired user—visitors can find it very difficult to determine the details they're supposed to enter into each field. The solution is to use the `<label>` tag, which ties a label to a specific field. The `<label>` tag represents another element that's easily styled with CSS rules.

File: **textonly.html (excerpt)**

```
<form method="post" action="textonly.html">
  <table>
    <tr>
      <td><label for="fullname">Name:</label></td>
      <td><input type="text" name="fullname" id="fullname"
          class="txt" /></td>
    </tr>
    <tr>
      <td><label for="email">Email Address:</label></td>
      <td><input type="text" name="email" id="email" class="txt"
          /></td>
```

```
      </tr>
      <tr>
        <td><label for="password1">Password:</label></td>
        <td><input type="password" name="password1" id="password1"
            class="txt" /></td>
      </tr>
      <tr>
        <td><label for="password2">Confirm Password:</label></td>
        <td><input type="password" name="password2" id="password2"
            class="txt" /></td>
      </tr>
      <tr>
        <td><label for="level">Membership Level:</label></td>
        <td><select name="level">
            <option value="silver">silver</option>
            <option value="gold">gold</option>
        </select></td>
      </tr>
    </table>
    <p>
      <input type="submit" name="btnSubmit" id="btnSubmit"
          value="Sign Up!" class="btn" />
    </p>
</form>
```

File: **textonly.css**

```
h1 {
  font: 1.2em Arial, Helvetica, sans-serif;
}
input.txt {
  color: #00008B;
  background-color: #E3F2F7;
  border: 1px inset #00008B;
  width: 200px;
}
input.btn {
  color: #00008B;
  background-color: #ADD8E6;
  border: 1px outset #00008B;
}
label {
  font : bold 0.9em  Arial, Helvetica, sans-serif;
}
```

Nothing terribly important to look at here, but the result can be seen in Figure 6.7. In addition to improving the usability of the form for text-only browsers, visual browsers will place the cursor in the corresponding field when the user clicks on one of the labels.

Figure 6.7. The form displays in the Web browser.

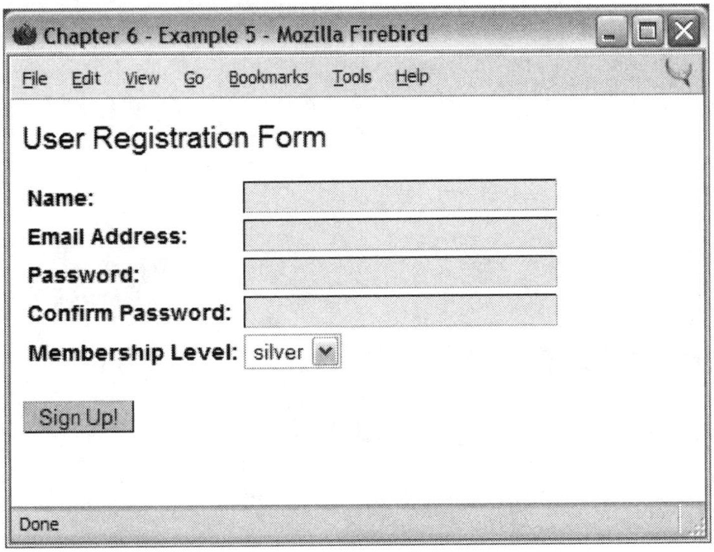

Discussion

The `<label>` tag makes it possible to indicate clearly what information users need to enter into a field. If the form is being read out to users by their screen readers, it may not be immediately obvious what a particular field is for. With a layout such as the one provided in this example, which uses a table to display the label in one cell and the field in another, it's especially important to use the `<label>` tag.

There are two ways in which you can use the `<label>` tag. If your form field is right next to the label, you can simply wrap the field and label with the tag:

```
<label>Name: <input type="text" name="fullname" id="fullname"
    class="txt" /></label>
```

If, as in our example above, you cannot wrap the label and field as they are not siblings in the document structure, you can use the `<label>` tag's `for` attribute instead. In this case, you must insert as a value the ID of the field that the label describes.

File: **textonly.html (excerpt)**

```
<tr>
  <td><label for="fullname">Name:</label></td>
  <td><input type="text" name="fullname" id="fullname"
       class="txt" /></td>
</tr>
```

Once you have your `<label>` tags in place, you can rest assured that those using screen readers will understand how to complete your form. You can also use CSS to style the `<label>` tag itself.

File: **textonly.css (excerpt)**

```
label {
  font: bold 0.9em  Arial, Helvetica, sans-serif;
}
```

How do I lay out a two-column form using CSS instead of a table?

Forms can be tricky to lay out without tables, however, the task is not impossible. Figure 6.8 shows a form layout that looks remarkably table-like, but if you examine the HTML code you won't find a table in sight!

Figure 6.8. This two-column form is laid out using CSS.

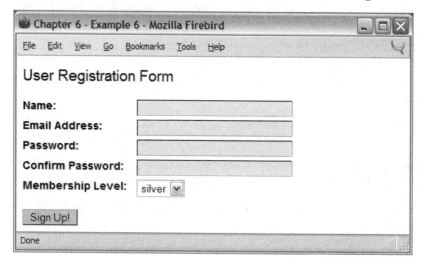

```
<!DOCTYPE html PUBLIC "-//W3C//DTD XHTML 1.0 Transitional//EN"
    "http://www.w3.org/TR/xhtml1/DTD/xhtml1-transitional.dtd">
<html xmlns="http://www.w3.org/1999/xhtml">
<head>
<title>Table-free form layout</title>
<meta http-equiv="content-type"
    content="text/html; charset=iso-8859-1" />
<link rel="stylesheet" type="text/css" href="tablefree.css" />
</head>
<body>
<h1>User Registration Form</h1>
<form method="post" action="tablefree.html">
  <p>
    <label for="fullname">Name:</label>
    <input type="text" name="fullname" id="fullname" class="txt"
        />
  </p>
  <p>
    <label for="email">Email Address:</label>
    <input type="text" name="email" id="email" class="txt" />
  </p>
  <p>
    <label for="password1">Password:</label>
    <input type="password" name="password1" id="password1"
        class="txt" />
  </p>
  <p>
    <label for="password2">Confirm Password:</label>
    <input type="password" name="password2" id="password2"
        class="txt" />
  </p>
  <p>
    <label for="level">Membership Level:</label>
    <select name="level">
      <option value="silver">silver</option>
      <option value="gold">gold</option>
    </select>
  </p>
  <p>
    <input type="submit" name="btnSubmit" id="btnSubmit"
        value="Sign Up!" class="btn" />
  </p>
</form>
</body>
</html>
```

File: **tablefree.css**

```css
h1 {
  font: 1.2em Arial, Helvetica, sans-serif;
}
input.txt {
  color: #00008B;
  background-color: #E3F2F7;
  border: 1px inset #00008B;
  width: 200px;
}
input.btn {
  color: #00008B;
  background-color: #ADD8E6;
  border: 1px outset #00008B;
}
form p {
  clear: left;
  margin: 0;
  padding: 0;
  padding-top: 5px;
}
form p label {
  float: left;
  width: 30%;
  font: bold 0.9em Arial, Helvetica, sans-serif;
}
```

Discussion

The example above creates a common form layout. As we saw earlier in this chapter, this is often achieved using a two-column table in which the label is placed in one cell, the field in another:

File: **textonly.html (excerpt)**

```html
<form method="post" action="textonly.html">
  <table>
    <tr>
      <td><label for="fullname">Name:</label></td>
      <td><input type="text" name="fullname" id="fullname"
           class="txt" /></td>
    </tr>
    <tr>
      <td><label for="email">Email Address:</label></td>
      <td><input type="text" name="email" id="email" class="txt"
           /></td>
```

```
      </tr>
      <tr>
        <td><label for="password1">Password:</label></td>
        <td><input type="password" name="password1" id="password1"
            class="txt" /></td>
      </tr>
      <tr>
        <td><label for="password2">Confirm Password:</label></td>
        <td><input type="password" name="password2" id="password2"
            class="txt" /></td>
      </tr>
      <tr>
        <td><label for="level">Membership Level:</label></td>
        <td><select name="level">
            <option value="silver">silver</option>
            <option value="gold">gold</option>
          </select></td>
      </tr>
    </table>
    <p>
      <input type="submit" name="btnSubmit" id="btnSubmit"
          value="Sign Up!" class="btn" />
    </p>
</form>
```

The reason we put the form within a table is to ensure that all the fields line up
neatly. Without the table, the fields would appear immediately after the label,
as can be seen in Figure 6.9.

Figure 6.9. This form is laid out without a table.

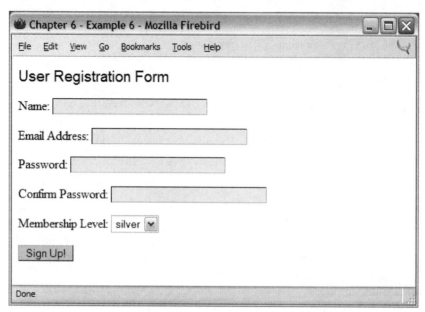

In the markup used to create the form shown in Figure 6.9, each form row is wrapped in a <p> tag. As you can see, without the table cells, the field appears immediately after the label:

File: **tablefree.html** (excerpt)

```
<form method="post" action="tablefree.html">
  <p>
    <label for="fullname">Name:</label>
    <input type="text" name="fullname" id="fullname" class="txt"
       />
  </p>
  <p>
    <label for="email">Email Address:</label>
    <input type="text" name="email" id="email" class="txt" />
  </p>
  ...
```

To recreate the effect of the table layout using CSS, we don't have to make any changes to our markup. We need merely apply some simple CSS:

File: **tablefree.css**

```css
form p {
  clear: left;
  margin: 0;
  padding: 0;
  padding-top: 5px;
}
form p label {
  float: left;
  width: 30%;
  font: bold 0.9em Arial, Helvetica, sans-serif;
}
```

What we are doing here is using the `<label>` tag to address our label. We then `float` it left and give it a `width` value.

As `float` takes an element out of the document flow, we need to give the paragraphs a `clear` property with the value `left`, to ensure that each paragraph starts below the `<label>` in the preceding paragraph. We also give our paragraphs a `padding-top` value, in order to space out the rows, and that's it!

How do I group related fields?

Large Web forms can be made much more usable if the visitor can ascertain which questions are related. What's the best way to show the relationships between information for users with standard browsers as well as those using text-only devices and screen readers?

Solution

You can group related fields using the `<fieldset>` and `<legend>` tags.

File: **fieldset.html (excerpt)**

```html
<form method="post" action="fieldset.html">
  <fieldset>
    <legend>Personal Information</legend>
    <p>
      <label for="fullname">Name:</label>
      <input type="text" name="fullname" id="fullname" class="txt"
        />
    </p>
    <p>
      <label for="email">Email Address:</label>
```

```
      <input type="text" name="email" id="email" class="txt" />
    </p>
    <p>
      <label for="password1">Password:</label>
      <input type="password" name="password1" id="password1"
          class="txt" />
    </p>
    <p>
      <label for="password2">Confirm Password:</label>
      <input type="password" name="password2" id="password2"
          class="txt" />
    </p>
  </fieldset>
  <fieldset>
    <legend>Address Details</legend>
    <p>
      <label for="address1">Address line one:</label>
      <input type="text" name="address1" id="address1" class="txt"
          />
    </p>
    <p>
      <label for="address2">Address line two:</label>
      <input type="text" name="address2" id="address2" class="txt"
          />
    </p>
    <p>
      <label for="city">Town / City:</label>
      <input type="text" name="city" id="city" class="txt" />
    </p>
    <p>
      <label for="zip">Zip / Post code:</label>
      <input type="text" name="zip" id="zip" class="txt" />
    </p>
  </fieldset>
  <p>
    <input type="submit" name="btnSubmit" id="btnSubmit"
        value="Sign Up!" class="btn" />
  </p>
</form>
```

File: **fieldset.css**

```
h1 {
  font: 1.2em Arial, Helvetica, sans-serif;
}
input.txt {
  color: #00008B;
```

```
    background-color: #E3F2F7;
    border: 1px inset #00008B;
    width: 200px;
}
input.btn {
    color: #00008B;
    background-color: #ADD8E6;
    border: 1px outset #00008B;
}
form p {
    clear: left;
    margin: 0;
    padding: 0;
    padding-top: 5px;
}
form p label {
    float: left;
    width: 30%;
    font: bold 0.9em Arial, Helvetica, sans-serif;
}
fieldset {
    border: 1px dotted #61B5CF;
    margin-top: 16px;
    padding: 10px;
}
legend {
    font: bold 0.8em Arial, Helvetica, sans-serif;
    color: #00008B;
    background-color: #FFFFFF;
}
```

You can see how the groupings are displayed by the browser in Figure 6.10.

Figure 6.10. Two sections in a form are created with the `<fieldset>` tag.

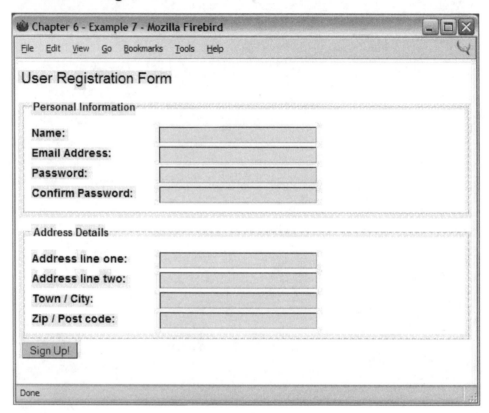

Discussion

The `<fieldset>` and `<legend>` tags are a great way to group related information in a form. These tags provide an easy means to group items visually, and are understood by screen readers and text-only devices, which can see that the tagged items are logically grouped together. This would not be the case if you simply wrapped the related items in a styled `<div>`; users of a standard browser would understand the relationship, but those who couldn't see the CSS would not.

To group form fields, simply wrap related fields with a `<fieldset>` tag and, immediately after your opening `<fieldset>` tag, add a `<legend>` tag containing a title for the group.

```
<fieldset>
  <legend>Personal Information</legend>
  <p>
    <label for="fullname">Name:</label>
    <input type="text" name="fullname" id="fullname" class="txt"
      />
  </p>
  <p>
    <label for="email">Email Address:</label>
    <input type="text" name="email" id="email" class="txt" />
  </p>
  <p>
    <label for="password1">Password:</label>
    <input type="password" name="password1" id="password1"
      class="txt" />
  </p>
  <p>
    <label for="password2">Confirm Password:</label>
    <input type="password" name="password2" id="password2"
      class="txt" />
  </p>
</fieldset>
```

<fieldset> and <legend> are displayed with a default style by the browsers, as are other HTML tags. The default style surrounds the grouped elements with a box, the legend tag appearing in the top left corner of that box. Figure 6.11 shows the <fieldset> and <legend> tags as they display in Firefox on Windows XP when they have not been styled with CSS.

Figure 6.11. These `fieldset` and `legend` tags are unstyled.

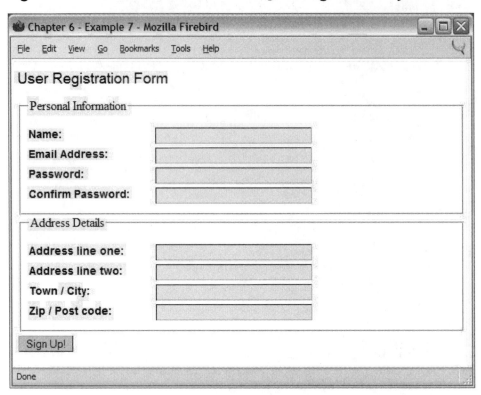

You can use CSS to style these tags, changing the padding, margins, color, and style of the border, as well as the style of the legend text.

File: **fieldset.css** (excerpt)

```
fieldset {
  border: 1px dotted #61B5CF;
  margin-top: 16px;
  padding: 10px;
}
legend {
  font: bold 0.8em Arial, Helvetica, sans-serif;
  color: #00008B;
  background-color: #FFFFFF;
}
```

How do I style accesskey hints?

Access keys allow users to jump quickly to a certain place in a document by pressing a combination of **Alt** (or equivalent) and another key. However, you have to let your users know what that other key is!

Solution

The operating system convention that indicates which letter of a key word is its access key is to underline the given letter. For example, **Alt-F** opens the File menu. This functionality is indicated by the underlining of the letter "F" in File in Figure 6.12.

Figure 6.12. The letter "F" in the word "File" is underlined.

You can use a similar technique on your site, underlining the correct letter to identify your access keys.

File: **accesskeys.html (excerpt)**

```
<fieldset>
  <legend><span class="akey">P</span>ersonal
    Information</legend>
  <p>
    <label for="fullname">Name:</label>
    <input type="text" name="fullname" id="fullname" class="txt"
      accesskey="p" />
  </p>
```

File: **accesskeys.css (excerpt)**

```
.akey {
  text-decoration: underline;
}
```

As you can see, the access key for each field set is underlined in Figure 6.13.

Figure 6.13. Access keys are indicated by the "P" in "Personal" and "A" in "Address."

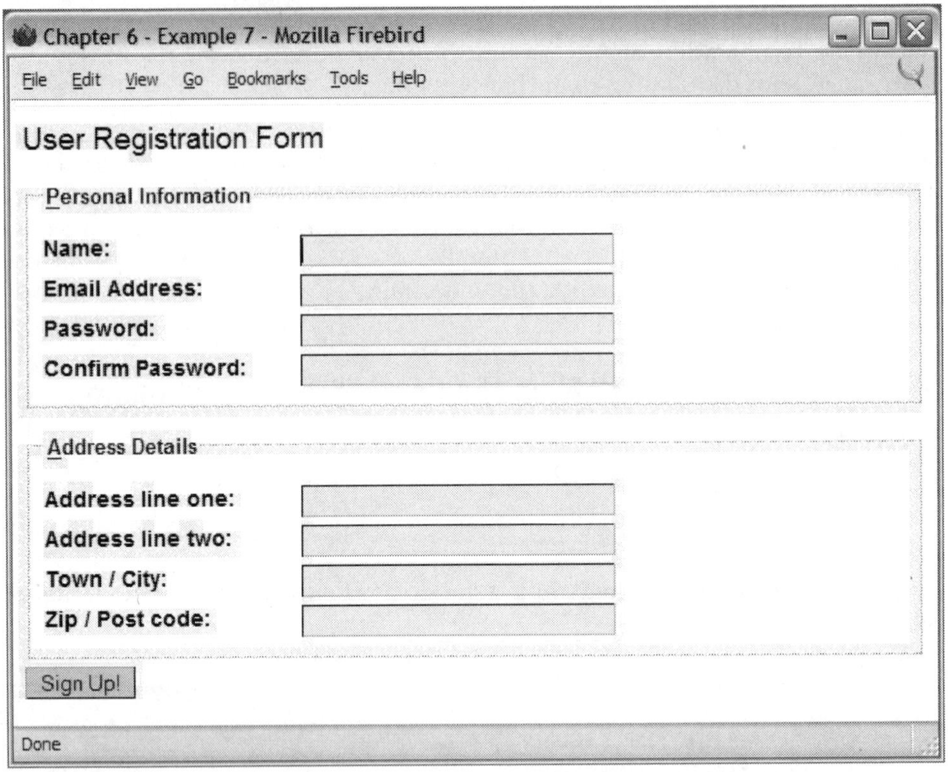

Discussion

Access keys can be very helpful to site users who have mobility problems and can't use a mouse. These visitors can use an access key to jump straight to the form; you could also offer an access key to enable users to jump to the search box, and so on. The convention of underlining the letter that corresponds to the access key will be familiar to a user who uses this functionality, even if other users don't know what it means.

To create access key functionality for a form field, you simply need to add the attribute `accesskey="x"` to your field, where *x* is the character you have chosen for the access key.

File: **accesskeys.html** (excerpt)

```
<p>
  <label for="fullname">Name:</label>
  <input type="text" name="fullname" id="fullname" class="txt"
    accesskey="p" />
</p>
```

I have made an access key for the first form element of each group; using the access key will focus that first form field so users can begin to complete the form. To highlight the access key, I've taken the first letter of the field set <legend> (e.g. the "P" in "Personal Details") and wrapped it in a span with a class of akey.

File: **accesskeys.html** (excerpt)

```
<legend><span class="akey">P</span>ersonal Information</legend>
```

The class akey simply sets the text-decoration property to underline.

File: **accesskeys.css** (excerpt)

```
.akey {
  text-decoration: underline;
}
```

 Keys in Browser may be Less Accessible than they Appear

IMPORTANT

When creating access keys, take care not to override default browser keyboard shortcuts!

How do I use different colored highlights in a select menu?

Earlier, you saw that it is possible to color the background of the select menu. But, is it possible to include in the menu several colors to highlight different options?

Solution

You can assign classes to menu options, to create multiple background colors within the drop-down. color and background-color are the only properties you can set for a menu item.

File: **select.html** (excerpt)

```html
<form method="post" action="example8.html">
  <p>
    <label for="color">Select your favorite color:</label>
    <select name="color" id="color">
      <option value="">Select One</option>
      <option value="blue" class="blue">blue</option>
      <option value="red" class="red">red</option>
      <option value="green" class="green">green</option>
      <option value="yellow" class="yellow">yellow</option>
    </select>
  </p>
  <p>
    <input type="submit" name="btnSubmit" id="btnSubmit"
        value="Send!" class="btn" />
  </p>
</form>
```

File: **select.css** (excerpt)

```css
.blue {
  background-color: #ADD8E6;
  color: #000000;
}
.red {
  background-color: #E20A0A;
  color: #ffffff;
}
.green {
  background-color: #3CB371;
  color: #ffffff;
}
.yellow {
  background-color: #FAFAD2;
  color: #000000;
}
```

Thanks to this code, the drop-down menu in Figure 6.14 looks very colorful indeed.

Figure 6.14. Options display within a select menu to which classes are applied.

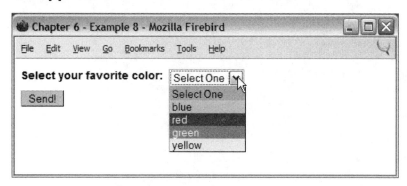

 Style with Substance

Use different background colors on sets of related options, or apply alternate row colors in your select menu.

 Safari has No Stripes

Again, Safari doesn't yet support background colors on form elements, so this solution will not work in that browser.

I have a form that allows users to enter data as if into a spreadsheet. How do I style this with CSS?

While laying out forms using CSS is possible—and recommended in most cases—there are some types of data that are better entered into a form within a table. A good example of this would be a situation in which users enter data into a spreadsheet-like Web application.

Users may already be accustomed to entering data into a spreadsheet using Microsoft Excel or another package. Keep this in mind as you design your application interface—mimicking familiar interfaces often helps users to feel comfortable with your application. Making your form look like a spreadsheet by laying it out in a table, and using CSS to format it, may be the way to go.

```
<form method="post" action="spreadsheet.html">
<table class="formdata" summary="This table contains a form to
    input the yearly income for years 1999 through 2002">
  <caption>Complete the Yearly Income 1999 - 2002</caption>
  <tr>
    <th></th>
    <th scope="col">1999</th>
    <th scope="col">2000</th>
    <th scope="col">2001</th>
    <th scope="col">2002</th>
  </tr>
  <tr>
    <th scope="row">Grants</th>
    <td><input type="text" name="grants1999" id="grants1999" />
    </td>
    <td><input type="text" name="grants2000" id="grants2000" />
    </td>
    <td><input type="text" name="grants2001" id="grants2001" />
    </td>
    <td><input type="text" name="grants2002" id="grants2002" />
    </td>
  </tr>
  <tr>
    <th scope="row">Donations</th>
    <td><input type="text" name="donations1999" id="donations1999"
        /></td>
    <td><input type="text" name="donations2000" id="donations2000"
        /></td>
    <td><input type="text" name="donations2001" id="donations2001"
        /></td>
    <td><input type="text" name="donations2002" id="donations2002"
        /></td>
  </tr>
  <tr>
    <th scope="row">Investments</th>
    <td><input type="text" name="investments1999"
        id="investments1999" /></td>
    <td><input type="text" name="investments2000"
        id="investments2000" /></td>
    <td><input type="text" name="investments2001"
        id="investments2001" /></td>
    <td><input type="text" name="investments2002"
        id="investments2002" /></td>
  </tr>
  <tr>
```

```
      <th scope="row">Fundraising</th>
      <td><input type="text" name="fundraising1999"
          id="fundraising1999" /></td>
      <td><input type="text" name="fundraising2000"
          id="fundraising2000" /></td>
      <td><input type="text" name="fundraising2001"
          id="fundraising2001" /></td>
      <td><input type="text" name="fundraising2002"
          id="fundraising2002" /></td>
   </tr>
   <tr>
      <th scope="row">Sales</th>
      <td><input type="text" name="sales1999" id="sales1999" /></td>
      <td><input type="text" name="sales2000" id="sales2000" /></td>
      <td><input type="text" name="sales2001" id="sales2001" /></td>
      <td><input type="text" name="sales2002" id="sales2002" /></td>
   </tr>
   <tr>
      <th scope="row">Miscellaneous</th>
      <td><input type="text" name="misc1999" id="misc1999" /></td>
      <td><input type="text" name="misc2000" id="misc2000" /></td>
      <td><input type="text" name="misc2001" id="misc2001" /></td>
      <td><input type="text" name="misc2002" id="misc2002" /></td>
   </tr>
   <tr>
      <th scope="row">Total</th>
      <td><input type="text" name="total1999" id="total1999" /></td>
      <td><input type="text" name="total2000" id="total2000" /></td>
      <td><input type="text" name="total2001" id="total2001" /></td>
      <td><input type="text" name="total2002" id="total2002" /></td>
   </tr>
</table>
<p><input type="submit" name="btnSubmit" id="btnSubmit"
      value="Add Data" /></p>
</form>
```

File: **spreadsheet.css**

```
table.formdata {
   border: 1px solid #5F6F7E;
   border-collapse: collapse;
}
table.formdata th {
   border: 1px solid #5F6F7E;
   background-color: #E2E2E2;
   color: #000000;
   text-align: left;
```

```
   font-weight: normal;
   padding: 2px 4px 2px 4px;
   margin: 0;
}
table.formdata td {
   margin: 0;
   padding: 0;
   border: 1px solid #E2E2E2;
}

table.formdata input {
   width: 80px;
   padding: 2px 4px 2px 4px;
   margin: 0;
   border: none;
}
```

The styled form, which looks very spreadsheet-like, is shown in Figure 6.15.

Figure 6.15. A form is styled in spreadsheet format.

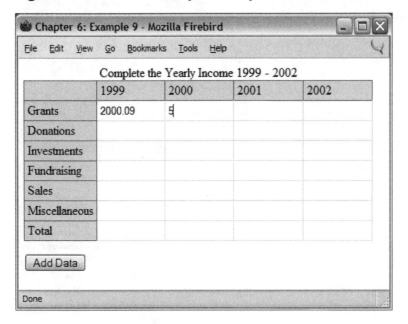

Discussion

The aim is to create a form that looks similar to a spreadsheet, such as the Excel spreadsheet shown in Figure 6.16. Recently, I created forms similar to this for a Web application that had many tables of data. What the client wanted was for the table to turn into an "editable table" when selected for editing—though it retained the appearance of the original data table, the contents could be edited by the user.

Figure 6.16. A spreadsheet displays in Excel.

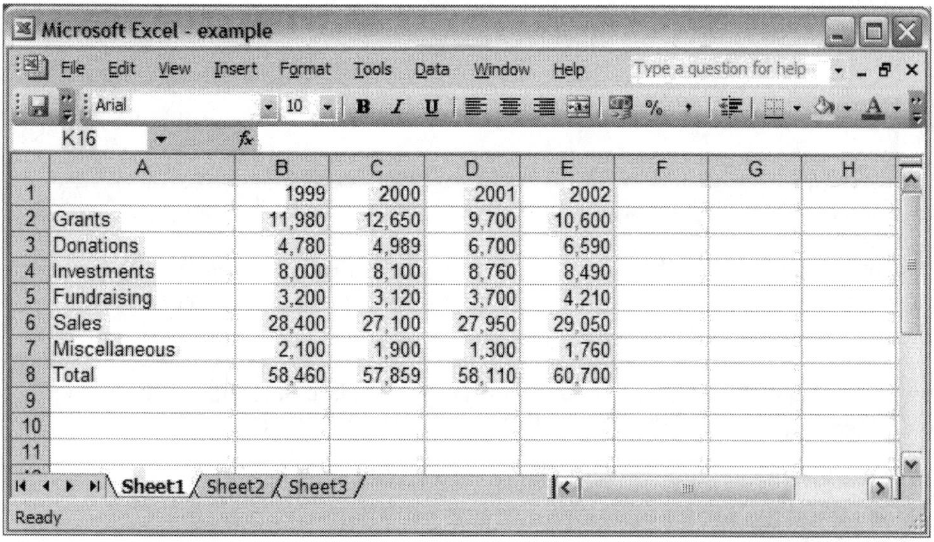

	A	B	C	D	E	F	G	H
1		1999	2000	2001	2002			
2	Grants	11,980	12,650	9,700	10,600			
3	Donations	4,780	4,989	6,700	6,590			
4	Investments	8,000	8,100	8,760	8,490			
5	Fundraising	3,200	3,120	3,700	4,210			
6	Sales	28,400	27,100	27,950	29,050			
7	Miscellaneous	2,100	1,900	1,300	1,760			
8	Total	58,460	57,859	58,110	60,700			
9								
10								
11								

The first step is to lay out the form within a structured table, using table headings (`<th>` tags) where appropriate, and adding a caption and summary for accessibility purposes. The complete code for this form is posted in the solution above and, before we add any CSS, the form should display as in Figure 6.17.

Figure 6.17. The unstyled form is ready for CSS formatting.

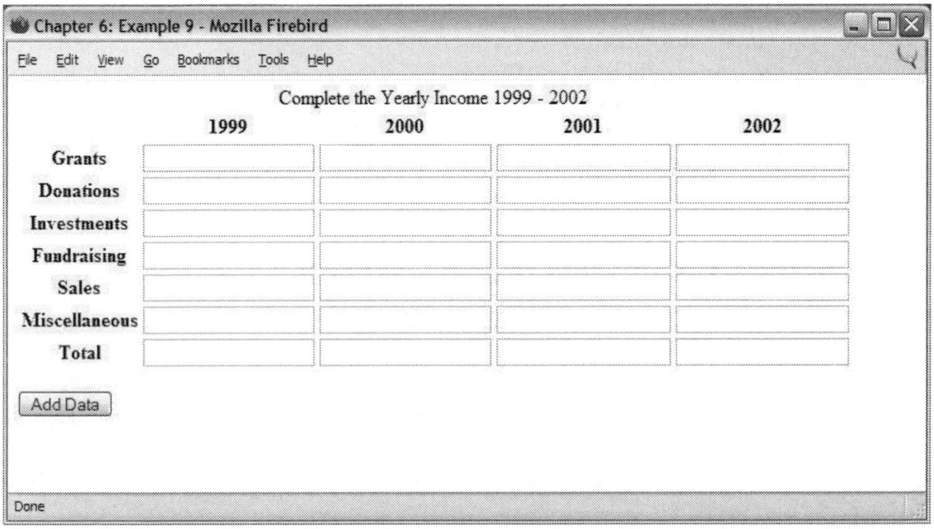

To create the CSS for this form, we must establish for the table a class that contains all the spreadsheet fields. I have given the table a class of `formdata`.

File: **spreadsheet.html** (excerpt)
```
<table class="formdata" summary="This table contains a form to
    input the yearly income for years 1999 through 2002">
```

In the style sheet, class `formdata` has a 1-pixel border in a dark, slate gray and the `border-collapse` property is set to `collapse`.

File: **spreadsheet.css** (excerpt)
```
table.formdata {
  border: 1px solid #5F6F7E;
  border-collapse: collapse;
}
```

Next, we can style the table headings. I've used the `<th>` tag for the top and left-hand column headings, so, to style these, all I need to do is address the `<th>` tags within a table of class `formdata`. The results are shown in Figure 6.18.

File: **calendar.css** (excerpt)
```
table.formdata th {
  border: 1px solid #5F6F7E;
  background-color: #E2E2E2;
```

```
  color: #000000;
  text-align: left;
  font-weight: normal;
  padding: 2px 4px 2px 4px;
  margin: 0;
}
```

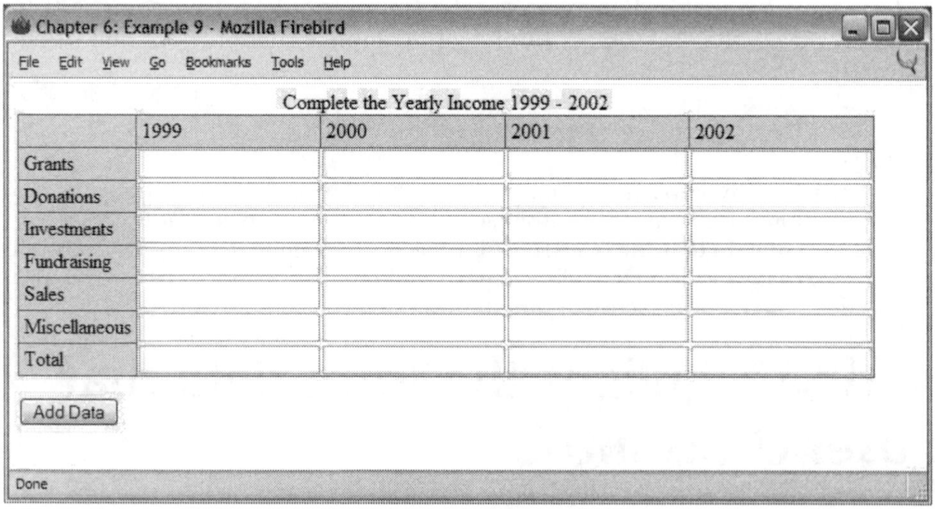

Figure 6.18. The form looks good after we style the `<table>` and `<th>` tags.

To produce the effect of an editable table, we need to hide the borders of the form fields and add borders to the table cells. As the only input tags within the table are the text fields that we want to style, we can simply address all `<input>` tags in the table with a class of `formdata`; this saves us having to add classes to all our fields.

We add a border to the `<td>` tag, and set the borders on the `input` tag to 0. We specify a width for the `<input>` tag, as we know the type of data that will be added won't need a large field, then add some padding so that text inserted into the form field does not bump up against the border.

File: **spreadsheet.css** (excerpt)

```
table.formdata td {
  margin: 0;
  padding: 0;
  border: 1px solid #E2E2E2;
```

```
}
table.formdata input {
  width: 80px;
  padding: 2px 4px 2px 4px;
  margin: 0;
  border-width: 0;
  border-style: none;
}
```

That's all there is to it. If you use this technique, make sure your users understand that the table is editable. Removing borders from form fields isn't going to help users if it means they can't work out how to complete the form—or don't even realize the form exists!

Borders May Not Collapse

Certain browsers do not support the `border-collapse` property. At the time of writing, neither Konqueror for KDE nor Safari on Mac OS X supported it. In those browsers, the form will not look quite so neat—the fields will be distinct from the cells. Despite this, however, the form is perfectly usable and not unattractive in these browsers.

How do I highlight the form field that the user clicks into?

Applications such as Excel highlight the focused form field when the user clicks on or tabs to it. Is it possible to create this effect in our Web form?

Solution

We can create this effect using pure CSS, thanks to the `:focus` pseudo-class, as I've shown in Figure 6.19. Unfortunately, this solution doesn't work in Internet Explorer.

File: **spreadsheet2.css (excerpt)**

```
table.formdata input {
  width: 80px;
  padding: 2px 4px 2px 4px;
  margin: 0;
  border: 2px solid #ffffff;
}
.formdata input:focus {
```

```
    border: 2px solid #000000;
}
```

Figure 6.19. Highlight the form field in focus in Firefox.

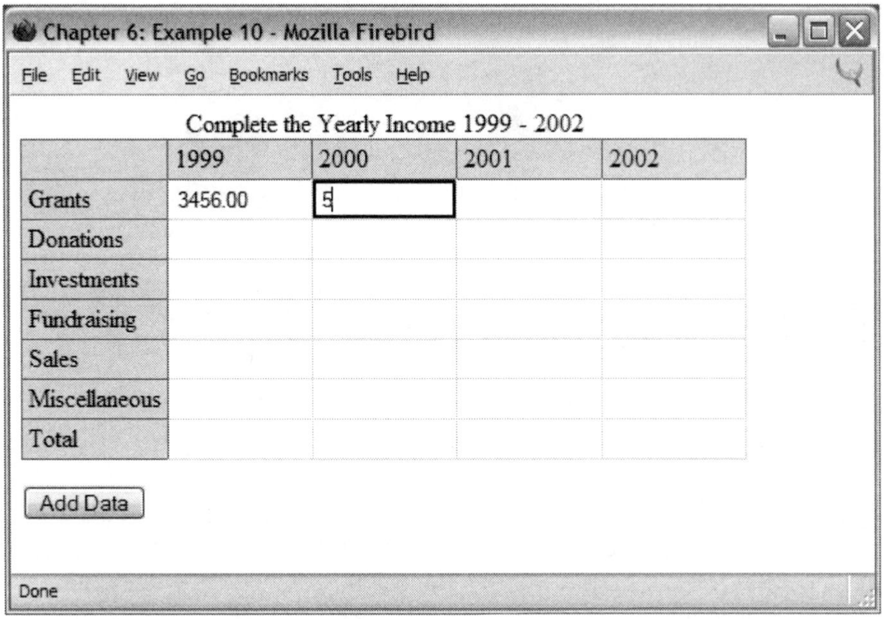

Discussion

This solution for adding a border, or changing the background color, of the form field when it receives focus is simple. In fact, it's as simple as adding the pseudo-class selector :focus to your style sheet to display a different style for the <input> tag when the user clicks into it.

Unfortunately, as I've already mentioned, Internet Explorer does not support the :focus pseudo-class, so this effect will not display for the majority of people who visit your site (unless you're the lucky person developing an intranet for a company that has Mozilla on every desktop).

There is a way around this problem that, unfortunately, requires a little JavaScript. In the head of the document, or in an external JavaScript file, declare the following functions.

File: **spreadsheet2.html** (excerpt)

```
<script language="javascript" type="text/javascript">
function hilite(obj) {
  obj.style.border = '2px solid #000000';
}

function delite(obj) {
  obj.style.border = '2px solid #ffffff';
}
</script>
```

In your document, you need to call these functions in the `onfocus` and `onblur` attributes of the `<input>` tags you wish to highlight.

File: **spreadsheet2.html** (excerpt)

```
<input type="text" name="grants1999" id="grants1999"
    onfocus="hilite(this);" onblur="delite(this);" />
```

Your field highlighting will now work in Internet Explorer as well as Mozilla-based browsers and any others that support the `:focus` pseudo-class.

For JavaScript Experts...

Simon Willison's article, *Simple Tricks for More Usable Forms*[1], on site-point.com, explains a neater technique for accomplishing the same effect using JavaScript that's a little more complex than that provided here.

Summary

In this chapter, we've looked at a variety of ways to style forms using CSS, from simply changing the look of form elements, to using CSS to lay forms out. We've seen how CSS can greatly enhance the appearance and usability of forms. We have also touched on the accessibility of forms for users of alternate devices, and we've seen how, by being careful when marking forms up, you can make it easier for all visitors to use your site or Web application.

---

[1] http://www.sitepoint.com/article/1273

7

Browser and Device Support

This chapter contains a wide range of solutions grouped under the somewhat loose heading of "browser and device support". But, the bottom line is that your sites need to be able to support the widest number of devices, browsers and users possible—and CSS can help you to do so.

Good use of CSS allows you to separate the structure and content of your documents from the presentation of the site. This means that visitors using devices that cannot render your design—either because they're limited from a technical standpoint, such as some PDA or phone browsers, or as a result of their own functional advantages, such as screen readers that speak your page's text for the benefit of visually impaired users—will still be able to access the content. However, you are still free to create beautiful designs for the majority of users who do have CSS-supporting browsers.

As well as discussing different browsers and devices, this chapter will help you learn some techniques to troubleshoot CSS bugs in those browsers that do support CSS. This chapter couldn't hope to cover every CSS bug known—even if it tried, it would likely be out of date before it was printed, as new bugs, and new bug fixes, appear all the time! What I have tried to do here is explain some of the main culprits that cause browser-related problems with CSS. Then, I've explored how those problems might be solved, where to go to get up-to-date advice, how to step through a problem and isolate exactly what causes it, and how to ask for help in a way that's likely to get you a useful answer.

This chapter also covers the use of alternate style sheets, style sheets for different media (such as print style sheets), and browser-based style sheet switching with the aid of JavaScript.

In which browsers should I test my site?

Once upon a time, Web designers only worried whether their sites looked good in Internet Explorer and Netscape Navigator; however, those days are long gone. While Internet Explorer currently has the largest share of the browser market, there are several other important desktop—and other—browsers in use, including screen readers, and browsers on PDAs and Web phones.

Solution

The answer is to test in as many browsers as you can. The types of browsers that you can install will depend on the operating systems to which you have access. Table 7.1 lists the major browsers that can be installed on Windows, Mac OS X, and Linux. At the very least, you're likely to want to test in Internet Explorer 5 and 6, a Mozilla-based browser, possibly Netscape 4, Opera, and, if your operating system allows it, a KHTML-based browser such as Konqueror or Safari.

Obscure and Obsolete Browsers

Older and more unusual browsers can be found at http://browsers.evolt.org/.

I only have access to one operating system. How can I test in more of these browsers?

Unless you have an entire test suite in your office, you'll probably find that you're unable to install certain browsers because they're operating-system specific.

Table 7.1. Popular Browsers

Browser (engine)	Win	Mac	Linux	Download From
Internet Explorer 5	✓			http://www.skyzyx.com/downloads/
Internet Explorer 5 for Mac		✓		http://www.apple.com/downloads/
Internet Explorer 6	✓			http://www.microsoft.com/windows/ie/
Netscape 4	✓	✓	✓	http://netscape.com/download/archive.html
Netscape 6 (Gecko beta)	✓	✓	✓	http://netscape.com/download/archive.html
Netscape 7 (Gecko)	✓	✓	✓	http://netscape.com/download/
Mozilla (Gecko)	✓	✓	✓	http://www.mozilla.org/
Firefox (Gecko)	✓	✓	✓	http://www.mozilla.org/firefox/
Camino (Gecko)		✓		http://www.mozilla.org/camino/
Galeon (Gecko)			✓	http://galeon.sourceforge.net/
Opera	✓	✓	✓	http://www.opera.com/
Safari (WebCore)		✓		http://www.apple.com/downloads/
Omniweb (Web-Core)		✓		http://www.omnigroup.com/omniweb/
Konqueror			✓	http://www.konqueror.org/
iCab		✓		http://www.icab.de/

Solution

There are a variety of solutions that will let you run an additional operating system on your computer, thereby giving you the ability to install and use the browsers developed for that operating system.

Windows

While there is currently no way to emulate a Mac on a Windows computer, there are various options for those who would like to be able to view sites in Linux-specific browsers.

Knoppix

Knoppix is a version of Linux that is run from a bootable CD. It doesn't install anything to your hard disk, and is therefore very useful if you simply want to see how your design looks in Linux. The Knoppix CD has KDE 3.1 as the desktop environment, which includes the Konqueror Web browser.

Knoppix is free to download and use; download it from http://www.knoppix.org/.

VMWare

VMWare Workstation is a powerful application that allows you to create "virtual computers" on your PC. You can get VMWare for Windows, which creates a Windows host machine upon which it installs virtual machines that run a variety of different operating systems. A Linux version of VMWare is also available, which runs virtual machines on a Linux host.

After creating a VMWare virtual machine, you simply install the operating system as normal—it runs completely independent of the host machine. You can use virtual machines to install older copies of Windows, as well as versions of Linux, so it's very useful if you need to be able to test on different platforms. VMWare is commercial software, however, the expense is far less than the cost of buying a new computer just to test on. So, if you frequently find that you need to test in other operating systems, this may be a good option for you. Find out more about VMWare at http://www.vmware.com/.

Figure 7.1. The author's site is displayed in multiple browsers and operating systems, using VMWare.

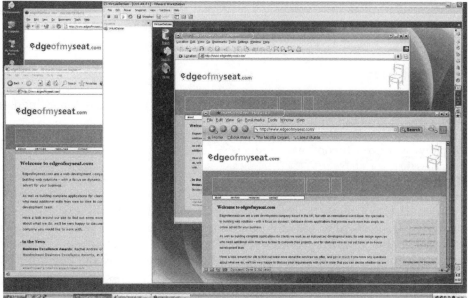

 Tip

Konqueror as Surrogate Safari

The KDE/Linux browser Konqueror uses the rendering engine KHTML, an updated version of which is used by Safari on Mac. There are differences between the two browsers, but the version of Konqueror that comes with KDE3.2 is close to Safari, as many changes made by the Safari team have been included in this version.

Dual Booting with Another Operating System

Another option, if you want to run another operating system, is to dual boot your computer. You can install Windows and Linux, then select which to boot into when you start up your machine. A good walkthrough of the process you'll need to use to get your dual boot system up and running can be found at http://www.aboutdebian.com/dualboot.htm.

Mac

Though not the most popular choice among Web users, Mac OS X is the one platform which cannot be emulated at present. Having one around is therefore almost essential for any serious Web designer, and the options for emulating other platforms on the Mac are surprisingly workable.

Virtual PC for Mac

Microsoft Virtual PC for Mac enables Mac users to install and run Windows applications. Find out more at:

http://www.microsoft.com/mac/products/virtualpc/virtualpc.aspx

KDE Darwin

A project that's currently under way aims to develop KDE for Mac OS X, thereby enabling Mac users to install and run Konqueror. This project was at pre-alpha stage at the time of writing; however, once it becomes more stable, it will be one way in which Mac users will be able to view their work on the Konqueror browser. Find out more at: http://kde.opendarwin.org/.

Linux

As with Windows, the cheapest option is usually to dual boot, but a number of tools exist for side-by-side testing with Windows browsers on the Linux desktop.

VMWare

A version of VMWare is available for Linux; it allows users to run a Linux host system and create VMWare virtual machines on which they can install other operating systems, such as Windows. For more details, see the above section about using VMWare with a Windows host.

Wine

Wine is an open source implementation of the Windows API, which runs on top of Linux. Installing Wine will enable you to run some Windows programs in Linux—with varying success! You can find out more about Wine at http://www.winehq.com/.

Far easier to install and configure than Wine itself is Crossover Office.[23] This commercial product incorporates Wine in creating a solution that allows customers to install Windows applications on Linux; one of the products that's currently supported is Internet Explorer 6.

Dual Booting

Similarly to Windows users, Linux users also have the option of dual booting their system as a way to install a version of Windows—as much as it may pain them to do so!

Is there a service that can show me how my site looks in various browsers?

Being able to use your site in a variety of browsers is the best way to check that it works well in all of them; however, unless you can set up a test suite in your office, there are likely to be some browsers to which you won't have access.

Solution

You can check your site's display and functioning in multiple browsers on multiple operating systems at Browser Cam.[24] You'll have to pay for this service, but if your testing is constrained to one operating system, Browser Cam can be a great way to get a feel for your site's behavior in browsers that you couldn't otherwise access. A sample results page can be seen in Figure 7.2.

---

[23] http://www.codeweavers.com/
[24] http://www.browsercam.com/

Figure 7.2. The author uses Browser Cam to test her own Website.

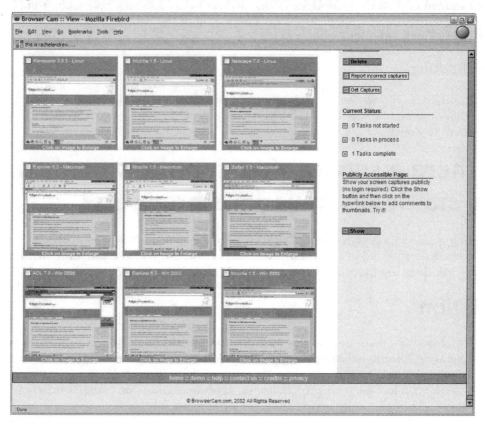

Discussion

In addition to Browser Cam, if you need to view your site in Safari, you can do so at iCapture,[25] which is currently a free service.

Another way to check that your site works in browsers to which you don't have access is to request a site check on a mailing list. Most Web design and development mailing lists are quite used to having users ask for people to check their sites, and you can return the favor by viewing other people's sites in the browsers that you use.

---

[25] http://www.danvine.com/icapture/

Can I install multiple versions of Internet Explorer in Windows?

There are major differences between Internet Explorer 6 and Internet Explorer 5 in terms of CSS rendering, but, unlike Netscape, users may only have one version of Internet Explorer installed. How can we test sites in older, but still used versions of IE?

Solution

It is now possible to run more than one version of Internet Explorer on your system. Download the standalone Internet Explorer ZIP files relevant to your system here: http://www.skyzyx.com/downloads/.

Once you've downloaded the files, you simply need to unzip them, then run them by double-clicking on the `iexplore.exe` file. In my experience, the browsers are prone to crashing, but they're fine simply for testing Websites. The standalone installs don't seem to affect any existing version of Internet Explorer that you may already have installed on your operating system, either.

In Figure 7.3, the three browsers running on my Windows XP machine (which has IE 6 installed by default) display a bug from a demo on Position is Everything.[27] The top left browser is IE 5.5; it displays the "phantom boxes" that the demo is presenting. To the right is IE 6, which renders the site correctly. At the bottom is IE 5, which, as you can see, displays the content using its different implementation of the box model. So, it's true! You *can* run three different versions of IE on the same machine!

---

[27] http://www.positioniseverything.net/explorer/inlinelist.html

Figure 7.3. Three versions of Internet Explorer run on one computer.

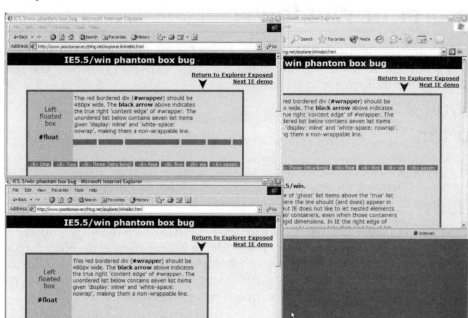

How do I test my site in a text-only browser?

Checking your site using a text-only browser is an excellent way to find out how accessible it really is. If you find it easy to navigate around your site using a text-only browser, it's likely that visitors using screen readers will also be able to do so.

Solution

You can view pages from your site using Lynx, a text-only browser, through the online Lynx Viewer at http://www.delorie.com/web/lynxview.html. While this is a useful test, Lynx is free to download and install—so, why not install a copy on your system? This provides the added advantage that it enables you to test pages before you upload them to the Web.

Linux/Unix

You may find that Lynx is already installed on your system; if not, you should be able to get a copy easily via your package management system. Or, simply download the source from http://lynx.isc.org/release/.

Windows

Installing Lynx on Windows used to be a tricky process, but now, an installer is available from http://www.csant.info/lynx.htm. Download and run the installer, which will also make Lynx available from your Start menu.

Mac OS X

Lynx for Mac OS X is available from the Apple Website.[31]

Discussion

Lynx behaves consistently across all platforms, and you'll need to learn a few simple commands in order to use it for Web browsing.

To open a Web page, hit **G** and enter the URL. Hit **Enter**, and Lynx will load that URL. If the site that you're trying to visit uses any form of cookies, Lynx will ask you if you wish to accept them. Type **Y** for yes, **N** for no, **A** to accept cookies from that site always, or **V** to ensure that you never accept cookies from that site.

Use the arrow keys to navigate using Lynx. The up and down arrow keys will let you jump from link to link. The right arrow key will follow the link that you're currently on, while the left arrow key will take you back.

---

[31] http://www.apple.com/downloads/macosx/unix_open_source/lynx.html

To complete a form, navigate to the form field using the down arrow key and, once you're there, type normally into the field.

You can use Lynx to view local files, which is useful during development. If you're running a local Web server, such as Apache or IIS, you can obviously just point Lynx to localhost URLs. Note, though, that the browser will also read an HTML file directly if you provide the path and filename.

For more information on how to use Lynx, hit **H** to bring up the help system, which you can navigate as you would any site.

Figure 7.4 shows a typical site displayed in Lynx.

Figure 7.4. View a site in Lynx.

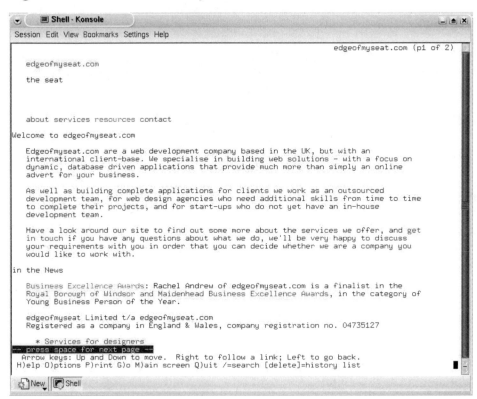

Tip

See Accessibility in Action

Spend some time visiting your favorite sites in a text-only browser—you'll soon start to appreciate how important it is to ensure that you have `alt` text on images, and a well structured document!

How do I test my site in a screen reader?

The best way to understand the experience of a user visiting your site with a screen reader is to try it out for yourself; however, the most popular and well known screen reader in use today, JAWS, is not only expensive, but also has a steep learning curve. What options do Web developers have to test their sites in a screen reader?

Solution

Currently, no screen readers are available for Mac OS X, although there are rumors that one is in the offing. Windows users can download IBM Home Page Reader,[32] which has a 30-day trial.

IBM Home Page Reader is an easy-to-use screen reader with which you can browse the Web and test your own sites. It really is worth taking the time to download the 30-day trial and navigate through your own—and other—sites. It's the best way to understand what it's like to have a Website read to you.

Linux and other UNIX users can download emacspeak,[33] the free screen reader for emacs.

How do I hide CSS from Netscape 4?

If you've created a site with a complex CSS layout, or which makes heavy use of CSS for styling forms, Netscape 4 probably won't handle it too well. Instead of trying to fix your site so that it works in Netscape 4—which might not be worthwhile if only a small proportion of your visitors use that browser—you can hide the style sheet from Netscape 4 altogether.

---

[32] http://www-3.ibm.com/able/solution_offerings/hpr.html
[33] http://emacspeak.sourceforge.net/

Solution

Netscape 4 does not recognize style sheets that have been imported, though it does recognize their linked counterparts. To link a style sheet, you'd use:

```
<link rel="stylesheet" href="layout.css" type="text/css" />
```

But, to import the style sheet, thereby "hiding" it from Netscape, use:

```
<style type="text/css" media="all">
@import "layout.css";
</style>
```

Discussion

Older browsers that do not display CSS at all are not really a problem—they will simply display the structured content of a page. The problem arises with browsers in which the implementation of CSS is incomplete; they may crash, or render the site in such a way as to make it unusable. The worst offender in this category, by far, is Netscape 4.

This method of importing the style sheet will hide the entire style sheet from Netscape 4, and from Internet Explorer 4 on Windows. While it's pretty unusual to encounter IE 4 on Windows today, there are still users with Netscape 4—in fact, developers who work in the education sector report that some libraries and schools still have this browser as the standard, as ridiculous as that may seem!

I used this method on my personal Website,[34] as I get so few visitors using older browsers like these. Though I didn't want to waste time optimizing the site for those browsers, nor did I want to crash anyone's browser or have the site display in a manner that made it unreadable. Hiding the style sheet was the answer. Figure 7.5 shows my site in Firefox and in Netscape 4.7.

---

[34] www.rachelandrew.co.uk

Figure 7.5. The author's site displays differently in Firefox than in Netscape 4.7.

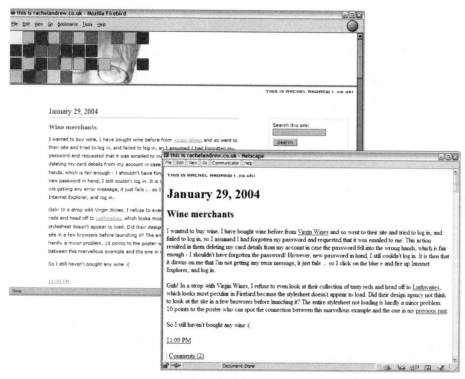

By styling your site with CSS, you can simply hide the style sheets from users whose browsers interpret CSS poorly.

 Tip

Score One More for Accessibility

If you have structured your site so that it's accessible, and users with text-only devices can read your content easily, then so can users who view the site without the style sheet.

How do I display different styles for Netscape 4?

Perhaps a reasonable proportion of your site's visitors use Netscape 4, and you want to avoid displaying an unformatted version of your site to them. Maybe your site works relatively well in the browser, but certain elements such as styled form fields cause a problem. How can you avoid serving styles suitable for Netscape 4 to newer browsers?

Solution

You can use the fact that Netscape 4 can only see linked, and not imported, style sheets to provide it with separate styles. This approach eradicates the need for you to use either JavaScript or server-side detection methods to serve an alternate style sheet. The following simple example illustrates one area in which Netscape 4 displays strangely.

File: **ns4—example.html** (excerpt)

```
<!DOCTYPE html PUBLIC "-//W3C//DTD XHTML 1.0 Transitional//EN"
 "http://www.w3.org/TR/xhtml1/DTD/xhtml1-transitional.dtd">
<html xmlns="http://www.w3.org/1999/xhtml">
<head>
<title>Different style sheet for NS4</title>
<meta http-equiv="content-type"
    content="text/html; charset=iso-8859-1" />
<link rel="stylesheet" type="text/css" href="ns4-example.css" />
</head>
<body>
<div id="content">
<p>...</p>
</div>
</body>
</html>
```

File: **ns4—example.css** (excerpt)

```
#content {
  background-color: #aaaaaa;
  color: #000000;
  padding: 0.2em 2em 0.2em 3em;
}
#content p {
```

```
  line-height: 1.6em;
  font-family: Verdana, Geneva, Arial, Helvetica, sans-serif;
  font-size: 80%;
}
```

Figure 7.6 shows this as displayed in Firefox (and other modern browsers), while Figure 7.7 shows what we see in Netscape 4.7.

Figure 7.6. The example code displays in Firefox.

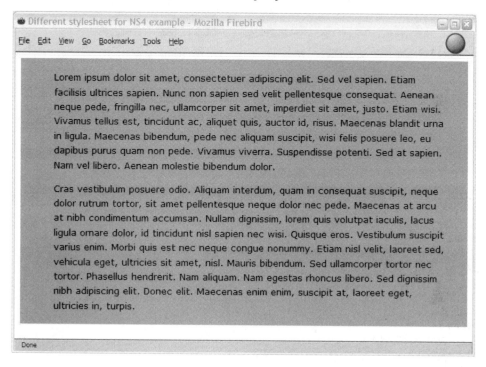

Figure 7.7. The example code displays in Netscape 4.7.

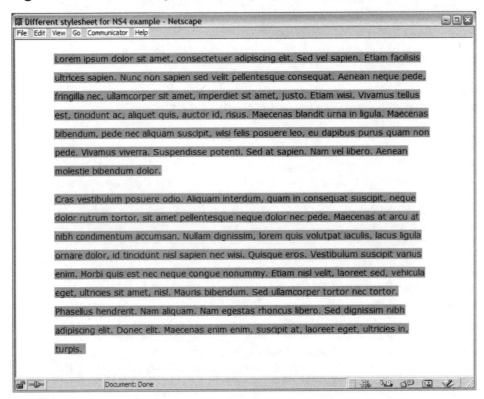

To correct this, first we change the method by which we attach the style sheet from linked to imported, as in the previous solution:

File: **ns4–example.html** (excerpt)

```
<style type="text/css" media="all">
@import "ns4-example.css";
</style>
```

This will have the effect of hiding the style sheet entirely from Netscape 4.

Create a new style sheet by saving the existing style sheet under a different name. Then, use a `<link>` tag to attach this new style sheet before the imported style sheet:

File: **ns4—example.html** (excerpt)

```
<head>
<title>Different style sheet for NS4</title>
<meta http-equiv="content-type"
    content="text/html; charset=iso-8859-1" />
<link rel="stylesheet" type="text/css"
    href="ns4-example-oldbrowsers.css" />
<style type="text/css" media="all">
@import "ns4-example.css";
</style>
</head>
```

You now have two identical style sheets attached via different methods—one is imported, the other linked. Modern browsers can see both style sheets; however, the values set in the second, imported style sheet will override any values set in the first. Netscape 4 can see only the first style sheet.

Open the first, linked style sheet. Netscape 4 did some very strange things with the background in Figure 7.7, so I changed the background color to transparent in this style sheet. The font size is comparatively larger in Netscape 4 due to differences in the ways the browsers size text, so I can also tweak the font sizes and line height here as I see fit.

File: **ns4—example-oldbrowsers.css** (excerpt)

```
#content {
  background-color: transparent;
  color: #000000;
  padding: 0.2em 2em 0.2em 3em;
}
#content p {
  line-height: 1.4em;
  font-family: Verdana, Geneva, Arial, Helvetica, sans-serif;
  font-size: 70%;
}
```

The resulting display in Netscape 4 is shown in Figure 7.8.

Figure 7.8. The document displays successfully in Netscape 4.7 after the linked style sheet is tweaked.

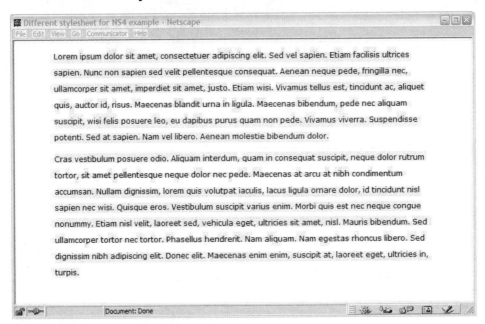

These changes to the linked style sheet do not affect the display of the document in recent browsers, because the imported style sheet contains all these properties, and it overrides the stylings defined in the linked version.

If you add any properties to the linked style sheet—perhaps to define the width of an element for Netscape 4—then you must add an overriding property in the imported style sheet to reflect the display you wish to maintain in modern browsers. Otherwise, the modern browsers will take the property from the linked style sheet and use it in rendering the page.

How do I add a message, which displays only in version 4 browsers, to explain why my site looks so plain?

If you have decided to hide your style sheet from version 4 browsers, or to implement only a very basic style sheet, you might like to indicate to users of these older browsers why your site looks so plain.

Solution

Add a hidden message by setting the CSS `display` property to `none`.

In your imported (new browser) style sheet, add the following class.

File: **ns4–example.css** (excerpt)

```css
.oldbrowsers {
  display: none;
}
```

At the very top of your document, insert the text that you want to show to users of older browsers. Place this text in a container (such as a paragraph) to which the `oldbrowsers` class is applied.

File: **ns4–example.html**

```html
<!DOCTYPE html PUBLIC "-//W3C//DTD XHTML 1.0 Transitional//EN"
    "http://www.w3.org/TR/xhtml1/DTD/xhtml1-transitional.dtd">
<html xmlns="http://www.w3.org/1999/xhtml">
<head>
<title>Different style sheet for NS4</title>
<meta http-equiv="content-type"
    content="text/html; charset=iso-8859-1" />
<link rel="stylesheet" type="text/css"
    href="ns4-example-oldbrowsers.css" />
<style type="text/css" media="all">
@import "ns4-example.css";
</style>
</head>
<body>
<div id="content">
  <p class="oldbrowsers">This site will look much better in a
```

```
    browser that supports Web standards, but it is accessible to
    any browser or Internet device.</p>
  <p>…</p>
</div>
</body>
</html>
```

If you used the method described in the previous solution to apply a different style sheet for Netscape 4 users, you can make the message more noticeable by styling it with CSS rules that are supported by Netscape 4.

File: **ns4–example-oldbrowsers.css** (excerpt)

```
.oldbrowsers {
  font-weight: bold;
  color: #FF4500;
  background-color: transparent;
}
```

The message will not appear in browsers that read the imported style sheet and that recognize `display: none`. However, the message will appear in a version 4 browser, as shown in Figure 7.9.

Figure 7.9. The message displays in Netscape 4.7.

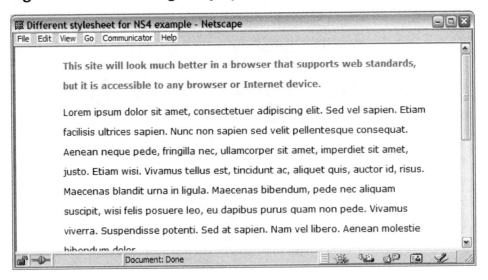

Discussion

This method of displaying a message to users of older browsers was popularized by the Web Standards Project (WaSP).[35]

The recommendation of the WaSP is to link your message to an information page that explains why you have hidden or scaled down your design for older browsers, and outlines the options as far as new browsers are concerned, along with download links to the latest versions of some of the more popular browsers.

Users of old browsers may be smarter than they appear

This technique became popular when there was a large percentage of Web users with older browsers who didn't realize that they could upgrade. Those who use old browsers these days are quite probably doing so because they have no choice—Netscape 4.7 is the browser installed on their school, work, or library machines. This makes the technique less useful; there is also the potential problem that your "old browser" message is likely to show up in search engines, be read out by screen readers, and display in limited PDA or phone devices that can't "upgrade" their browsers.

How do I hide CSS from other browsers?

You might have discovered that certain CSS rules, or sets of rules, simply break in newer browsers as a result of bugs in the browsers themselves. How can we hide CSS in order to cope with bugs in browsers that, otherwise, display our CSS well?

Solution

The exact solution to this problem will depend on the problem itself, and which browser you wish to hide your CSS from. As no browser has a perfect implementation of CSS, it is possible to use what are, in effect, bugs in particular browsers to hide entire style sheets—or certain properties—from those browsers. I've covered some of the most commonly used hacks here.

---

[35] http://www.webstandards.org/act/campaign/buc/tips.html

The Box Model Hack

Internet Explorer 5 and 5.5 interpret the CSS box model incorrectly. A correct implementation of the CSS box model will add to the specified width of a block any padding and borders applied to that block to produce the actual visible width. So, a <div> that's 200 pixels wide, which has 20 pixels of padding on both the right and the left, and a 5-pixel border, will actually have a total width of 250 pixels. In the world of Internet Explorer 5, however, this <div> will be 200 pixels wide *including* the borders and padding. As you can imagine, this will make a mess of any CSS layout that relies on the precise widths of page elements.

This problem can be seen clearly in Figure 7.10. The top browser is Internet Explorer 5, which, with its incorrect implementation of the box model, displays the <div> 50 pixels narrower than does Internet Explorer 6. The latter browser uses a correct implementation of the box model.

File: **box-model-hack.html (excerpt)**

```
<!DOCTYPE html PUBLIC "-//W3C//DTD XHTML 1.0 Transitional//EN"
    "http://www.w3.org/TR/xhtml1/DTD/xhtml1-transitional.dtd">
<html xmlns="http://www.w3.org/1999/xhtml">
<head>
<title>Box Model Hack</title>
<meta http-equiv="content-type"
    content="text/html; charset=iso-8859-1" />
<link rel="stylesheet" type="text/css" href="box-model-hack.css"
    />
</head>
<body>
<div id="mybox">
<p>This div has a width of 200 pixels, padding of 20 pixels and a
   border of 5 pixels.</p>
</div>
</body>
</html>
```

File: **box-model-hack.css**

```
#mybox {
  padding: 20px;
  border: 5px solid #000000;
  background-color: #00BFFF;
  width: 200px;
}
```

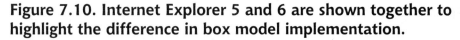

Figure 7.10. Internet Explorer 5 and 6 are shown together to highlight the difference in box model implementation.

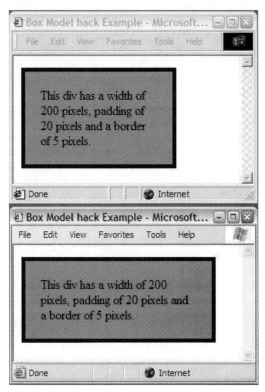

To make IE 5 display the box with the same width as newer browsers that accurately comply with box model implementation, we need to specify a width of 250 pixels for the box in IE 5/5.5 *only*.

To achieve this, we can take advantage of a bug in the IE 5/5.5 CSS parser, using a method developed by Tantek Çelik.[36]

File: **box-model-hack2.css**

```
#mybox {
  padding: 20px;
  border: 5px solid #000000;
  background-color: #00BFFF;
}
```

[36] http://tantek.com/CSS/Examples/boxmodelhack.html

```
#mybox {
  width: 250px;
  voice-family: "\"}\"";
  voice-family: inherit;
  width: 200px;
}
html > body #mybox {
  width: 200px;
}
```

With this style sheet, the two browsers agree on the width of the box, as you can see in Figure 7.11.

Figure 7.11. Internet Explorer 5 and 6 both display the box at the same width once we apply the filter.

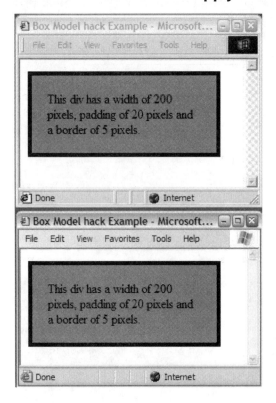

This trick works because, with the hack in place, IE 5/5.5 does not see the second or third occurrences of the width property, and therefore renders the box at the first specified width (250 pixels). Standards-compliant browsers render the box at the second, correct width (200 pixels). The final declaration deals with browsers that have the same parsing bug as IE 5/5.5 but that implement a correct box model, ensuring that they display the correct width. This has become known as the "be nice to Opera 5" rule, as it's one of the browsers affected.

There are other versions of this hack, but when people refer to using "the box model hack," they're generally talking about this or a very similar variation.

The High Pass Filter

Another filter[1] developed by Tantek Çelik can be used if you wish to hide style sheets entirely from browsers that do not fully implement CSS parsing. The filter effectively hides the style sheet from older browsers, including IE 5.5 and below, Netscape 4 and below, and IE Mac 4.5 and below. You can use the filter to display unstyled content to all these browsers, similar to the use of the @import method to hide CSS from version 4 browsers discussed above.

The HTML page simply uses a linked style sheet:

File: **high-pass-filter.html** (excerpt)

```
<link rel="stylesheet" type="text/css" href="high-pass-filter.css"
   />
```

This style sheet contains two @import declarations:

File: **high-pass-filter.css**

```
@import "null?\"\{";
@import "high-pass-filter-compliant.css";
```

Create a style sheet named null (not null.css), which is empty, apart from a comment:

File: **null**

```
/* this is an empty style sheet —
   see http://tantek.com/CSS/Examples/highpass.html */
```

Then, create a style sheet that contains all your CSS—the second style sheet imported above.

---

[1] These hacks are often referred to as filters since they "filter out" particular browsers, allowing the remaining browsers to be targeted by particular CSS property declarations.

File: **high-pass-filter-compliant.css**

```
body {
  font: 11px/22px Verdana, Geneva, Arial, Helvetica, sans-serif;
  background-image: url(peppers_bg.jpg);
  background-repeat: no-repeat;
  background-position: 20px 20px;
}
#content {
  margin-left: 220px;
  margin-top: 40px;
  margin-right: 80px;
}
```

Figure 7.12 shows the document in Firefox and IE 5. As you can see, IE 5 displays the document unstyled.

Figure 7.12. The document displays differently in Firefox and Internet Explorer 5.

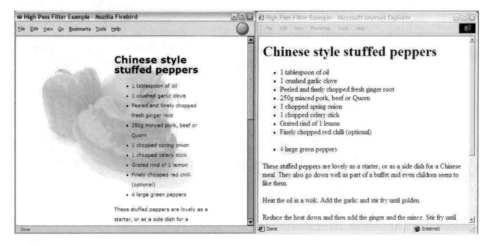

Discussion

The hacks in this solution are frequently seen on Websites and within example style sheets that are made available for download, so you may well come across them in your work. There are also a whole range of hacks and filters that deal with specific browsers. This information changes all the time as new browser versions are released, and new hacks discovered, so it's worth bookmarking a site that has an up-to-date hacks list and checking there for new information if you experience a problem with a specific browser.

My favorite sites for this type of information are:

❏ CSS Filters on Dithered.com

http://www.dithered.com/css_filters/

❏ The CSS Hack category on the CSS-Discuss Wiki

http://css-discuss.incutio.com/?page=CssHack

IMPORTANT

Use Only as Needed

Before you use a CSS hack, make sure that it really is the only way you can achieve the effect you want. Sometimes, you can work around a bug by changing your approach slightly; at other times, the difference doesn't really matter and the site still looks reasonably good in the buggy browsers.

CSS hacks make your code less readable, and can hurt the forwards compatibility of your site. Avoid them if you can.

Commenting Hacks

Once you've decided that you really must use a hack, be sure to comment it properly. When you come back to the site at a later date, you may not remember why you implemented the hack, and anyone who takes over from you or works on your team may become confused by one of the less common hacks if they can't see what it is at a glance.

File: **box-model-hack2.css (excerpt)**

```
/* box model hack -
    see http://tantek.com/CSS/Examples/boxmodelhack.html */
#mybox {
  width: 250px;
  voice-family: "\"}\"";
  voice-family: inherit;
  width: 200px;
}
html > body #mybox {
  width: 200px;
}
```

Choosing a Hack

When you're selecting a CSS hack to use, try to find something that works because of some lack of support in the browser from which you want to hide the CSS. That way, you're unlikely to have any problems when a newer browser is released.

It is unlikely that a new browser with, for example, the bug exploited by the High Pass Filter, would be released. Thus, using the High Pass Filter is unlikely to result in a newer browser being unable to display the styles.

Why does my site look different in Internet Explorer 6 than it does in Mozilla?

You're developing a site using XHTML and CSS, testing in IE 6, and it all seems to be going well... Then, you look at the layout with Mozilla and realize it's displaying very differently to the way it's rendering in Internet Explorer. What's going on?

Solution

IE bugs aside, the most likely issue is that Internet Explorer is rendering your document in **Quirks Mode**. Many modern browsers have two rendering modes. Quirks Mode renders documents according to the buggy implementations of older browsers such as Netscape 4 and Internet Explorer 4 and 5. Standards or Compliance Mode renders documents as per the W3C specifications.

☐ Documents that use older DOCTYPEs, are poorly formed, or have no DOC-TYPE at all, display using Quirks Mode.

☐ Documents that are using strict HTML or XHTML DOCTYPEs render using Compliance Mode.

However, it's not quite as simple as that. For example, if you include anything at all above the statement of the DOCTYPE—a blank line, or even the XML declaration—Internet Explorer will render in Quirks Mode. Figure 7.13 shows the following document rendered in both Mozilla Firefox (at the top) and Internet Explorer 6 (at the bottom).

Figure 7.13. Internet Explorer in Quirks Mode renders the same document differently than Firefox in Compliance Mode.

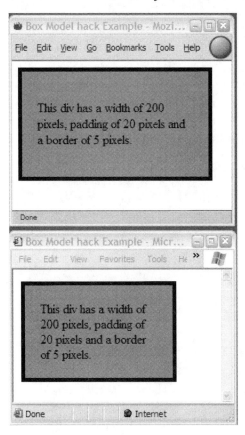

File: **doctype-quirks.html**

```
<?xml version="1.0" encoding="iso-8859-1"?>
<!DOCTYPE html PUBLIC "-//W3C//DTD XHTML 1.0 Transitional//EN"
    "http://www.w3.org/TR/xhtml1/DTD/xhtml1-transitional.dtd">
<html xmlns="http://www.w3.org/1999/xhtml">
<head>
<title>DOCTYPE Example</title>
<meta http-equiv="content-type"
    content="text/html; charset=iso-8859-1" />
<link rel="stylesheet" type="text/css" href="box-model-hack.css"
    />
</head>
<body>
```

```
<div id="mybox">
  <p>This div has a width of 200 pixels, padding of 20 pixels and
    a border of 5 pixels.</p>
</div>
</body>
</html>
```

If you read about the box model hack above, you might realize that Internet Explorer 6 here is rendering the page with the broken CSS Box Model implementation used by IE 5/5.5. This happens as a result of the inclusion of the <?xml declaration above the DOCTYPE. If you delete this from the document, so that the DOCTYPE declaration is the first thing on the page, Internet Explorer will render in Compliance Mode, as shown in Figure 7.14.

File: **doctype-compliance.html**

```
<!DOCTYPE html PUBLIC "-//W3C//DTD XHTML 1.0 Transitional//EN"
    "http://www.w3.org/TR/xhtml1/DTD/xhtml1-transitional.dtd">
<html xmlns="http://www.w3.org/1999/xhtml">
<head>
<title>DOCTYPE Example</title>
<meta http-equiv="content-type"
    content="text/html; charset=iso-8859-1" />
<link rel="stylesheet" type="text/css" href="box-model-hack.css"
    />
</head>
<body>
<div id="mybox">
  <p>This div has a width of 200 pixels, padding of 20 pixels and
    a border of 5 pixels.</p>
</div>
</body>
</html>
```

Figure 7.14. Internet Explorer and Firefox render the page in Compliance Mode.

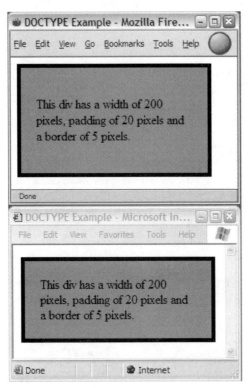

Discussion

If you're building a new site, I recommend that you aim to meet the requirements of Compliance Mode, whichever DTD you're working to. New browsers will be likely to support the W3C standards and will render pages using those standards whether or not they support any DOCTYPE switching.

If you continue to design for older browsers, relying on Quirks Mode in their newer counterparts, you may find that you site doesn't work in a browser that doesn't have a Quirks Mode. It's better to work in Compliance Mode in the new browsers and deal with the older browsers using the fixes we've already discussed, as these are a known entity—the latest version of Mozilla is not!

The following DOCTYPEs should force the browsers that support DOCTYPE switching—IE 6, Mozilla, IE 5 Mac, and Opera 7—into Compliance Mode. Remember that even a comment above the DOCTYPE statement will switch IE 6 back into Quirks Mode.

HTML 4.01 Transitional

```
<!DOCTYPE HTML PUBLIC "-//W3C//DTD HTML 4.01 Transitional//EN"
    "http://www.w3.org/TR/html4/loose.dtd">
```

HTML 4.01 Frameset

```
<!DOCTYPE HTML PUBLIC "-//W3C//DTD HTML 4.01 Frameset//EN"
    "http://www.w3.org/TR/html4/frameset.dtd">
```

HTML 4.01 Strict

```
<!DOCTYPE HTML PUBLIC "-//W3C//DTD HTML 4.01//EN"
    "http://www.w3.org/TR/html4/strict.dtd">
```

XHTML 1.0 Transitional

```
<!DOCTYPE html PUBLIC "-//W3C//DTD XHTML 1.0 Transitional//EN"
    "http://www.w3.org/TR/xhtml1/DTD/xhtml1-transitional.dtd">
```

XHTML 1.0 Frameset

```
<!DOCTYPE html PUBLIC "-//W3C//DTD XHTML 1.0 Frameset//EN"
    "http://www.w3.org/TR/xhtml1/DTD/xhtml1-frameset.dtd">
```

XHTML 1.0 Strict

```
<!DOCTYPE html PUBLIC "-//W3C//DTD XHTML 1.0 Strict//EN"
    "http://www.w3.org/TR/xhtml1/DTD/xhtml1-strict.dtd">
```

XHTML 1.1

```
<!DOCTYPE html PUBLIC "-//W3C//DTD XHTML 1.1//EN"
    "http://www.w3.org/TR/xhtml11/DTD/xhtml11.dtd">
```

A full list of DOCTYPEs, and their effects on various browsers, is available at http://gutfeldt.ch/matthias/articles/doctypeswitch/table.html.

I think I've found a CSS bug! What do I do?

We all find ourselves in situations in which our CSS just will not work! You've tried every solution you can think of, yet, some random bit of text continues to appear and disappear in IE 6, or part of your layout spreads across half the content in Safari. Before it drives you mad, take a deep breath and relax. There is a solution!

Solution

This is a solution that helps you find the solution!

1. **Take a break.**

    Once we designers have gotten frustrated battling a problem, to apply any kind of rational process to finding a solution is difficult at best. So, take a break. Go for a walk, tidy your desk, or do some housework. If you're at work with boss looking over your shoulder so that you can't even get to the coffee machine in peace, work on something else—answer some mail, tidy up some content. Do anything to take your mind off the problem for a while.

2. **Validate your style sheet and document.**

    If you haven't already done so, your next step should be to validate the CSS and the (X)HTML document. Errors in your CSS or markup may well cause problems and, even if they don't, they often make it more difficult for you to find a solution.

3. **Isolate the problem.**

    Can you get your bug to occur in isolation from the rest of your document? As CSS bugs often display only when a certain group of conditions is met, trying to find out exactly where the problem occurs may help you work out how it can be fixed. Try and reproduce the problem on a document that doesn't contain the rest of your layout.

4. **Search the Web.**

If what you have is a bug, it's likely that someone else has seen it before. There are plenty of great sites that detail browser bugs and explain how to get around them. I always check the following list of sites when I'm up against a problem:

CSS Pointers Group   http://css.nu/pointers/bugs.html

Position is   http://www.positioniseverything.net/
Everything

Category Browser   http://css-discuss.incutio.com/?page=CategoryBrowserBug
Bug on the css-d wiki

Also, search the css-discuss archives,[43] and don't forget Google!

5. **Ask for help.**

If you haven't managed to find a solution as you've moved through the above steps, ask for help. Even the most experienced developers hit problems that they just can't see past. Sometimes, just talking through the issue with a bunch of people who haven't been staring at it all week can help you resolve the problem, or come up with new ideas to test—even if no-one has an immediate solution.

When you post to a forum or mailing list, remember these rules of thumb:

❑ If the list or forum has archives, search them first, just in case you're about to ask one of those questions that's asked at least once a day.

❑ Make sure that your CSS and HTML validates; otherwise, the answer you'll get is most likely to be, "go and validate your document and see if that helps."

❑ Upload an example to a location to which you can link. If you manage to reproduce the problem outside a complex layout, so much the better—this will make it easier for others to work out what's going on.

❑ Explain what you've tried so far in the message. This saves the recipients of your message from pursuing those same dead-ends again, and shows that you've attempted to fix the problem yourself before asking for help.

---

[43] http://www.css-discuss.org/

❑ Give your message a descriptive subject line. People are more likely to read a post entitled, "Duplicate boxes appearing in IE5" than one that screams, "HELP!" Good titles also make the list archives more useful, as people can see at a glance the titles of posts in a thread.

❑ Be polite and to the point.

❑ Be patient while you wait for answers. If you don't receive a reply after a day or so, and it's a busy list, it is usually acceptable to post again with the word "REPOST" in the subject line. Posts can be overlooked in particularly large boards, and this is a polite way to remind users that you have not received any assistance with your problem.

❑ When you receive answers, try implementing the poster's suggestions. Don't get upset or angry if the recommendations don't work, or you feel that the poster is asking you to try very basic things. I've seen threads go on for many posts with different posters weighing in to help someone solve a problem, and continuing the discussion until a solution is solved. Give people a chance to help!

❑ If you find a solution—or you don't, and decide instead to change your design to avoid the problem—post back to the thread to explain what worked and what didn't. This shows good manners towards those who helped you, but will also help anyone who searches the archive for information on the same problem. It's very frustrating to search an archive and find several possible solutions to a problem, but to not know which (if any) was successful!

Many Web design and development mailing lists are used by people who are very knowledgeable about CSS. In my opinion, the best CSS-specific list is css-discuss.[44] It's a high-traffic list, but the people on it are very helpful, and you can pick up a lot just by reading the posts and browsing the archives.

See the next solution for a real-world walkthrough of a common bug, and the process required to find a solution and fix it.

---

[44] http://www.css-discuss.org/

Some of my content is appearing and disappearing in Internet Explorer 6! What should I do?

I recently added some images to a page on my business Website, which lists the books that I've been involved with. As my default browser is Firefox, the page looked absolutely fine (see Figure 7.15); then, I checked it in Internet Explorer 6. What I saw was the page displayed in Figure 7.16—two paragraphs of text were missing in action! If I refreshed the page, or scrolled, the text reappeared, but something very odd seemed to be going on!

Figure 7.15. The document displays in Firefox as expected.

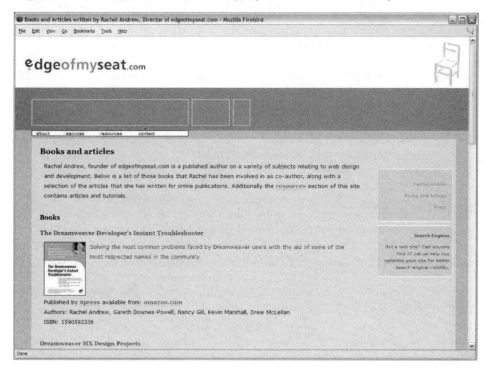

Figure 7.16. The document renders poorly in Internet Explorer 6.

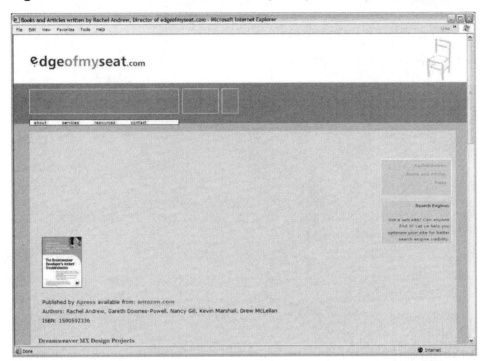

Solution

First, I checked my document at the W3C markup validator[45] and my CSS at the W3C CSS Validator.[46] I wanted to make sure that there was no problem within my document, or the CSS, that would cause IE 6 to behave strangely.

Isolating the Problem

In this particular design, each book is described within a `<div>` container with a class of `cBlock`. Within `cBlock`, I have a paragraph with a class of `booktext`, an image, and a normal paragraph. The style sheet sets up various margins and padding, floats the image to the left, and makes sure that the normal paragraph is clear of the floated image.

[45] http://validator.w3.org
[46] http://jigsaw.w3.org/css-validator/

```
<h1>Books and articles</h1>
<p>Rachel Andrew, founder of edgeofmyseat.com …</p>
<h2>Books</h2>
<h3>The Dreamweaver Developer's Instant Troubleshooter</h3>
<div class="cBlock">
  <p class="booktext">
    <img src="img/instant_troubleshooter.jpg" width="100"
        height="124" alt="Cover" />
    Solving the most common problems faced by Dreamweaver users
    with the aid of some of the most respected names in the
    community.
  </p>
  <p>
    Published by <a href="http://www.apress.com">Apress</a>
    available from: <a href="http://www.amazon.com/exec/obidos/ASI
N/1590592336/edgeofmyseat-20">amazon.com</a><br />
    Authors: Rachel Andrew, Gareth Downes-Powell, Nancy Gill,
    Kevin Marshall, Drew McLellan<br />
    ISBN: 1590592336
  </p>
</div>
```

```
.cBlock {
  margin-top: 10px;
}
.cBlock p.booktext {
  padding-left: 30px;
  padding-right: 20px;
  padding-top: 10px;
  color: #4E475F;
  background-color: transparent;
  clear: none;
}
.cBlock img {
  float: left;
  margin: 0 10px 4px 0;
  border: 1px solid #4E475F;
}
.cBlock p {
 clear: both;
}
```

I discovered that if I removed the `float` property from the image, the problem disappeared, so I was pretty sure that was the source of the problem. However, I wanted to keep the floated image as it was—without it, as shown in Figure 7.17, the text would not display to the right of the image.

Figure 7.17. Removing the float property fixes the disappearing text problem.

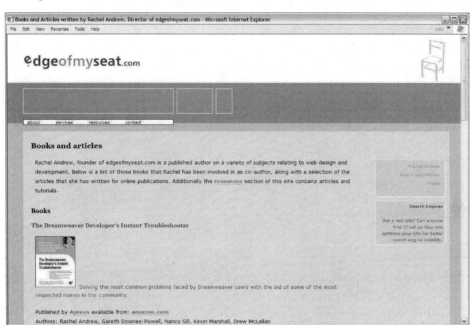

Searching the Web

As I knew what caused the problem, I could then go and see whether I could find any details on this bug, or a method to fix it. My layout wasn't very complicated, so I figured that if I was seeing this, other people would have seen it, too.

On the Website "Position is Everything" I found details of the IE6 Peekaboo Bug:[47] "A liquid box has a float inside, and content that appears alongside that float. All is well, until it's viewed in IE6. 'Wah? Where's my content?!' You reload the page, and nothing. When you scroll down, or perhaps switch to another window, upon returning to the 'scene of the crime' there it all is, fat 'n sassy!"

That sounded just like my bug! And, the page gave me some information on how to get rid of it.

---

[47] http://www.positioniseverything.net/explorer/peekaboo.html

I decided to try out the newest method on the page, "The Holly Hack." This seemed to be the one that would have the least impact on my layout, which worked in other browsers; the problem manifested only in IE 6.

This method points to a hack that's used to cure another IE6–specific problem.[48] Looking down the page, I found the CSS that seemed as if it should fix the problem, so I added it to my style sheet.

```
.cBlock {
  margin-top: 10px;
}
.cBlock p.booktext {
  padding-left: 30px;
  padding-right: 20px;
  padding-top: 10px;
  color: #4E475F;
  background-color: transparent;
  clear: none
}
.cBlock img {
  float: left;
  margin: 0 10px 4px 0;
  border: 1px solid #4E475F;
}

/* Hide from IE5-mac. Only IE-win sees this.
The Holly Hack -
http://www.positioniseverything.net/explorer/threepxtest.html
Used to combat the IE6 Peekaboo Bug
\*/
* html .cBlock img {
  margin-right: 10px;
}
* html p {
  height: 1%;
  margin-left: 0;
}
/* End hide from IE5/mac
End Holly Hack*/

.cBlock p {
  clear: both;
}
```

---

[48] http://www.positioniseverything.net/explorer/threepxtest.html

Upon testing the page again in IE 6, I saw that the problem had indeed vanished. I then checked the site in other browsers, just to be sure that it didn't cause any unwanted side-effects. It's always a good idea to test your site again after implementing a hack. Even though sites that demonstrate these hacks tend to be kept up-to-date, and users will let the owners know if a solution is found to cause issues in any browser, there may be problems that haven't been uncovered yet—or, you may have made a mistake as you implemented the hack.

What do the error and warning messages in the W3C Validator mean?

Validating your documents and CSS is an important step to ensure that your site renders correctly in standards-complaint browsers. Sometimes, however, the error and warning messages can be very confusing.

Solution

You can validate your (X)HTML documents online at the W3C Validator.[49]

CSS documents likewise have the W3C CSS Validator.[50]

With both CSS and (X)HTML documents, start at the top. Sometimes, you'll run a document through the validator and get a huge long list of errors. However, when you fix the first error that the validator has encountered, many of the subsequent errors often disappear. This is especially likely to happen in an (X)HTML document. If you have forgotten to close a tag correctly, the validator believes that the tag is still open, and it will give you a whole list of errors to tell you that element X is not allowed within element Y. Close the offending tag and those errors will disappear.

A related problem is found in documents with an HTML DTD, where the developer has closed a tag using XML syntax, like this:

```
<link rel="stylesheet" href="stylesheet.css" type="text/css" />
```

If you've done this in a document that doesn't have an XHTML DOCTYPE, you'll receive errors indicating that there is a closing HEAD element in the wrong

---

[49] http://validator.w3.org/
[50] http://jigsaw.w3.org/css-validator/

place. To make the document obey the HTML standard, simply remove the slash from the tag:

```
<link rel="stylesheet" href="stylesheet.css" type="text/css">
```

Errors Versus Warnings

A CSS document is not valid CSS if it contains errors, including the use of invalid syntax, missing semicolons, and so on. You will need to fix these errors to have a valid document, and also, to ensure that your style sheet behaves as expected.

If your style sheet is error-free, it will validate. A valid document, however, may still contain warnings when it's run through the validator. Whether you take notice of these warnings or not is entirely up to you. The most common warning is that you have failed to specify a background color with your color. If this warning appears because you're expecting the background color or image of the parent element to show through, you can always get the same effect—without the warning—by specifying:

```
background-color: transparent;
```

It is worth looking at the warnings just in case they highlight something that you've missed, which may cause a problem to your users.

How do I create style sheets for specific devices, such as screen readers or WebTV?

It's possible to show different CSS to different browsers, but what about other devices?

Solution

The CSS specification includes a specification for **media types**, which allow a Web page author to restrict a style sheet, or section of a style sheet, to a given medium.

You can tag a style sheet with any of these media types when you use it. For example, for a linked style sheet:

```
<link rel="stylesheet" type=text/css" href="aural.css"
    media="aural" />
```

In-page style sheets can also be tagged this way:

```
<style type="text/css" media="all">
…
</style>
```

In both these examples, the `media` attribute has a value of the media type for which the style sheet has been created. This style sheet will then only be used by devices that support that media type.

Discussion

The following list of media types is taken from the CSS2 specification.[51]

all   Suitable for all devices

aural   Intended for speech synthesizers

braille   Intended for Braille tactile feedback devices

embossed   Intended for Braille printers

handheld   Intended for handheld devices

print   Intended for pages, opaque material, and for documents viewed on screen in print preview mode

projection   Intended for projected presentations

screen   Intended primarily for color computer screens

tty   Intended for media using a fixed-pitch character grid, such as teletypes, terminals, or portable devices with limited display capabilities

tv   Intended for television-type devices

---

[51] http://www.w3.org/TR/REC-CSS2/media.html#media-types

In addition to the `media` attribute described above, there is another method for specifying media types that allows you to address multiple media types within one style sheet. It's called the **media at-rule**.

Here's an example. In this style sheet, printed documents will print with a font size of 10 points, while on the screen, the font will display at a size of 12 points. Both print and screen devices will display the text in black.

```
@media print {
  body {
    font-size: 10pt;
  }
}
@media screen {
  body {
    font-size: 12px;
  }
}
@media screen, print {
  body {
    color: #000000;
  }
}
```

Currently, there are very few devices that fully support the media types you would expect them to. The only media type that Netscape 4 recognizes is `screen`. If you're using multiple linked style sheets to deal with different media types, you must have a style sheet linked with `media="screen"` in order to reach Netscape 4.

The media type that is most usefully supported by modern browsers is the print media type. The next solution discusses how you can use this media type to create print versions of your pages.

Tip

Don't Start from Scratch

If you're creating a style sheet for a new media type, the easiest way to get started is to save a copy of your existing style sheet under a new name. That way, you already have all your selectors at hand, and can simply change the styles that you have created for each.

How do I create a print style sheet?

Web pages rarely print well, as techniques designed to make something look good on a screen are different to those used to create something that will print well. However, it is possible to use the CSS media types to provide a style sheet for use when the document is printed.

Solution

We can create a special print style sheet for our visitors:

File: **print-stylesheet.html**

```
<!DOCTYPE html PUBLIC "-//W3C//DTD XHTML 1.0 Transitional//EN"
 "http://www.w3.org/TR/xhtml1/DTD/xhtml1-transitional.dtd">
<html xmlns="http://www.w3.org/1999/xhtml">
<head>
<title>Print Style Sheet</title>
<meta http-equiv="content-type"
    content="text/html; charset=iso-8859-1" />
<link rel="stylesheet" type="text/css" href="main.css"
    title="default" />
<link rel="stylesheet" type="text/css" href="print.css"
    media="print" />
</head>
<body>
<div id="banner"></div>
<div id="content">
  <h1>Chinese style stuffed peppers</h1>
  <p>These stuffed peppers are lovely as a starter, or as a side
    dish for a Chinese meal. They also go down well as part of a
    buffet and even children seem to like them.</p>
  <h2>Ingredients</h2>
  ...
</div>
<div id="navigation">
  <ul id="mainnav">
    <li><a href="#">Recipes</a></li>
    <li><a href="#">Contact Us</a></li>
    <li><a href="#">Articles</a></li>
    <li><a href="#">Buy Online</a></li>
  </ul>
</div>
```

```
</body>
</html>
```

```css
body, html {
  margin: 0;
  padding: 0;
}
#navigation {
  width: 200px;
  font: 90% Arial, Helvetica, sans-serif;
  position: absolute;
  top: 41px;
  left: 0;
}
#navigation ul {
  list-style: none;
  margin: 0;
  padding: 0;
  border: none;
}
#navigation li {
  border-bottom: 1px solid #ED9F9F;
  margin: 0;
}
#navigation li a:link, #navigation li a:visited {
  display: block;
  padding: 5px 5px 5px 0.5em;
  border-left: 12px solid #711515;
  border-right: 1px solid #711515;
  color: #ffffff;
  background-color: #b51032;
  text-decoration: none;
}
#navigation li a:hover {
  color: #ffffff;
  background-color: #711515;
}
#content {
  margin-left: 260px;
  margin-right: 60px;
}
#banner {
  height: 40px;
  background-color: #711515;
  border-bottom: 1px solid #ED9F9F;
```

```
    text-align: right;
    padding-right: 20px;
    margin-top: 0;
}
#banner ul {
    margin: 0;
    padding: 0;
}
#banner li {
    display: inline;
}
#banner a:link, #banner a:visited {
    font: 80% Arial, Helvetica, sans-serif;
    color: #ffffff;
    background-color: transparent;
}
#content p, #content li {
    font: 80%/1.6em Arial, Helvetica, sans-serif;
}
#content p {
    margin-left: 1.5em;
}
#content h1, #content h2 {
    font: 140% Georgia, "Times New Roman", Times, serif;
    color: #B51032;
    background-color: transparent;
}
#content h2 {
    font: 120% Georgia, "Times New Roman", Times, serif;
    padding-bottom: 3px;
    border-bottom: 1px dotted #ED9F9F;
}
```

File: **print.css**

```
body, html {
    margin: 0;
    padding: 0;
}
#navigation {
    display: none;
}
#content {
    margin-left: 20pt;
    margin-right: 30pt;
}
#banner {
```

```
  display: none;
}
#content p, #content li {
  font: 12pt/20pt "Times New Roman", Times, serif;
}
#content p {
  margin-left: 20pt;
}
#content h1, #content h2 {
  font: 16pt Georgia, "Times New Roman", Times, serif;
  color: #4b4b4b;
  background-color: transparent;
}
#content h2 {
  font: 14pt Georgia, "Times New Roman", Times, serif;
  padding-bottom: 2pt;
  border-bottom: 1pt dotted #cccccc;
}
```

Discussion

Creating a print style sheet, particularly if your page has many graphics, can be very helpful to your visitors. Printing pages from a site that has many graphics can be costly in terms of printer ink, and slow on older printers. Additionally, some sites really don't print out well at all, due to the color combinations or layouts used. For example, Figure 7.18 shows a page that has a simple two-column CSS layout, with navigation in the sidebar, and a main content area that contains a recipe. Figure 7.19 shows this layout in Print Preview, indicating how it would be printed.

In Figure 7.19, we can see the practical differences between the on-screen and print displays. As a standard A4 sheet is reasonably narrow, by the time the print display has accounted for the menu, it only has half the total width of the page left in which to display the text. This may mean that long recipes need to be printed on two pages, rather than one.

Traditionally, sites offer print versions of documents that they expect users to print. However, this solution requires the maintenance of more than one version of the document—and users have to be savvy enough to find and click the print button on the page, rather than simply printing the page using the browser's print button. With the CSS method, when visitors use their browser's print functionality, the print style sheet will automatically come into play.

Figure 7.18. A two-column layout displays in the browser.

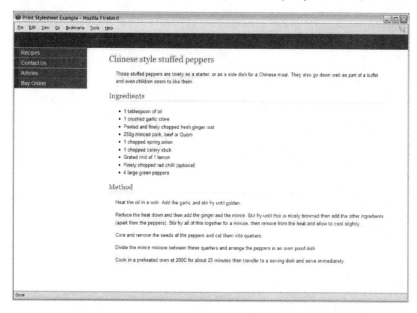

Figure 7.19. The layout appears in Print Preview.

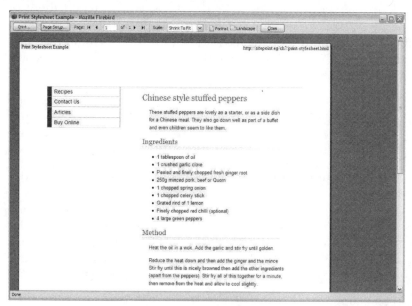

Linking a Print Style Sheet

Open your existing main style sheet and save it as `print.css`. This will become your print style sheet. Link this style sheet to your document with the print media type.

```
<link rel="stylesheet" type="text/css" href="print.css"
    media="print" />
```

Creating the Print Styles

If you've saved your existing style sheet as `print.css`, you can use this to decide what needs to be changed in order to create the print style sheet.

In my layout, the navigation is contained within a `<div>`; the section in the style sheet for that element is as follows:

File: **main.css (excerpt)**

```
#navigation {
  width: 200px;
  font: 90% Arial, Helvetica, sans-serif;
  position: absolute;
  top: 41px;
  left: 0;
}
```

The first thing I want to do is hide the navigation, as it isn't useful in the print version of the document. To do this, replace the properties in the above section of the style sheet with `display: none`:

File: **print.css (excerpt)**

```
#navigation {
  display: none;
}
```

You can then remove any navigation rules that apply to elements within the `#navigation` element.

We can also make the content area wider, so that it takes up all the available space. Find the section for the `#content` element in your style sheet:

File: **main.css (excerpt)**

```
#content {
  margin-left: 260px;
```

```
    margin-right: 60px;
}
```

Change the left margin to a lesser value, as you no longer need to leave space for the navigation. It's also a good idea to switch from pixels (a screen unit) to points (a print unit), as we discussed in "Should I use pixels, points, ems or something else for font sizes?" in Chapter 2.

File: **print.css** (excerpt)

```
#content {
    margin-left: 20pt;
    margin-right: 30pt;
}
```

If you check your document in Print Preview, as shown in Figure 7.20, or print it using the browser, you'll find that the navigation has gone and the content now fills the space much more effectively.

Figure 7.20. The page prints more cleanly after we remove the navigation.

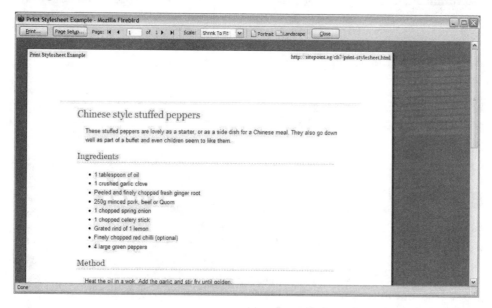

The line at the top is the bottom border of the banner. We can hide this banner just as we hid the navigation. First, we must find the section for #banner in the style sheet.

File: **main.css** (excerpt)

```css
#banner {
  height: 40px;
  background-color: #711515;
  border-bottom: 1px solid #ED9F9F;
}
```

Once again, set the banner to `display: none` and delete the remaining rules associated with this ID:

File: **print.css** (excerpt)

```css
#banner {
  display: none;
}
```

Finally, we can format the text. For print purposes, I'd normally turn any colored text to grayscale, unless it was important that the text stayed colored.

We can also use print-friendly points to size our text. As we discussed in "Should I use pixels, points, ems or something else for font sizes?" in Chapter 2, point measurements are designed for print and can help you to apply a reliable font size across different systems.

Additionally, you might like to use a serif font for your printed text, as serif fonts are generally considered easier to read on paper:

File: **print.css** (excerpt)

```css
#content p, #content li {
  font: 12pt/20pt "Times New Roman", Times, serif;
}
#content p {
  margin-left: 20pt;
}
#content h1, #content h2 {
  font: 16pt Georgia, "Times New Roman", Times, serif;
  color: #4b4b4b;
  background-color: transparent;
}
#content h2 {
  font: 14pt Georgia, "Times New Roman", Times, serif;
  padding-bottom: 2pt;
  border-bottom: 1pt dotted #cccccc;
}
```

The much more plain, but much more readable print layout is shown in its final form in Figure 7.21.

Figure 7.21. The completed style sheet is displayed in Print Preview.

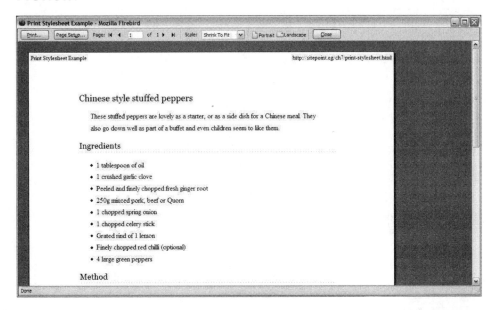

Print Style Sheets and Table Layouts

Print style sheets are easy to implement on CSS layouts, but you can also create effective print style sheets for table-based layouts, particularly if you use CSS to set the widths of table cells. You can then hide cells that contain navigation just as we hid the navigation `<div>` in the above CSS layout.

Some browsers allow users to choose a style sheet. How do I add alternate style sheets to my site?

Some modern browsers allow the user to view a list of the style sheets attached to a document, and select the one they want to use to view the site. This facility can be very helpful to people who struggle to read text if it is low contrast, or need a very large text size, for example.

Solution

Link your alternate style sheet with `rel="alternate stylesheet"`, and use a title. Users will see the title in the browser's menu, so, using a title that's descriptive, such as "high contrast" or "large text," is most helpful. You should also give your default style sheet a title.

File: **alternate-stylesheets.html** (excerpt)

```
<link rel="stylesheet" type="text/css" href="main.css"
    title="default" />
<link rel="stylesheet" type="text/css" href="print.css"
    media="print" />
<link rel="alternate stylesheet" type="text/css"
    href="largetext.css" title="large text" />
```

File: **largetext.css**

```
body, html {
  margin: 0;
  padding: 0;
  font-size: 140%;
}
#navigation {
  width: 280px;
  font: 90% Arial, Helvetica, sans-serif;
  position: absolute;
  top: 41px;
  left: 0;
}
#navigation ul {
  list-style: none;
  margin: 0;
  padding: 0;
  border: none;
}
#navigation li {
  border-bottom: 1px solid #ED9F9F;
  margin: 0;
}
#navigation li a:link, #navigation li a:visited {
  display: block;
  padding: 5px 5px 5px 0.5em;
```

```
  border-left: 12px solid #711515;
  border-right: 1px solid #711515;
  color: #ffffff;
  background-color: #b51032;
  text-decoration: none;
}
#navigation li a:hover {
  color: #ffffff;
  background-color: #711515;
}
#content {
  margin-left: 320px;
  margin-right: 60px;
}
#banner {
  height: 40px;
  background-color: #711515;
  border-bottom: 1px solid #ED9F9F;
  text-align: right;
  padding-right: 20px;
  margin-top: 0;
}
#banner ul {
  margin: 0;
  padding: 0;
}
#banner li {
  display: inline;
}
#banner a:link, #banner a:visited {
  font: 80% Arial, Helvetica, sans-serif;
  color: #ffffff;
  background-color: transparent;
}
#content p, #content li {
  font: 80%/1.6em Arial, Helvetica, sans-serif;
}
#content p {
  margin-left: 1.5em;
}
#content h1, #content h2 {
  font: 140% Georgia, "Times New Roman", Times, serif;
  color: #B51032;
  background-color: transparent;
}
#content h2 {
```

```
  font: 120% Georgia, "Times New Roman", Times, serif;
  padding-bottom: 3px;
  border-bottom: 1px dotted #ED9F9F;
}
```

In Figure 7.22, you can see how the page looks when the user selects the alternate style sheet. Note the style switching menu at the bottom of the window.

Figure 7.22. Switching to the "large text" style sheet in Firefox is easy.

Discussion

Utilizing this browser functionality is easy, and allows you to add further valuable support for your users with a minimum of effort. Typically, it takes very little time to create a style sheet that displays large fonts or has a high contrast color scheme. Simply save the existing style sheet and tweak the fonts, colors, and layout if necessary.

Unfortunately, browser support for this feature is still limited, and does not exist at all in Internet Explorer. However, users who find this functionality beneficial may choose an alternate browser specifically to have access to these features. In the next solution, we'll look at a way to mimic this functionality for those browsers that do not offer it as standard.

Tip

Look how Thoughtful I Am!

As very few sites utilize this feature at present, it would be a good idea to let your users know that you offer alternate style sheets. Perhaps include the information on a separate page that explains how to use the site, and is clearly linked from the home page.

How do I make a style sheet switcher?

The above solution for alternate style sheets is all very well for those who use a browser that supports the functionality, but, what about everyone else? Internet Explorer has the largest user base and it doesn't support alternate style sheets! How can we empower those users to select the style sheet that's most appropriate to their needs?

Solution

Add a JavaScript style switcher to enable users to select their style.

File: **alternate-stylesheets-js.html (excerpt)**

```
<link rel="stylesheet" type="text/css" href="main.css"
    title="default" />
<link rel="stylesheet" type="text/css" href="print.css"
    media="print" />
<link rel="alternate stylesheet" type="text/css"
    href="largetext.css" title="large text" />
<script language="javascript" type="text/javascript"
    src="switcher.js"></script>
</head>
<body>
<div id="banner">
  <ul id="styleswitch">
    <li><a href="javascript:;"
        onclick="setActiveStyleSheet('default'); return false;"
      >Default Style</a></li>
    <li><a href="javascript:;"
        onclick="setActiveStyleSheet('large text'); return false;"
```

```
      >Large Text</a></li>
   </ul>
</div>
```

File: **switcher.js**

```javascript
/*
Paul Sowden's JavaScript switcher as detailed on:
http://www.alistapart.com/articles/alternate/
*/

function setActiveStyleSheet(title) {
  var i, a, main;
  for(i=0; (a = document.getElementsByTagName("link")[i]); i++) {
    if(a.getAttribute("rel").indexOf("style") != -1 &&
        a.getAttribute("title")) {
      a.disabled = true;
      if(a.getAttribute("title") == title) a.disabled = false;
    }
  }
}

function getActiveStyleSheet() {
  var i, a;
  for(i=0; (a = document.getElementsByTagName("link")[i]); i++) {
    if(a.getAttribute("rel").indexOf("style") != -1 &&
        a.getAttribute("title") && !a.disabled)
      return a.getAttribute("title");
  }
  return null;
}

function getPreferredStyleSheet() {
  var i, a;
  for(i=0; (a = document.getElementsByTagName("link")[i]); i++) {
    if(a.getAttribute("rel").indexOf("style") != -1
        && a.getAttribute("rel").indexOf("alt") == -1
        && a.getAttribute("title")
        ) return a.getAttribute("title");
  }
  return null;
}

function createCookie(name,value,days) {
  if (days) {
    var date = new Date();
    date.setTime(date.getTime()+(days*24*60*60*1000));
```

```
      var expires = "; expires="+date.toGMTString();
  }
  else expires = "";
  document.cookie = name+"="+value+expires+"; path=/";
}

function readCookie(name) {
  var nameEQ = name + "=";
  var ca = document.cookie.split(';');
  for(var i=0;i < ca.length;i++) {
    var c = ca[i];
    while (c.charAt(0)==' ') c = c.substring(1,c.length);
    if (c.indexOf(nameEQ) == 0)
      return c.substring(nameEQ.length,c.length);
  }
  return null;
}

window.onload = function(e) {
  var cookie = readCookie("style");
  var title = cookie ? cookie : getPreferredStyleSheet();
  setActiveStyleSheet(title);
}

window.onunload = function(e) {
  var title = getActiveStyleSheet();
  createCookie("style", title, 365);
}

var cookie = readCookie("style");
var title = cookie ? cookie : getPreferredStyleSheet();
setActiveStyleSheet(title);
```

You can see the new style selection links in Figure 7.23.

Figure 7.23. Change the style sheet with JavaScript.

Discussion

Adding a JavaScript style switcher to your site gives all users with JavaScript support the ability to choose the style sheet that best suits their needs.

In this solution, I've used JavaScript functions from an A List Apart article.[52] After you save the functions into your site as `switcher.js`, all you need do is link in the file, and add links or buttons to call the JavaScript.

File: **alternate-stylesheets-js.html** (excerpt)

```
<script language="javascript" type="text/javascript"
    src="switcher.js"></script>
```

File: **alternate-stylesheets-js.html** (excerpt)

```
<ul id="styleswitch">
  <li><a href="javascript:;"
      onclick="setActiveStyleSheet('default'); return false;"
    >Default Style</a></li>
```

[52] http://www.alistapart.com/articles/alternate/

```
  <li><a href="javascript:;"
       onclick="setActiveStyleSheet('large text'); return false;"
    >Large Text</a></li>
  </ul>
```

The `setActiveStyleSheet` function selects the style sheet that's applied. By calling it with the title of the desired style sheet, we can allow users to select style sheets from within the browser. As such, this method can be used in conjunction with that described in the previous solution: visitors who are able to change style sheets using their browser can still do so; others can use the JavaScript style switcher.

You can also use this method to swap the site's color scheme, and even to change the layout of your site, if you used CSS to position site elements.

 Tip

Server-Side Solutions

It's also possible to change the style sheet by writing out the link to the selected style sheet using server-side code, such as PHP. Examples of the methods you can use to achieve this are linked from the css-discuss Wiki.[53]

How do I use alternate style sheets without duplicating code?

In the examples above, we changed very few properties within the main style sheet to create our alternate style sheet. Do we actually need to create a whole new style sheet, or is it possible to alter only those styles that *need* to be changed?

Solution

Create multiple style sheets: a base style sheet for properties that never change, a default style sheet containing the properties that will change, and a style sheet containing the alternate version of those properties.

File: **alternate-stylesheets-js2.html (excerpt)**

```
<link rel="stylesheet" type="text/css" href="main2.css" />
<link rel="stylesheet" type="text/css" href="defaulttext.css"
    title="default" />
<link rel="stylesheet" type="text/css" href="print.css"
```

[53] http://css-discuss.incutio.com/?page=StyleSwitching

```
      media="print" />
<link rel="alternate stylesheet" type="text/css"
      href="largetext2.css" title="large text" />
```

File: **main2.css**

```css
body, html {
  margin: 0;
  padding: 0;
}
#navigation {
  font: 90% Arial, Helvetica, sans-serif;
  position: absolute;
  left: 0;
  top: 41px;
}
#navigation ul {
  list-style: none;
  margin: 0;
  padding: 0;
  border: none;
}
#navigation li {
  border-bottom: 1px solid #ED9F9F;
  margin: 0;
}
#navigation li a:link, #navigation li a:visited {
  display: block;
  padding: 5px 5px 5px 0.5em;
  border-left: 12px solid #711515;
  border-right: 1px solid #711515;
  background-color: #B51032;
  color: #FFFFFF;
  text-decoration: none;
}
#navigation li a:hover {
  background-color: #711515;
  color: #FFFFFF;
}
#banner {
  background-color: #711515;
  border-bottom: 1px solid #ED9F9F;
  text-align: right;
  padding-right: 20px;
  margin-top: 0;
}
#banner ul {
```

```
  margin: 0;
}
#banner li {
  display: inline;
}
#banner a:link, #banner a:visited {
  font: 80% Arial, Helvetica, sans-serif;
  color: #ffffff;
  background-color: transparent;
}
#content p, #content li {
  font: 80%/1.6em Arial, Helvetica, sans-serif;
}
#content p {
  margin-left: 1.5em;
}
#content h1, #content h2 {
  font: 140% Georgia, "Times New Roman", Times, serif;
  color: #B51032;
  background-color: transparent;
}
#content h2 {
  font: 120% Georgia, "Times New Roman", Times, serif;
  padding-bottom: 3px;
  border-bottom: 1px dotted #ED9F9F;
}
```

File: **defaulttext.css**

```
#navigation {
  width: 200px;
}
#content {
  margin-left: 260px;
  margin-right: 60px;
}
#banner {
  height: 40px;
}
```

File: **largetext2.css**

```
body, html {
  font-size: 1.4em;
}
#navigation {
  width: 280px;
}
```

```
#content {
  margin-left: 320px;
  margin-right: 60px;
}
#banner {
  height: 60px;
}
```

Discussion

To create the `largefonts.css` file that I used in the previous two examples, I changed very few properties in the original style sheet.

I changed the base font size:

File: **main.css** (excerpt)

```
body, html {
  margin: 0;
  padding: 0;
}
```

File: **largetext.css** (excerpt)

```
body, html {
  margin: 0;
  padding: 0;
  font-size: 1.4em;
}
```

I also tweaked the layout slightly to make room for much larger text. In particular, I altered the #banner, #content, and #navigation elements:

File: **main.css** (excerpt)

```
#navigation {
  width: 200px;
  font: 90% Arial, Helvetica, sans-serif;
  position: absolute;
  top: 41px;
  left: 0;
}
#content {
  margin-left: 260px;
  margin-right: 60px;
}
```

```
#banner {
  height: 40px;
  background-color: #711515;
 border-bottom: 1px solid #ED9F9F;
 text-align: right;
 padding-right: 20px;
 margin-top: 0;
}
```

File: **largetext.css** (excerpt)

```
#navigation {
  width: 280px;
  font: 90% Arial, Helvetica, sans-serif;
  position: absolute;
  top: 61px;
  left: 0;
}
#content {
  margin-left: 320px;
  margin-right: 60px;
}
#banner {
  height: 60px;
  background-color: #711515;
  border-bottom: 1px solid #ED9F9F;
  text-align: right;
  padding-right: 20px;
}
```

To avoid making a copy of the entire style sheet in order to create the large-text.css file, you can remove from the main style sheet those properties that you know you will need to swap. Place them in a new style sheet that determines the default font size; your large-text style sheet need contain only the changed version of those properties.

Similarly, if you are using this method to change your site's color scheme, you can put all the properties that relate to color into separate style sheets, and swap only those. This way, you avoid having to maintain several different versions of what is, essentially, the same style sheet.

Tip

Flexible Layouts Mean Simpler Style Sheets

If your layout is a flexible one in which you have avoided setting elements in pixel widths, you may be able to get away with simply altering the base font size to effect a change in text size. The example above addresses a design that does have some fixed width elements, however, as most designers are likely to have to deal with containers of a fixed width at some stage in their careers.

Summary

This chapter has covered a wide range of solutions to problems that you may not yet have experienced. This will almost certainly be the case if you have not yet designed sites that use CSS, rather than tables, for positioning. It's at that point that the more interesting browser bugs start to rear their ugly heads, and testing in a wide range of browsers, and browser versions, becomes very important indeed.

What I hope to have shown you is how I go about testing sites, finding bugs, and getting help. I've also aimed to broaden your options in terms of displaying your pages appropriately for different users. If you're reading through this book chapter by chapter, you might find that much of this information makes more sense in light of Chapter 8, which deals with the use of CSS for layout.

8

CSS Positioning and Layout

Tables or CSS? There is little that generates more heated debate within the Web design and development community. But, whether you believe that the use of tables for layout will immediately send you to Web design hell to be beaten forever with a red hot (standards-compliant) poker, or you have a more flexible view that, sometimes, the minimal use of tables for layout can be the best way to accomplish particular tasks, skills in CSS positioning are fast becoming a necessity for every Web designer who wants to stay up-to-date.

This chapter will introduce the basics of CSS layout, and will explore useful tricks and techniques that you can use to create unique and beautiful sites. These are the essential building blocks—starting points for your creativity. If you work through the chapter from beginning to end, you'll start by gaining a grasp of some of the fundamentals that you'll need to know to be able to create workable CSS layouts. The chapter then progresses to more detailed layout examples; if you're already comfortable with the basics, simply dip into these solutions to find the specific technique you need.

How do I decide when to use a class and when to use an ID?

At first glance, classes and IDs seem to be used in much the same way: you can assign CSS properties to both classes and IDs, and apply them to change the way (X)HTML elements look. But, in which circumstances are classes best applied, and what about IDs?

Solution

The most important rule, where classes and IDs are concerned, is that an ID must be only used *once* in a document, as it identifies the element to which it is applied. Once you have assigned an ID to an element, you cannot use it again within that document.

Classes, on the other hand, may be used as many times as you like within the same document. Therefore, if you have on a page a feature that you wish to repeat, a class is the ideal choice.

You can apply both a class and an ID to any given element. For example, you might apply a class to all text input fields on a page; if you want to be able to address those fields using JavaScript, they'll each need an ID, too. However, no styles need be assigned to that ID.

You can apply more than one class to an element, but one ID only is allowable.

I tend to use IDs for the main, structural, positioned elements of the page, so I often end up with IDs such as `header`, `content`, `nav`, and `footer`.

Can I make an inline element display as if it were block-level, and vice-versa?

Sometimes, we need to use HTML elements differently than the way they're treated, by default, in the browser.

Solution

In Figure 8.1, you can see that we can force a `<div>` tag to display as an inline element and a link to display as a block.

Figure 8.1. The block-level element is displayed inline, while the inline element is displayed as a block.

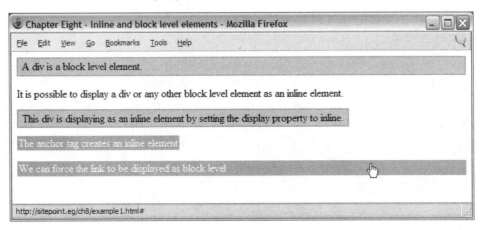

File: **inline-block.html**

```
<!DOCTYPE html PUBLIC "-//W3C//DTD XHTML 1.0 Transitional//EN"
    "http://www.w3.org/TR/xhtml1/DTD/xhtml1-transitional.dtd">
<html xmlns="http://www.w3.org/1999/xhtml">
<head>
<title>Inline and block level elements</title>
<meta http-equiv="content-type"
    content="text/html; charset=iso-8859-1" />
<style type="text/css">
#one {
  background-color: #CCCCCC;
  color: #000000;
  border: 2px solid #AAAAAA;
  padding: 2px 6px 2px 6px;
}
#two {
  background-color: #CCCCCC;
  color: #000000;
  border: 2px solid #AAAAAA;
  padding: 2px 6px 2px 6px;
  display: inline;
```

```
}
a:link, a:visited {
  background-color: #ACACAC;
  color: #FFFFFF;
  text-decoration: none;
  padding: 1px 2px 1px 2px;
}
a.block:link, a.block:visited {
  display: block;
}
</style>
</head>
<body>
<div id="one">A div is a block level element.</div>
  <p>It is possible to display a div or any other block level
    element as an inline element.</p>
  <div id="two">This div is displaying as an inline element by
    setting the display property to inline.</div>
  <p><a href="#">The anchor tag creates an inline element</a></p>
  <p><a href="#" class="block">We can force the link to be
    displayed as block level</a></p>
</body>
</html>
```

Discussion

Block-level elements are distinguished from inline elements in that they may contain inline elements as well as other block-level elements. They're also formatted differently than inline elements—block-level elements occupy a rectangular area of the page, by default spanning the entire width of the page, whereas inline elements flow along lines of text, and wrap to fit inside the blocks that contain them. HTML tags treated as block-level elements by default include headings (<h1>, <h2>, <h3>, ...), paragraphs (<p>), lists (<ul>, <ol>), and various containers (<div>, <blockquote>).

In the example above, we can see a <div> that displays as normal. As it is a block level element, it takes up the full width of the parent element, which, in this case, is the <body>. If it were contained within another <div>, or a table cell, it would stretch only to the width of that element.

If we don't want the <div> to behave this way, we can set it to display inline by applying the following CSS property:

```
display: inline;
```

In the same way, we can cause an inline element to display as if it were a block-level element. In the above example, note that the `<a>` tag displays as an inline element by default. We often want it to display as a block—for example, when creating a navigation bar using CSS. To achieve this, set the `display` property of the element to `block`. In our example, this causes the gray box that contains the linked text to expand to fill the screen.

How do margins and padding work in CSS?

What is the difference between the properties, and how do they affect elements?

Solution

The margin properties add space to the outside of an element. You can set margins individually:

```
margin-top: 1em;
margin-right: 2em;
margin-bottom: 0.5em;
margin-left: 3em;
```

You can also set margins using a shorthand property:

```
margin: 1em 2em 0.5em 3em;
```

If all the margins are to be equal, simply use a rule like this:

```
margin: 1em;
```

This rule applies a 1-em margin to all sides of the element.

Figure 8.2 shows what a block element looks like when it has margins added to it. The code for this page is as follows:

File: **margin.html**

```
<!DOCTYPE html PUBLIC "-//W3C//DTD XHTML 1.0 Transitional//EN"
    "http://www.w3.org/TR/xhtml1/DTD/xhtml1-transitional.dtd">
<html xmlns="http://www.w3.org/1999/xhtml">
<head>
<title>Margins</title>
<meta http-equiv="content-type"
```

```
        content="text/html; charset=iso-8859-1" />
<style type="text/css">
p {
  border: 2px solid #AAAAAA;
  background-color: #EEEEEE;
}
p.margintest {
  margin: 40px;
}
</style>
</head>
<body>
<p>This paragraph should be displayed in the default style of…</p>
<p>This is another paragraph that has the default browser…</p>
<p class="margintest">This paragraph has a 40 pixel margin…</p>
</body>
</html>
```

Figure 8.2. The CSS code applies margins to an element.

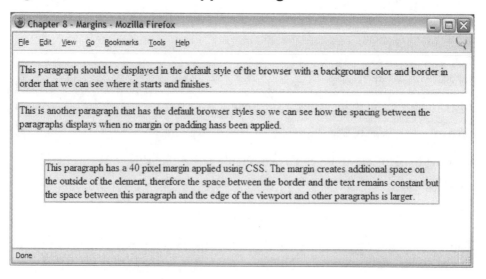

The padding properties, meanwhile, add space *inside* the element—between its borders and its content. You can set padding individually for the top, right, bottom, and left sides of an element:

```
padding-top: 1em;
padding-right: 1.5em;
```

```
padding-bottom: 0.5em;
padding-left: 2em;
```

You can also apply padding using this shorthand property:

```
padding: 1em 1.5em 0.5em 2em;
```

As with margins, if the padding is to be equal all the way around an element, you can simply use:

```
padding: 1em;
```

Figure 8.3, which results from the following code, shows what a block looks like with padding applied. Compare it to Figure 8.2 to see the difference between margins and padding.

File: **padding.html**

```
<!DOCTYPE html PUBLIC "-//W3C//DTD XHTML 1.0 Transitional//EN"
    "http://www.w3.org/TR/xhtml1/DTD/xhtml1-transitional.dtd">
<html xmlns="http://www.w3.org/1999/xhtml">
<head>
<title>Padding</title>
<meta http-equiv="content-type"
    content="text/html; charset=iso-8859-1" />
<style type="text/css">
p {
  border: 2px solid #AAAAAA;
  background-color: #EEEEEE;
}
p.paddingtest {
  padding: 40px;
}
</style>
</head>
<body>
<p>This paragraph should be displayed in the default style …</p>
<p>This is another paragraph that has the default browser …</p>
<p class="paddingtest">This paragraph has 40 pixels of …</p>
</body>
</html>
```

Figure 8.3. Padding is applied to an element in CSS.

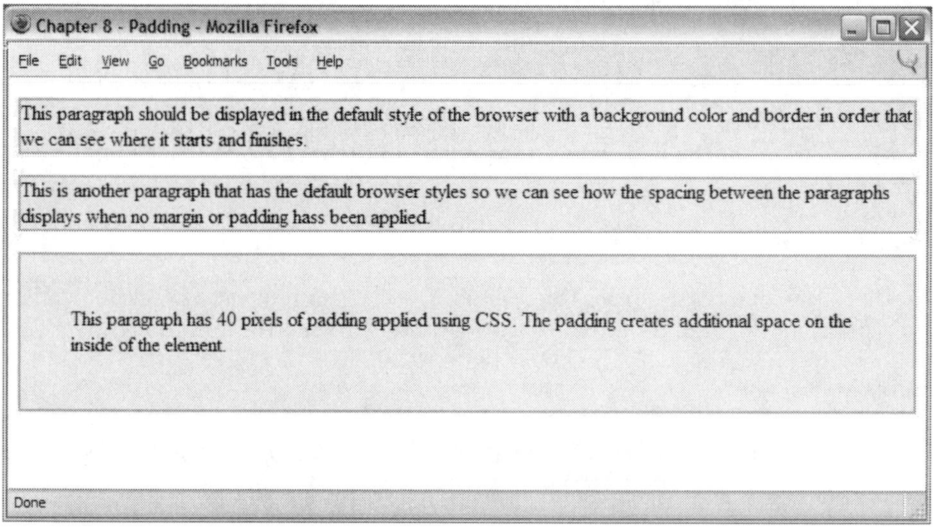

Discussion

The above solution demonstrates the basics of margins and padding. As we've seen, the margin properties create space between the element to which they are applied and surrounding elements, whereas padding creates space inside the elements to which it is applied.

If you're applying margins and padding to a fixed-width element, they will be added to the specified width to produce the total width for that element. So, if your element has a width of 400 pixels, and you add 40 pixels' worth of padding on all sides, you'll make the element 480 pixels wide. Add 20 pixels of margins to that, and the element will occupy a width of 520 pixels (a visible width of 480 pixels with 20 pixels of spacing on either side). If you have a very precise layout, you'll need to remember to calculate your element sizes carefully, to include any added margins and padding.

In Internet Explorer versions 5 and 5.5, padding (and borders) are interpreted as being included within the specified width of the element; in these browsers, the element just described would remain 400 pixels in width with the padding included, and adding margins would reduce the visible width of the element. One workaround for this peculiarity is to apply padding to a parent element, rather than using margin on the element in question. Alternatively, you can use the box model hack described in Chapter 7.

How do I get text to wrap around an image without using the HTML `align` attribute?

With HTML it is possible to wrap text around an image using the `align` attribute. This attribute is now deprecated, but there is a CSS equivalent!

Solution

Use the CSS `float` property to float an image to the left or right, as shown in Figure 8.4.

Here's the code for this page:

File: **float.html**

```
<!DOCTYPE html PUBLIC "-//W3C//DTD XHTML 1.0 Transitional//EN"
    "http://www.w3.org/TR/xhtml1/DTD/xhtml1-transitional.dtd">
<html xmlns="http://www.w3.org/1999/xhtml">
<head>
<title>Float</title>
<meta http-equiv="content-type"
    content="text/html; charset=iso-8859-1" />
<style type="text/css">
.leftimg {
  float: left;
}
</style>
</head>
<body>
<h1>Chinese style stuffed peppers</h1>
<img src="peppers1.jpg" width="319" height="255" alt="peppers"
    class="leftimg" />
<p>These stuffed peppers are lovely as a starter...</p>
</body>
</html>
```

Figure 8.4. Float an image to the left using the `float` property.

Discussion

The `float` property takes the element out of the document flow and "floats" it against the edge of the block level element that contains it. Other block-level elements will then ignore the floated element and render as if it isn't there. Inline elements such as content, however, will make space for it, which is why we can use `float` to have our text wrap around an image.

In the example above, the image displayed on a white background, and that white space around it created a gap between the edge of the image and the text. If we add a border to that image, as in Figure 8.5, we can see that the text is bumped right up against the side of the image.

Figure 8.5. Text renders against an image.

To create space between the image and the text, we need to add a margin to the image. As the image is aligned against the left margin, we'll probably only want to add right and bottom margins to move the text away from the image slightly.

File: **float2.html** (excerpt)

```
.leftimg {
  float: left;
  border: 2px solid #000000;
  margin-right: 20px;
  margin-bottom: 6px;
}
```

Figure 8.6 shows the resulting display, with extra space around the floated image.

Figure 8.6. The addition of right and bottom margins to an image improves the display.

How do I stop the next element moving up when I use float?

Floating an image or other element causes it to be ignored by block-level elements, although the text and inline images contained in those elements will appear to wrap around the floated element. How can you force elements to display below the floated element?

Solution

The CSS property clear allows you to clear an element of any floated elements. In the following example, we apply this property with a value of both to the first paragraph following the list of ingredients.

```
<!DOCTYPE html PUBLIC "-//W3C//DTD XHTML 1.0 Transitional//EN"
    "http://www.w3.org/TR/xhtml1/DTD/xhtml1-transitional.dtd">
<html xmlns="http://www.w3.org/1999/xhtml">
<head>
<title>float and clear</title>
<meta http-equiv="content-type"
    content="text/html; charset=iso-8859-1" />
<style type="text/css">
.rightimg {
  float: right;
  margin-left: 20px;
  margin-bottom: 6px;
}
.clear {
  clear: both;
}
p, ul {
  border: 2px solid #000000;
}
</style>
</head>
<body>
<h1>Chinese style stuffed peppers</h1>
<img src="peppers1.jpg" width="319" height="255" alt="peppers"
    class="rightimg" />
<ul>
  <li>1 tablespoon of oil</li>
  <li>1 crushed garlic clove</li>
  <li>Peeled and finely chopped fresh ginger root</li>
  <li>250g minced pork, beef or Quorn</li>
  <li>1 chopped spring onion</li>
  <li>1 chopped celery stick</li>
  <li>Grated rind of 1 lemon</li>
  <li>Finely chopped red chilli (optional)</li>
  <li>4 large green peppers</li>
</ul>
<p class="clear">These stuffed peppers are lovely as a ...</p>
...
```

```
</body>
</html>
```

As shown in Figure 8.7, the paragraph is pushed down so that it begins below the floated image.

Figure 8.7. The first paragraph is clear of the floated image.

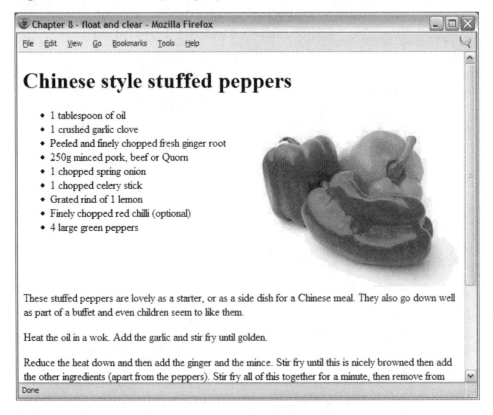

Discussion

The `float` property takes an element out of the flow of the document; the block level elements that appear after it will simply ignore the floated element. The effect of this can be seen more clearly if we apply a border to the elements in our document. This is illustrated in Figure 8.8, which adds a 2-pixel border to the `<ul>` and `<p>` tags in the page.

Figure 8.8. A 2-pixel border is applied to the `<ul>` and `<p>` tags.

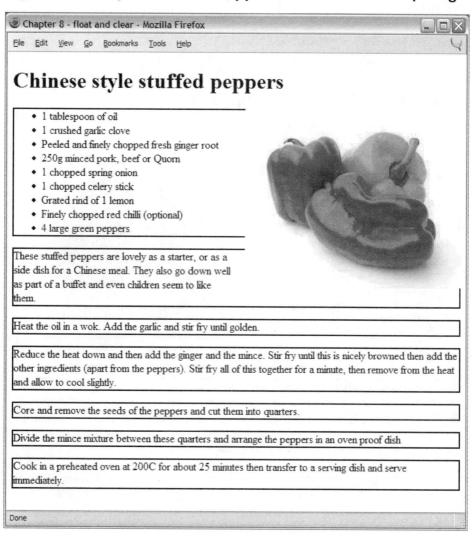

As you can see, the floated image basically sits on top of the block elements. The text within those elements wraps around it, but the actual elements themselves will ignore the fact that the float is there. This means that, in our example, the paragraph after the list of ingredients wraps around the image, if the height of the ingredients list is less than that of the image.

Figure 8.9. Use the `clear` property to clear the paragraph from the float.

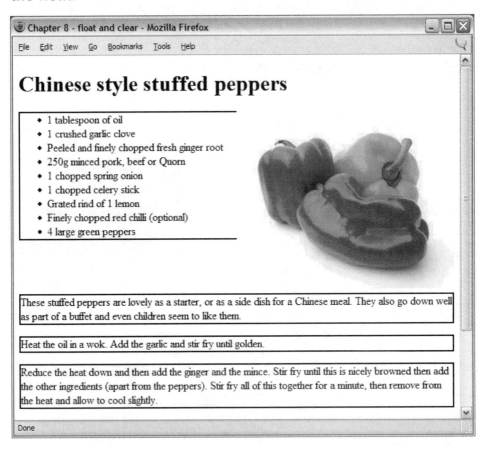

To get the paragraph to begin at a point below that at which the image finishes, we can use the `clear` property:

File: **`float-clear.html` (excerpt)**

```
.clear {
  clear: both;
}
```

We then apply this CSS class to the first <p> tag after the ingredients list:

File: **float-clear.html** (excerpt)

```
<p class="clear">These stuffed peppers are lovely as a starter, or
    as a side dish for a Chinese meal. They also go down well as
    part of a buffet and even children seem to like them.</p>
```

If we leave the borders in place and reload the document as in Figure 8.9, we can see that the paragraph now begins below the pepper image; its border does not run behind the image at all.

The `clear` property can also have values of `left` or `right`, which are useful if you want to clear an element only from left or right floats, respectively. The value you are most likely to use, though, is `both`. Both `float` and `clear` can trigger bugs, particularly in Internet Explorer. We discussed one of these bugs in Chapter 7.

How do I align my logo and strapline to the left and right without using a table?

If you've ever used tables for layout, you'll know how easy it is to create the type of effect shown in Figure 8.10 with a two-column table. This method allows you to align the contents of the left-hand table cell to the left, and those of the right-hand cell to the right. The same end result is achievable using CSS.

Figure 8.10. The logo and strapline are aligned left and right using CSS.

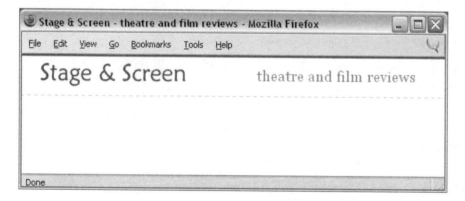

Solution

We can use float to create this type of layout.

File: **strapline-align.html**

```
<!DOCTYPE html PUBLIC "-//W3C//DTD XHTML 1.0 Transitional//EN"
    "http://www.w3.org/TR/xhtml1/DTD/xhtml1-transitional.dtd">
<html xmlns="http://www.w3.org/1999/xhtml">
<head>
<title>Stage &amp; Screen - theatre and film reviews</title>
<meta http-equiv="content-type"
    content="text/html; charset=iso-8859-1" />
<link rel="stylesheet" type="text/css" href="strapline-align.css"
    />
</head>
<body>
<div id="header">
  <img src="stage-logo.gif" width="187" height="29"
      alt="Stage &amp; Screen" class="logo" />
  <span class="strapline">theatre and film reviews</span>
</div>
</body>
</html>
```

File: **strapline-align.css**

```
body {
  margin: 0;
  padding: 0;
  background-color: #FFFFFF;
  color: #000000;
  font-family: Arial, Helvetica, sans-serif;
  border-top: 2px solid #2A4F6F;
}
#header {
  border-top: 1px solid #778899;
  border-bottom: 1px dotted #B2BCC6;
  height: 3em;
}
#header .strapline {
  font: 120% Georgia, "Times New Roman", Times, serif;
  color: #778899;
  background-color: transparent;
  float: right;
  margin-right: 2em;
  margin-top: 0.5em;
```

```
}
#header .logo {
  float: left;
  margin-left: 1.5em;
  margin-top: 0.5em;
}
```

Discussion

The `float` property allows us easily to align the elements in our header to either side of the viewport. Before adding the float, our elements will display next to each other, as in Figure 8.11.

Figure 8.11. The elements display at their default position.

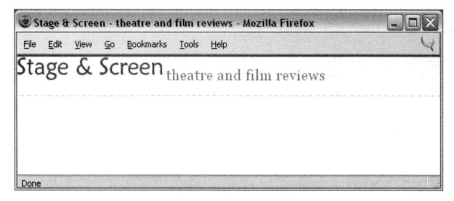

The elements appear side by side because the HTML that marks them up dictates nothing about their position on the page. Thus, they appear one after the other.

File: **strapline-align.html (excerpt)**

```
<div id="header">
  <img src="stage-logo.gif" width="187" height="29"
      alt="Stage &amp; Screen" class="logo" />
  <span class="strapline">theatre and film reviews<span>
</div>
```

By floating the class `logo` to the left and `strapline` to the right, we can move the elements to the left and right of the screen, as shown in Figure 8.12.

Figure 8.12. The application of `float` makes the elements display as desired.

IMPORTANT

Floated Text and Width

Inline elements, such as the logo in this example, can be floated without our having to specify a width in the CSS. However, if you're going to float a block-level element, you must specify a width for that element to prevent it taking up the full width of the parent block.

To provide some space around the elements, let's add a margin to the top and left of the logo, and the top and right of the strapline.

File: **strapline-align.css** (excerpt)

```
#header .strapline {
  font: 120% Georgia, "Times New Roman", Times, serif;
  color: #778899;
  background-color: transparent;
  float: right;
  margin-right: 2em;
  margin-top: 0.5em;
}
#header .logo {
  float: left;
  margin-left: 1.5em;
  margin-top: 0.5em;
}
```

One thing to be aware of when using this technique is that, once you have floated all the elements within a container, that container will no longer be "held open" by anything, so it will collapse to zero height. To demonstrate this point, I've added a large border to my header in Figure 8.13. The elements here have not been floated, so the header surrounds the elements.

Figure 8.13. The example shows the size of the header when elements are not floated.

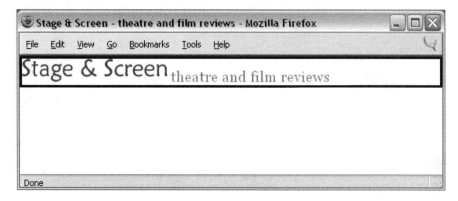

Once I float the elements right and left, the header loses its height, because the elements have been taken out of the document flow. The thick black line at the top of Figure 8.14 is actually the header's border, but it's collapsed, as the block has no flowed content.

Figure 8.14. The header collapsed.

To avoid this problem, you can set an explicit `height` for the block:

File: **strapline-align.css** (excerpt)

```
#header {
  border-top: 1px solid #778899;
  border-bottom: 1px dotted #B2BCC6;
```

```
    height: 3em;
}
```

The block now occupies the desired area of the page, as shown in Figure 8.15.

Figure 8.15. The page displays normally after a `height` is set for the header `<div>`.

When you're setting heights in this kind of situation, keep in mind the potential impact that user-altered text sizes may have on your layout. You should be able to set a height that will expand to accommodate larger text sizes without risking the floated element coming out of the box.

How do I set an item's position on the page using CSS?

It is possible to specify exactly where on the page an element should be displayed.

Solution

With CSS, you can place an element on the page by positioning it from the top, right, bottom or left using **absolute positioning**. The two blocks shown in Figure 8.16 have been placed with absolute positioning.

Figure 8.16. The boxes are positioned using absolute positioning.

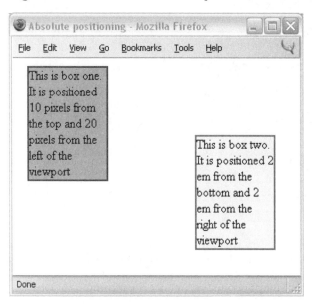

The code for this page is as follows:

File: **position.html**

```
<!DOCTYPE html PUBLIC "-//W3C//DTD XHTML 1.0 Transitional//EN"
 "http://www.w3.org/TR/xhtml1/DTD/xhtml1-transitional.dtd">
<html xmlns="http://www.w3.org/1999/xhtml">
<head>
<title>Absolute positioning</title>
<meta http-equiv="content-type"
    content="text/html; charset=iso-8859-1" />
<link rel="stylesheet" type="text/css" href="position.css" />
</head>
<body>
<div id="box1">This is box one. It is positioned 10 pixels from
  the top and 20 pixels from the left of the viewport</div>
<div id="box2">This is box two. It is positioned 2 em from the
  bottom and 2 em from the right of the viewport</div>
</body>
</html>
```

File: **position.css**

```
#box1 {
  position: absolute;
```

```
    top: 10px;
    left: 20px;
    width: 100px;
    background-color: #B0C4DE;
    border: 2px solid #34537D
}
#box2 {
    position: absolute;
    bottom: 2em;
    right: 2em;
    width: 100px;
    background-color: #FFFAFA;
    border: 2px solid #CD5C5C;
}
```

Discussion

Setting an element's `position` property to `absolute` removes it completely from the document flow. As an example, if I add several paragraphs of text to the example document shown above, the two boxes will sit on top of the content, as shown in Figure 8.17.

Figure 8.17. The content ignores the positioned boxes.

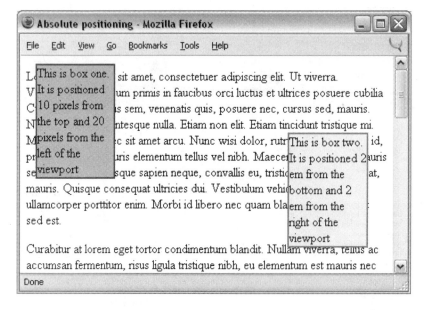

In the markup that I used to produce this display, the paragraphs follow the the absolute-positioned <div>s; however, because the <div>s have been removed from the document flow, the paragraphs begin at the top corner just as they would if the boxes did not exist.

As we'll see in "How do I create a liquid, two-column layout with the menu on the left, and the content on the right?", we can create space for absolutely-positioned areas by placing them within the margins or padding of other elements.

What may not be obvious from this example is that elements need not be positioned relative to the edges of the document (although this is quite common). Elements can also be positioned within other elements with the same degree of precision.

Figure 8.18. Box two is positioned within box one.

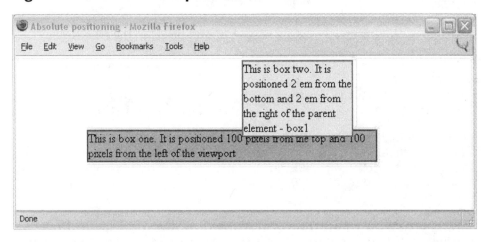

Figure 8.18 depicts a layout containing two boxes. In this example, box two is nested inside box one. Because box one is positioned using CSS, absolute positioning of box two sets its position relative to the edges of box one.

File: **position2.html (excerpt)**

```
<div id="box1">This is box one. It is positioned 100 pixels from
    the top and 100 pixels from the left of the viewport
    <div id="box2">This is box two. It is positioned 2 em from the
        bottom and 2 em from the right of the parent element - box1
    </div>
</div>
```

File: **position2.css**

```
#box1 {
  position: absolute;
  top: 100px;
  left: 100px;
  width: 400px;
  background-color: #B0C4DE;
  border: 2px solid #34537D
}
#box2 {
  position: absolute;
  bottom: 2em;
  right: 2em;
  width: 150px;
  background-color: #FFFAFA;
  border: 2px solid #CD5C5C;
}
```

To demonstrate this further, add a `height` of 300 pixels to the CSS for box1.

File: **position3.css (excerpt)**

```
#box1 {
  position: absolute;
  top: 100px;
  left: 100px;
  width: 400px;
  height: 300px;
  background-color: #B0C4DE;
  border: 2px solid #34537D
}
```

You'll then see box2 render entirely within box1, as shown in Figure 8.19, rather than appearing to stick out the top of it. This happens because box2 is positioned with respect to the bottom and right edges of box1.

Figure 8.19. box2 renders within box1.

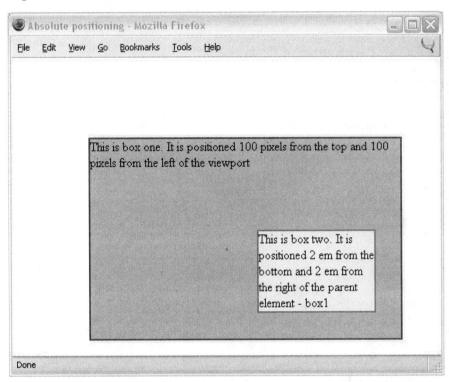

Positioning Starts with the Parent

It's important to note that the parent element (**box1**) must be positioned using CSS for the child element (**box2**) to base its position on that parent. This means the parent element must have its **position** property set to **absolute** (or **relative**, as we'll see later in this chapter).

If the parent element's **position** property is not set, then the child's position will be based on the edges of the document—not those of the parent element.

How do I center a block on the page?

A common page layout has a fixed-width, centered box that contains the page content, as shown in Figure 8.20. How can we center this box on the page using CSS?

Figure 8.20. A fixed-width box can be centered using CSS.

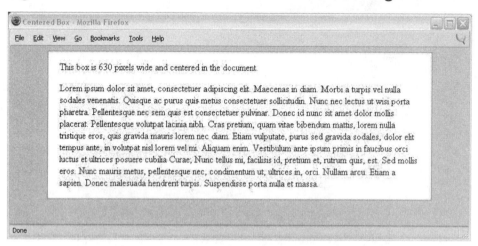

Solution

You can use CSS to center a fixed-width box by setting its left and right margins to auto.

File: **center.html**

```
<!DOCTYPE html PUBLIC "-//W3C//DTD XHTML 1.0 Transitional//EN"
    "http://www.w3.org/TR/xhtml1/DTD/xhtml1-transitional.dtd">
<html xmlns="http://www.w3.org/1999/xhtml">
<head>
<title>Centered Box</title>
<meta http-equiv="content-type"
    content="text/html; charset=iso-8859-1" />
<link rel="stylesheet" type="text/css" href="center.css" />
</head>
<body>
<div id="content">
  <p>This box is 630 pixels wide and centered in the document.</p>
  <p>Lorem ipsum dolor sit amet, consectetuer adipiscing …</p>
</div>
</body>
</html>
```

File: **center.css**

```
body {
  background-color: #CCD3D9;
```

```
    color: #000000;
    text-align: center;
}
#content {
    width: 630px;
    margin-left: auto;
    margin-right: auto;
    border: 2px solid #A6B2BC;
    background-color: #FFFFFF;
    color: #000000;
    padding: 0 20px 0 20px;
    text-align: left;
}
```

Discussion

This technique allows you to center a box easily, and is ideal if you need to center a content block on a page.

When we set both the left and right margins to auto, we are asking the browser to calculate the margins necessary to make them equal, thereby centering the box. In "How do I create a fixed-width, centered, two-column layout?", we'll see how to create a layout inside a container that has been centered in this way.

The example code provided here contains additional CSS that works around a bug in IE 5.x that prevents the margins from centering content. By setting text-align: center on the body, then setting it back again (text-align: left) on the content <div>, we are able to work around the problem, allowing the layout to center in these browsers as well.

How do I create a liquid, two-column layout with the menu on the left, and the content on the right?

Web page layouts like that shown in Figure 8.21, which display a menu on the left and a large content area to the right, are very common. Let's discover how to build this layout using CSS.

Figure 8.21. The liquid two-column layout is built using CSS.

Solution

File: **2col.html**

```
<!DOCTYPE html PUBLIC "-//W3C//DTD XHTML 1.0 Transitional//EN"
    "http://www.w3.org/TR/xhtml1/DTD/xhtml1-transitional.dtd">
<html xmlns="http://www.w3.org/1999/xhtml">
<head>
<title>Stage &amp; Screen - theatre and film reviews</title>
<meta http-equiv="content-type"
    content="text/html; charset=iso-8859-1" />
<link rel="stylesheet" type="text/css" href="2col.css" />
</head>
<body>
<div id="header">
  <img src="stage-logo.gif" width="187" height="29"
      alt="Stage &amp; Screen" class="logo" />
  <span class="strapline">theatre and film reviews</span>
```

```
</div>
<div id="content">
  <h1>Welcome to Stage &amp; Screen</h1>
  <p>Lorem ipsum dolor sit amet, consectetuer adipiscing …</p>
</div>
<div id="nav">
  <ul>
    <li><a href="#">Play Reviews</a></li>
    <li><a href="#">Film Reviews</a></li>
    <li><a href="#">Post a Review</a></li>
    <li><a href="#">About this site</a></li>
    <li><a href="#">Contact Us</a></li>
  </ul>
  <h2>Latest Reviews</h2>
  <ul>
    <li><a href="#">The Passion of The Christ</a></li>
    <li><a href="#">Finding Nemo</a></li>
    <li><a href="#">Stomp</a></li>
    <li><a href="#">The Lion King 3</a></li>
  </ul>
</div>
</body>
</html>
```

File: **2col.css**

```
body {
  margin: 0;
  padding: 0;
  background-color: #FFFFFF;
  color: #000000;
  font-family: Arial, Helvetica, sans-serif;
  border-top: 2px solid #2A4F6F;
}
#header {
  border-top: 1px solid #778899;
  border-bottom: 1px dotted #B2BCC6;
  height: 3em;
}
#header .strapline {
  font: 120% Georgia, "Times New Roman", Times, serif;
  color: #778899;
  background-color: transparent;
  float: right;
  margin-right: 2em;
  margin-top: 0.5em;
}
```

```
#header .logo {
  float: left;
  margin-left: 1.5em;
  margin-top: 0.5em;
}
#nav {
  position: absolute;
  top: 5em;
  left: 1em;
  width: 14em;
}
#nav ul {
  list-style: none;
  margin-left: 1em;
  padding-left: 0;
}
#nav li {
  font-size: 80%;
  border-bottom: 1px dotted #B2BCC6;
  margin-bottom: 0.3em;
}
#nav a:link, #nav a:visited {
  text-decoration: none;
  color: #2A4F6F;
  background-color: transparent;
}
#nav a:hover {
  color: #778899;
}
#nav h2 {
  font: 110% Georgia, "Times New Roman", Times, serif;
  color: #2A4F6F;
  background-color: transparent;
  border-bottom: 1px dotted #cccccc;
}
#content {
  margin-left: 16em;
  margin-right: 2em;
}
h1 {
  font: 150% Georgia, "Times New Roman", Times, serif;
}
#content p {
  font-size: 80%;
  line-height: 1.6em;
```

```
    padding-left: 1.2em;
}
```

Discussion

Our starting point for this layout is the header that we created in "How do I align my logo and strapline to the left and right without using a table?"

Here, we've added some content to that layout; it resides within a `<div>` with the ID content. The navigation for the page comprises two unordered lists contained in a `<div>` with the ID nav. As you'd expect, without any positioning applied, these blocks will display below the heading in the order in which they appear in the document (see Figure 8.22). At this point, the CSS looks like this:

File: **2col.css (excerpt)**

```
body {
  margin: 0;
  padding: 0;
  background-color: #FFFFFF;
  color: #000000;
  font-family: Arial, Helvetica, sans-serif;
  border-top: 2px solid #2A4F6F;
}
#header {
  border-top: 1px solid #778899;
  border-bottom: 1px dotted #B2BCC6;
  height: 3em;
}
#header .strapline {
  font: 120% Georgia, "Times New Roman", Times, serif;
  color: #778899;
  background-color: transparent;
  float: right;
  margin-right: 2em;
  margin-top: 0.5em;
}
#header .logo {
  float: left;
  margin-left: 1.5em;
  margin-top: 0.5em;
}
```

Figure 8.22. The content and navigation have no positioning information.

Size and Position the Menu

Let's use absolute positioning to position the menu just under the heading bar, and give it a comfortable width:

File: **2col.css (excerpt)**

```
#nav {
  position: absolute;
  top: 5em;
  left: 1em;
```

```
  width: 14em;
}
```

As you can see from Figure 8.23, this code causes the menu to appear over the content text, as the absolute positioning we've applied has removed it from the flow of the document.

Figure 8.23. The menu has been positioned absolutely.

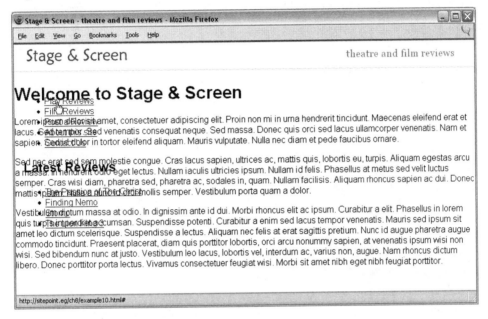

Positioning the Content

As we're aiming to maintain a liquid layout, we don't want to assign fixed width to the content and, in fact, we don't need to. The problem with the content is that it appears in the space required by the menu. To solve this problem, we can simply apply a large left-hand margin to the content area to allow space for the menu. The results are shown in Figure 8.24:

```
#content {
  margin-left: 16em;
  margin-right: 2em;
}
```

Figure 8.24. The margins are added to the content.

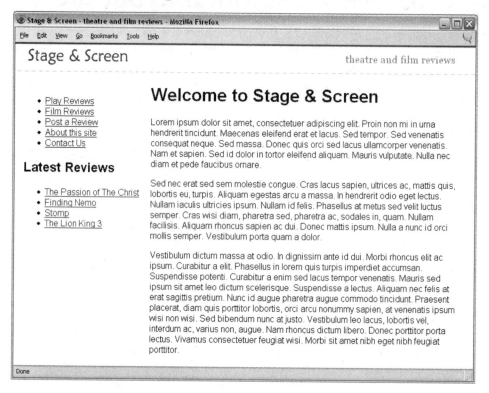

Now that all the elements are laid out neatly, we can work on the style of individual elements, using CSS to create the layout we saw back in Figure 8.21. The completed CSS style sheet is given at the start of this solution.

Tip

Ems for Positioning Text Layouts

I used ems to position the elements in this layout. The em unit will resize as the text resizes, which should help us avoid any problems with overlapping text if the user resizes the font in their browser. For layouts that are predominantly text-based, the em is an excellent choice for setting the widths of boxes and margins. However, care should be taken if your design involves many images. Images do not resize with the altered text size, so you may prefer to use pixels for positioning elements in cases where you need precise control over the elements' locations on the page.

Can I reverse this layout and put the menu on the right?

Can the technique presented in the previous solution be used to create a layout in which the menu is positioned on the right?

Solution

Exactly the same technique can be used! You'll need to position your menu from the top and right, and give the content area a large right margin so that the menu has sufficient space in which to display. The result is shown in Figure 8.25.

Figure 8.25. A two-column layout can be built so that the menu appears on the right.

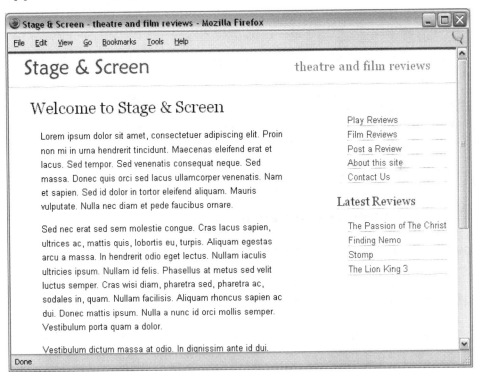

Discussion

To position the menu on the right does not require us to change the markup of the original document at all. All we need to do is change the positioning properties for #nav and the margins on #content:

File: **2col-reverse.css**

```
#nav {
  position: absolute;
  top: 5em;
  right: 1em;
  width: 14em;
}
#content {
  margin-left: 2em;
  margin-right: 16em;
}
```

The advantage of using absolute positioning can be seen clearly here. It doesn't matter where our menu appears in the markup: the use of absolute positioning means it will be removed from the document flow and we can place it wherever we like on the page. This can be of great benefit for accessibility purposes, as it allows us to place some of the less important items (such as lists of links to other sites, advertising, etc.) right at the end of the document code. This way, those who employ screen readers to use the site won't have to hear these unnecessary items read aloud each time they access a page. Yet you, as the designer, are still able to position these items wherever you like for visual effect.

How do I create a fixed-width, centered, two-column layout?

How can you create a two-column layout that's contained within a centered <div> on the page?

Solution

Creating a two-column, fixed-width, centered layout is slightly trickier than a fixed-width, left-aligned or liquid layout, as you don't have an absolute reference point from the left- or right-hand side of the browser window to position the elements horizontally. There are a couple of different ways to deal with this complication in order to achieve the kind of layout shown in Figure 8.26.

Figure 8.26. The fixed-width, centered layout.

Whichever layout method you chose, the HTML code is the same:

File: **2col-fixedwidth.html**

```
<!DOCTYPE html PUBLIC "-//W3C//DTD XHTML 1.0 Transitional//EN"
    "http://www.w3.org/TR/xhtml1/DTD/xhtml1-transitional.dtd">
<html xmlns="http://www.w3.org/1999/xhtml">
<head>
<title>Recipe for Success</title>
<meta http-equiv="content-type"
    content="text/html; charset=iso-8859-1" />
<link href="2col-fixedwidth.css" rel="stylesheet" type="text/css"
    />
</head>
<body>
<div id="wrapper">
  <div id="content">
    <h1>Welcome</h1>
    <p>The Recipe for Success web site brings you exciting and
```

```
    easy to use recipes from around the world.</p>
  <p>…</p>
</div>
<div id="navigation">
  <ul id="mainnav">
    <li><a href="#">Recipes</a>
      <ul class="subnav">
        <li><a href="#">Starters</a></li>
        <li><a href="#">Main Courses</a></li>
        <li><a href="#">Desserts</a></li>
      </ul>
    </li>
    <li><a href="#">Contact Us</a></li>
    <li><a href="#">Articles</a></li>
    <li><a href="#">Buy Online</a></li>
  </ul>
</div>
<div id="footer">Copyright &copy; 1999 - 2004 Recipe for
  success</div>
</div>
</body>
</html>
```

The first, and simplest option to achieve the desired layout is to use **relative positioning** to place the content and navigation elements within the centered block:

File: **2col-fixedwidth.css**

```
body {
  margin: 0;
  padding: 0;
  font-family: Verdana, Arial, Helvetica, sans-serif;
  background-color: #FFFFFF;
  text-align: center;
}
#wrapper {
  position: relative;
  text-align: left;
  width: 760px;
  margin-right: auto;
  margin-left: auto;
  padding: 122px 0 0 0;
  background-image: url(recipe_header.jpg);
  background-repeat: no-repeat;
  background-position: left top;
  border-left: 2px solid #722100;
```

```
    border-right: 2px solid #722100;
    border-bottom: 2px solid #722100;
}
#content {
    margin-left: 230px;
    padding: 20px 10px 0 0;
}
#content p {
    font-size: 80%;
    line-height: 1.8em;
    padding-left: 2em;
}
#content h1 {
    font: normal 180% Georgia, "Times New Roman", Times, serif;
    color: #B51032;
    background-color: transparent;
}
#content h2 {
    font-size: 120%;
    color: #940D1E;
    background-color: transparent;
    border-bottom: 1px dotted #FF9006;
}
#navigation {
    position: absolute;
    top: 122px;
    left: 0;
    width: 180px;
}
#navigation ul {
    list-style: none;
    margin: 0;
    padding: 0;
    border: none;
}
#navigation li {
    width: 180px;
    border-bottom: 1px solid #ED9F9F;
    margin: 0;
    padding: 0;
    font-size: 80%;
    vertical-align: bottom;
}
#navigation a:link, #navigation a:visited {
    display: block;
    padding: 5px 5px 5px 0.5em;
```

```
   border-left: 12px solid #722100;
   border-right: 1px solid #722100;
   background-color: #B51032;
   color: #FFFFFF;
   text-decoration: none;
}
#navigation a:hover {
   background-color: #722100;
   color: #FFFFFF;
}
#navigation ul.subnav {
   margin-left: 12px;
}
#navigation ul.subnav li {
   border-bottom: 1px solid #722100;
   width: 168px;
}
#navigation ul.subnav a:link, #navigation ul.subnav a:visited {
   background-color: #ED9F9F;
   color: #722100;
}
#footer {
   padding: 0 0 10px 255px;
   font-size: 70%;
   color: #AAAAAA;
   background-color: transparent;
}
```

An alternative that gives the exact same result is to simply float the navigation and content against the left and right sides of the centered block, respectively:

File: **2col-fixedwidth-float.css**

```
body {
   margin: 0;
   padding: 0;
   font-family: Verdana, Arial, Helvetica, sans-serif;
   background-color: #FFFFFF;
   text-align: center;
}
#wrapper {
   text-align: left;
   width: 760px;
   margin-right: auto;
   margin-left: auto;
   padding: 122px 0 0 0;
   background-image: url(recipe_header.jpg);
```

```
    background-repeat: no-repeat;
    background-position: left top;
    border-left: 2px solid #722100;
    border-right: 2px solid #722100;
    border-bottom: 2px solid #722100;
}
#content {
    width: 520px;
    float: right;
    padding: 20px 10px 0 0;
}
#content p {
    font-size: 80%;
    line-height: 1.8em;
    padding-left: 2em;
}
#content h1 {
    font: normal 180% Georgia, "Times New Roman", Times, serif;
    color: #B51032;
    background-color: transparent;
}
#content h2 {
    font-size: 120%;
    color: #940D1E;
    background-color: transparent;
    border-bottom: 1px dotted #FF9006;
}
#navigation {
    float: left;
    width: 180px;
}
#navigation ul {
    list-style: none;
    margin: 0;
    padding: 0;
    border: none;
}
#navigation li {
    width: 180px;
    border-bottom: 1px solid #ED9F9F;
    margin: 0;
    padding: 0;
    font-size: 80%;
    vertical-align: bottom;
}
#navigation a:link, #navigation a:visited {
```

```
  display: block;
  padding: 5px 5px 5px 0.5em;
  border-left: 12px solid #722100;
  border-right: 1px solid #722100;
  background-color: #B51032;
  color: #FFFFFF;
  text-decoration: none;
}
#navigation a:hover {
  background-color: #722100;
  color: #FFFFFF;
}
#navigation ul.subnav {
  margin-left: 12px;
}
#navigation ul.subnav li {
  border-bottom: 1px solid #722100;
  width: 168px;
}
#navigation .subnav a:link, #navigation ul.subnav a:visited {
  background-color: #ED9F9F;
  color: #722100;
}
#footer {
  clear: both;
  padding: 0 0 10px 255px;
  font-size: 70%;
  color: #AAAAAA;
  background-color: transparent;
}
```

Discussion

For the purposes of this discussion, we'll ignore purely aesthetic style properties such as borders, colors, and fonts so that we may concentrate on the layout.

Both versions of this layout begin with a centered <div>, similar to "How do I center a block on the page?". This <div> is given the ID wrapper.

File: **2col-fixedwidth.css** or **2col-fixedwidth-float.css** (excerpt)

```
body {
  margin: 0;
  padding: 0;
  text-align: center;
  …
```

```
}
#wrapper {
  text-align: left;
  width: 760px;
  margin-right: auto;
  margin-left: auto;
  ...
}
```

The results are shown in Figure 8.27.

Figure 8.27. The content is centered on the page.

We then add to the block a background image to act as the page heading. We use padding to allow the required space, which renders as shown in Figure 8.28.

File: **2col-fixedwidth.css** or **2col-fixedwidth-float.css** (excerpt)

```
#wrapper {
  text-align: left;
  width: 760px;
  margin-right: auto;
  margin-left: auto;
  padding: 122px 0 0 0;
```

```
background-image: url(recipe_header.jpg);
background-repeat: no-repeat;
background-position: left top;
...
}
```

Figure 8.28. Add a header image and borders to #wrapper.

Now, in "How do I create a liquid, two-column layout with the menu on the left, and the content on the right?" we saw that we could use absolute positioning to control the navigation, and apply enough margin to the content of the page so that the two blocks would not overlap. The only difference in this layout is that we need to position the navigation within the centered `wrapper` block, so we cannot give it an absolute position on the page.

Instead of `absolute`, you can set an element's `position` property to `relative`, which doesn't take the element out of the document flow the way absolute positioning does, but instead lets you shift the element from the starting point of its default position on the page. If you don't provide coordinates to shift the element, it will actually stay exactly where the browser would normally position it. Unlike an element that doesn't have a `position` value specified, however, a `relative`-positioned element will provide a new **positioning context** for any absolute-positioned elements within it.

In plain English, an element with `position: absolute` contained within an element with `position: relative` will base its position on the edges of that parent element, not on the edges of the browser window. This is exactly what we need to position the navigation within the centered block in this example.

So the first step is to set the `position` property of `wrapper` to `relative`:

File: **2col-fixedwidth.css** (excerpt)

```
#wrapper {
  position: relative;
  text-align: left;
  width: 760px;
  margin-right: auto;
  margin-left: auto;
  padding: 122px 0 0 0;
  background-image: url(recipe_header.jpg);
  background-repeat: no-repeat;
  background-position: left top;
  …
}
```

We can then use absolute positioning to set the location of the `navigation` block:

File: **2col-fixedwidth.css** (excerpt)

```
#navigation {
  position: absolute;
  top: 122px;
  left: 0;
  width: 180px;
}
```

And finally we add a margin to the main content of the page to make space for the newly-positioned navigation area:

File: **2col-fixedwidth.css** (excerpt)

```
#content {
  margin-left: 230px;
  padding: 20px 10px 0 0;
}
```

As long as the content of the page occupies more vertical space than the navigation, this layout will work just fine. Unfortunately, since the `navigation` block is absolute positioned, it doesn't affect the height of the `wrapper` block, so if the content is shorter than the navigation, the wrapper block will not be tall enough to contain the navigation.

The alternative method of using floated blocks to achieve our design goals is more complex, but it overcomes the limitation just mentioned. First, we float the `navigation` block left and the `content` block right.

File: **2col-fixedwidth-float.css** (excerpt)

```
#navigation {
  float: left;
  width: 180px;
}
#content {
  width: 520px;
  float: right;
  padding: 20px 10px 0 0;
}
```

Figure 8.29. Float the navigation left and the content right.

As you can see in Figure 8.29, the border of the `wrapper` block now cuts through the page content. This occurs because we floated most of the block's contents, removing them from the document flow. The only element inside `wrapper` that is still within the document flow is the `footer` block, which can be seen here in the bottom left corner of the `wrapper` block, where it has been pushed by the floated blocks.

By setting the `clear` property of the `footer` block to `both`, the footer will drop down below both of the floated blocks, thereby forcing `wrapper` to accommodate both the navigation and the content—no matter which is taller.

File: **2col-fixedwidth-float.css** (excerpt)

```
#footer {
  clear: both;
  ...
}
```

Figure 8.30. The footer is set to `clear: both.`

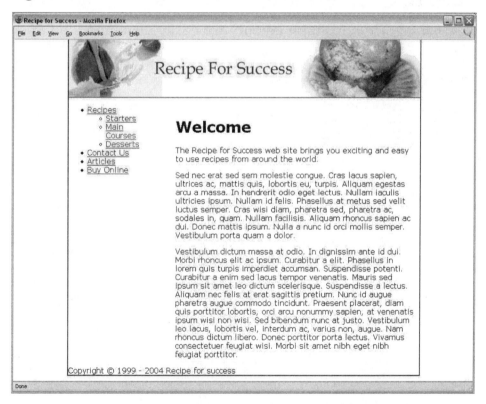

With the completed layout shown in Figure 8.30 in place, you can style the remaining elements as you wish. You may recognize the menu—it's the one we saw in "Can I use CSS and lists to create a navigation system with sub-navigation?" in Chapter 4. The completed examples in the code archive use the same style rules as we developed in that solution for the menu. You can, however, style the elements in many other ways.

How do I create a three-column CSS layout?

Many designs fall into a three-column model. As demonstrated in Figure 8.31, you might need a column for navigation, one for content, and one for additional items such as advertising or highlighted content on the site. How can this type of layout be accomplished using CSS?

Figure 8.31. Three-column layouts are easily developed in CSS.

Solution

A three-column, liquid layout is easily created using a simple technique similar to that we used previously for the two-column layout in "How do I create a liquid, two-column layout with the menu on the left, and the content on the right?".

File: **3col.html**

```
<!DOCTYPE html PUBLIC "-//W3C//DTD XHTML 1.0 Transitional//EN"
    "http://www.w3.org/TR/xhtml1/DTD/xhtml1-transitional.dtd">
<html xmlns="http://www.w3.org/1999/xhtml">
<head>
<title>Recipe for Success</title>
<meta http-equiv="content-type"
    content="text/html; charset=iso-8859-1" />
<link rel="stylesheet" type="text/css" href="3col.css" />
</head>
<body>
<div id="content">
  <h1>Recipe for Success</h1>
  <p>…</p>
</div>
<div id="side1">
  <h3>Search the Recipes</h3>
  <form method="post" action="">
    <input type="text" name="textfield" class="txt" /><br />
    <input type="submit" name="Submit" value="Submit" />
  </form>
  <ul>
    <li><a href="#">About Us</a></li>
    <li><a href="#">Recipes</a></li>
    <li><a href="#">Articles</a></li>
    <li><a href="#">Buy Online</a></li>
    <li><a href="#">Contact Us</a></li>
  </ul>
</div>
<div id="side2">
  <h3>Please Visit our Sponsors</h3>
  <div class="adbox"><p>Lorem ipsum dolor sit amet, …</p></div>
  <div class="adbox"><p>Sed mattis, orci eu porta …</p></div>
  <div class="adbox"><p>Quisque mauris nunc, mattis …</p></div>
</div>
</body>
</html>
```

```css
body {
  margin: 0;
  padding: 0;
  background-image: url(tomato_bg.jpg);
  background-repeat: no-repeat;
  background-color: #FFFFFF;
}
p {
  font: 80%/1.8em Verdana, Geneva, Arial, Helvetica, sans-serif;
  padding-top: 0;
  margin-top: 0;
}
form {
  margin: 0;
  padding: 0;
}
#content {
  margin: 66px 260px 0px 240px;
  padding: 10px;
}
#content h1 {
  text-align: right;
  padding-right: 20px;
  font: 150% Georgia, "Times New Roman", Times, serif;
  color: #901602;
}
#side1 {
  position: absolute;
  width: 200px;
  top: 30px;
  left: 10px;
  padding: 70px 10px 10px 10px;
}
#side2 {
  position: absolute;
  width: 220px;
  top: 30px;
  right: 10px;
  padding: 70px 10px 10px 10px;
  border-left: 1px dotted #cccccc;
  background-image: url(sm-tomato.jpg);
  background-position: top right;
  background-repeat: no-repeat;
}
#side2 h3 {
```

```
  font: 110% Georgia, "Times New Roman", Times, serif;
  margin: 0;
  padding-bottom: 4px;
}
.adbox {
  padding: 2px 4px 2px 6px;
  margin: 0 0 10px 0;
  border: 1px dotted #B1B1B1;
  background-color: #F4F4F4;
}
#side1 h3 {
  font: 110% Georgia, "Times New Roman", Times, serif;
  color: #621313;
  background-color: transparent;
  margin: 0;
  padding-bottom: 4px;
}
#side1 .txt {
  width: 184px;
  background-color: #FCF5F5;
  border: 1px inset #901602;
}
#side1 ul {
  list-style: none;
  margin-left: 0;
  padding-left: 0;
  width: 184px;
}
#side1 li {
  font: 80% Verdana, Geneva, Arial, Helvetica, sans-serif;
  margin-bottom: 0.3em;
  border-bottom: 1px solid #E7AFAF;
}
#side1 a:link, #side1 a:visited {
  text-decoration: none;
  color: #901602;
  background-color: transparent;
}
#side1 a:hover {
  color: #621313;
}
```

Discussion

This layout uses a simple technique to create three-column layouts. We start with the unstyled XHTML document shown in Figure 8.32, which has three <div>s: one with ID content, one with ID side1, and one with ID side2.

Figure 8.32. The XHTML document is unstyled.

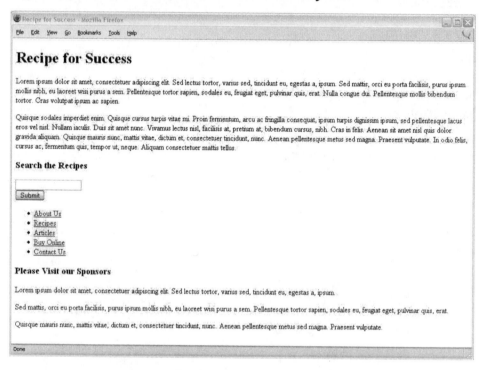

We create the three columns using the following CSS fragments. We place both the left- and right-hand columns with absolute positioning—side1 is positioned from the left edge of the page, side2 from the right. We add some significant top padding to these columns to make room for background images to act as headings.

File: **3col.css** (excerpt)

```
#side1 {
  position: absolute;
  width: 200px;
  top: 30px;
```

```
  left: 10px;
  padding: 70px 10px 10px 10px;
}
```

```
#side2 {
  position: absolute;
  width: 220px;
  top: 30px;
  right: 10px;
  padding: 70px 10px 10px 10px;
  ...
}
```

Figure 8.33. The three columns appear with the initial CSS positioning.

The content area simply sits between the two absolute-positioned columns, with margins applied to give them the room they need:

```
#content {
  margin: 66px 260px 0px 240px;
```

```
    padding: 10px;
}
```

Figure 8.33 shows what the page looks like with these initial positioning tasks complete.

With our three columns in place, we can simply style the individual elements as required for the design in question. I've used background images on the body and on side2 to add the tomato images seen in Figure 8.31.

Figure 8.34. An alternative three-column layout is created using CSS.

An Alternative Method for Three-Column Layouts

The above method is a robust way to create a three-column layout, and it's the one I'd choose under most circumstances. However, there are a variety of other ways to create this type of layout. If you require a three-column layout in which all three columns are the same height (e.g. if you have borders or background colors you wish to line up), then the example shown in Figure 8.34, based on the layout developed by Douglas Livingstone,[1] may serve you better.

File: **3col-alt.html**

```
<!DOCTYPE html PUBLIC "-//W3C//DTD XHTML 1.0 Transitional//EN"
    "http://www.w3.org/TR/xhtml1/DTD/xhtml1-transitional.dtd">
<html xmlns="http://www.w3.org/1999/xhtml">
<head>
<title>Recipe for Success</title>
<meta http-equiv="content-type"
    content="text/html; charset=iso-8859-1" />
<link rel="stylesheet" type="text/css" href="3col-alt.css" />
</head>
<body>
<div id="wrapper">
  <div id="header"><h1>Recipe for Success</h1></div>
  <div id="outer">
    <div id="inner">
      <div id="side1">
        <h3>Search the Recipes</h3>
        <form method="post" action="">
          <input type="text" name="textfield" class="txt" /><br />
          <input type="submit" name="Submit" value="Submit" />
        </form>
        <ul>
          <li><a href="#">About Us</a></li>
          <li><a href="#">Recipes</a></li>
          <li><a href="#">Articles</a></li>
          <li><a href="#">Buy Online</a></li>
          <li><a href="#">Contact Us</a></li>
        </ul>
      </div>
      <div id="content">
        <h2>Welcome to Recipe for Success</h2>
        <p>…</p>
      </div>
      <div id="side2">
```

[1] http://www.redmelon.net/tstme/3cols2/

```
          <h3>Visit our Sponsors</h3>
          <div class="adbox"><p>Lorem ipsum dolor sit …</p></div>
          <div class="adbox"><p>Sed mattis, orci eu …</p></div>
        </div>
        <div class="clear"></div>
      </div>
    </div>
    <div id="footer"><p>&copy; Recipe for Success 2000 - 2004</p>
    </div>
  </div>
</body>
</html>
```

File: **3col-alt.css**

```css
body {
  margin: 0;
  padding: 0;
}
h2, h3 {
  margin-top: 0;
}
form {
  margin: 0;
  padding: 0;
}
p {
  font: 80%/1.8 Verdana, Geneva, Arial, Helvetica, sans-serif;
  margin-top: 0;
}
#wrapper {
  min-width: 400px;
  width: 100%;
}
#outer {
  border-left: 165px solid #FFFFFF; /* left column background */
  border-right: 200px solid #FCF5F5;/* right column background */
  background-color: #FAFAFA;         /* center column background */
}
#inner {
  margin: 0;
  width: 100%;
}
#header {
  background-color: #FFFFFF;
  color: #901602;
  border-bottom: 1px dotted #CCCCCC;
```

```
}
#header h1 {
  font: 150% Georgia, "Times New Roman", Times, serif;
  text-align: right;
  margin-right: 1em;
}
#side1 {
  width: 160px;                      /* left column width */
  margin-left: -160px;               /* -ive left column width */
  float: left;
  position: relative;
  z-index: 10;
  padding-left: 5px;
}
#side1 h3 {
  width: 150px;
  font: 110% Georgia, "Times New Roman", Times, serif;
  color: #621313;
  background-color: transparent;
  margin-bottom: 0;
  padding-bottom: 4px;
}
#side1 .txt {
  width: 150px;
  background-color: #FCF5F5;
  border: 1px inset #901602;
}
#side1 ul {
  width: 150px;
  list-style: none;
  margin-left: 0;
  padding-left: 0;
}
#side1 li {
  font: 80% Verdana, Geneva, Arial, Helvetica, sans-serif;
  margin-bottom: 0.3em;
  border-bottom: 1px solid #E7AFAF;
}
#side1 a:link, #side1 a:visited {
  text-decoration: none;
  color: #901602;
  background-color: transparent;
}
#side1 a:hover {
  color: #621313;
}
```

```
#side2 {
  width: 200px;                    /* right column width */
  margin-right: -200px;            /* -ive right column width */
  float: left;
  position: relative;
  z-index: 11;
}
#side2 h3 {
  font: 110% Georgia, "Times New Roman", Times, serif;
  color: #621313;
  background-color: transparent;
  margin-bottom: 0;
  padding-bottom: 4px;
  padding-left: 0.2em;
}
#side2 p {
  padding-left: 10px;
}
.adbox {
  padding: 2px 4px 2px 6px;
  margin: 0 0.5em 10px 0.5em;
  border: 1px dotted #B1B1B1;
  background-color: #FFFFFF;
}
#content {
  float: left;
  width: 100%;
  position: relative;
  z-index: 12;
}
#content h2 {
  font: 130% Georgia, "Times New Roman", Times, serif;
  color: #901602;
  margin-left: 1em;
}
#content p {
  margin-left: 3em;
  margin-right: 2em;
}
#footer {
  background-color: #F4F4F4;
  width: 100%;
  position: relative;
  z-index: 13;
  border-top: 1px dotted #B1B1B1;
}
```

```
#footer p {
  padding-left: 1em;
}
.clear {
  clear: both;
}

/* Mozilla bug workarounds */
#outer > #inner {
  border-bottom: 1px solid transparent;
}
#side1 {
  margin-right: 1px;
}
#side2 {
  margin-left: 1px;
}
#content {
  margin: 0 -3px 0 -2px;
}
```

This layout works by floating all three columns (the left-hand navigation, the center content, and the right-hand advertisements) to the left, so that they effectively stack against the left-hand side of the screen. These three blocks reside within a container that provides the solid background colors for the columns using thick borders: its left border provides a background for the left column, its right border provides a background for the right column, and its content area provides the background for the center content column:

File: **3col-alt.css** (excerpt)

```
#outer {
  border-left: 165px solid #FFFFFF; /* left column background */
  border-right: 200px solid #FCF5F5;/* right column background */
  background-color: #FAFAFA;         /* center column background */
}
```

In order to get side1 and side2 to sit on top of outer's borders (instead of within them), we assign these blocks negative left and right margins, respectively, equal to their widths:

File: **3col-alt.css** (excerpt)

```
#side1 {
  width: 160px;                /* left column width */
  margin-left: -160px;         /* -ive left column width */
  float: left;
```

```
  position: relative;
  z-index: 10;
}
```

File: **3col-alt.css** (excerpt)

```
#side2 {
  width: 200px;                    /* right column width */
  margin-right: -200px;            /* -ive right column width */
  float: left;
  position: relative;
  z-index: 11;
}
```

In order for the outer block to provide full-height backgrounds for all three columns, it needs to be as tall as the tallest of these three. Since our columns are all floated, we use an empty <div> with class clear just before the closing tag of outer to which we apply the CSS clear property:

File: **3col-alt.css** (excerpt)

```
.clear {
  clear: both;
}
```

Unfortunately, Mozilla browsers have a few bugs to do with margins and borders that affect floated elements when they are stacked in this way. Our style sheet must therefore end with a number of rules that work around these bugs without seriously affecting the display:

File: **3col-alt.css** (excerpt)

```
/* Mozilla bug workarounds */
#outer > #inner {
  border-bottom: 1px solid transparent;
}
#side1 {
  margin-right: 1px;
}
#side2 {
  margin-left: 1px;
}
#content {
  margin: 0 -3px 0 -2px;
}
```

While technically interesting, this layout is not particularly easy to work with, as the slightest change can often set off a cascade of browser bugs and wreck the layout. Additionally, the stacking order of the floated columns relies on the order they appear in the document, so you don't have the same flexibility with your HTML markup as you do when using absolute positioning.

For all these reasons, I'd recommend you use the first method for three-column layouts where possible, as it's far more robust than the float technique. However, if you find that layout unsuitable, this solution represents an alternative way to tackle the problem.

How do I add a footer that works well, using CSS?

If you've tried to add a footer to your CSS layout, you may well have encountered a problem. If the content is shorter than the browser window, the footer will move up under the content, instead of sticking to the bottom of the window, as in Figure 8.35. How can we get the look we want using CSS?

Figure 8.35. The footer is positioned using CSS.

Solution

This is a bit of a tricky one, but most browsers can be persuaded to force the <body> element to be at least the same height as the browser window, even when it doesn't contain enough content to justify that height. You can then use absolute positioning to stick the footer to the bottom of that block.

File: **footer.html**

```
<!DOCTYPE html PUBLIC "-//W3C//DTD XHTML 1.0 Transitional//EN"
    "http://www.w3.org/TR/xhtml1/DTD/xhtml1-transitional.dtd">
<html xmlns="http://www.w3.org/1999/xhtml">
<head>
<title>Stage &amp; Screen - theatre and film reviews</title>
<meta http-equiv="content-type"
    content="text/html; charset=iso-8859-1" />
<link rel="stylesheet" type="text/css" href="footer.css" />
</head>
<body>
<div id="contents">
  <div id="header">
    <img src="stage-logo.gif" width="187" height="29"
        alt="Stage &amp; Screen" class="logo" />
    <span class="strapline">theatre and film reviews</span>
  </div>
  <div id="content">
    <h1>Welcome to Stage &amp; Screen</h1>
    <p>...</p>
  </div>
  <div id="nav">
    <ul>
      <li><a href="#">Play Reviews</a></li>
      <li><a href="#">Film Reviews</a></li>
      <li><a href="#">Post a Review</a></li>
      <li><a href="#">About this site</a></li>
      <li><a href="#">Contact Us</a></li>
    </ul>
    <h2>Latest Reviews</h2>
    <ul>
      <li><a href="#">The Passion of The Christ</a></li>
      <li><a href="#">Finding Nemo</a></li>
      <li><a href="#">Stomp</a></li>
      <li><a href="#">The Lion King 3</a></li>
    </ul>
  </div>
  <div id="footer"><p>Copyright &copy; 2003 - 2004 Stage &amp;
```

```
      Screen</p></div>
</div>
</body>
</html>
```

```css
body {
  margin: 0;
  padding: 0;
  background-color: #FFFFFF;
  color: #000000;
  font-family: Arial, Helvetica, sans-serif;
}
html, body, #contents {
  min-height: 100%;
  width: 100%;
  height: 100%;
}
html>body, html>body #contents {
  height: auto;
}
#contents {
  position: absolute;
  top: 0;
  left: 0;
}
#header {
  border-top: 1px solid #778899;
  border-bottom: 1px dotted #B2BCC6;
  height: 3em;
}
#header .strapline {
  font: 120% Georgia, "Times New Roman", Times, serif;
  color: #778899;
  background-color: transparent;
  float: right;
  margin-right: 2em;
  margin-top: 0.5em;
}
#header .logo {
  float: left;
  margin-left: 1.5em;
  margin-top: 0.5em;
}
#nav {
  position: absolute;
```

```
    top: 5em;
    left: 1em;
    width: 14em;
}
#nav ul {
    list-style: none;
    margin-left: 1em;
    padding-left: 0;
}
#nav li {
    font-size: 80%;
    border-bottom: 1px dotted #B2BCC6;
    margin-bottom: 0.3em;
}
#nav a:link, #nav a:visited {
    text-decoration: none;
    color: #2A4F6F;
    background-color: transparent;
}
#nav a:hover {
    color: #778899;
}
#nav h2 {
    font: 110% Georgia, "Times New Roman", Times, serif;
    color: #2A4F6F;
    background-color: transparent;
    border-bottom: 1px dotted #cccccc;
}
#content {
    margin-left: 16em;
    margin-right: 2em;
    margin-bottom: 3em;
}
h1 {
    font: 150% Georgia, "Times New Roman", Times, serif;
}
#content p {
    font-size: 80%;
    line-height: 1.6em;
    padding-left: 1.2em;
}
#footer {
    position: absolute;
    bottom: 0;
    width: 100%;
    border-top: 1px dotted #AAAAAA;
```

```
  background-color: #CCCCCC;
  color: #626262;
  font-size: 70%;
}
#footer p {
  margin: 0.5em 0 1em 2em;
  padding: 0;
}
```

Discussion

I've taken as my starting point a two-column liquid layout to which I want to add a footer. The first thing to do is to add the `footer` `<div>` to the document, and style it using CSS. It's the final element in the document and with just some basic style properties assigned, as you'd expect, it sits just below the content.

File: **footer.html** (excerpt)

```
<div id="footer"><p>Copyright &copy; 2003 - 2004 Stage &amp;
    Screen</p></div>
```

File: **footer.css** (excerpt)

```
#footer {
  ...
  width: 100%;
  border-top: 1px dotted #AAAAAA;
  background-color: #CCCCCC;
  color: #626262;
  font-size: 70%;
}
#footer p {
  margin: 0.5em 0 1em 2em;
  padding: 0;
}
```

If the content is longer than the viewport, this works fine. However, as you can see in Figure 8.36, if it's shorter than the viewport, the footer comes away from the bottom of the browser window.

Figure 8.36. The footer falls just below the content.

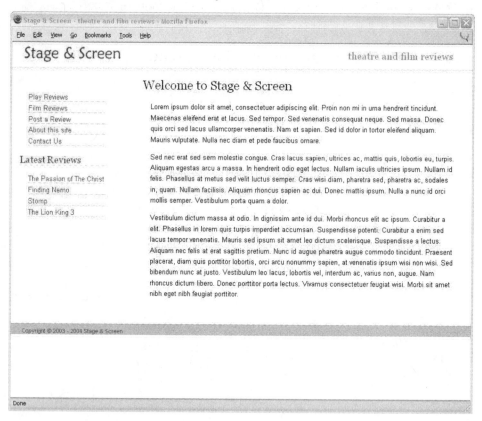

If you're comfortable with absolute positioning, your first instinct might be to position the footer at the bottom of the document:

File: **.php (excerpt)**

```
#footer {
  position: absolute;
  bottom: 0;
  width: 100%;
  border-top: 1px dotted #AAAAAA;
  background-color: #CCCCCC;
  color: #626262;
  font-size: 70%;
}
```

But rather than the bottom of the document, the footer will go to the bottom of the browser window. When the user scrolls down, the footer will scroll along with the rest of the page, as seen in Figure 8.37.

Figure 8.37. The footer overlays the content.

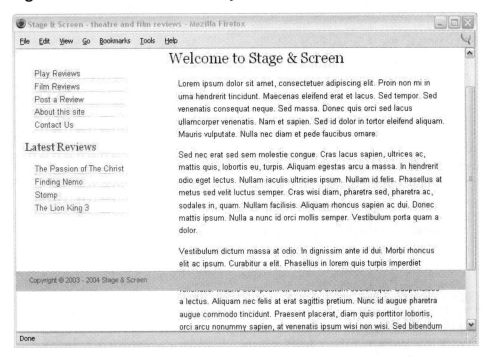

By adding positioning to the footer, however, we are part of the way to achieving our end result. We just need two more things to complete the effect:

❏ The footer must be placed at the bottom of the *document*, not the bottom of the browser window.

❏ The document must be at least as tall as the browser window.

The first is easy to achieve. Simply put the footer, along with the rest of the page, inside a `<div>` with its `position` property set to `absolute`. The footer will then stick to the bottom of this `<div>`, which is the bottom of the document.

File: **footer.css** (excerpt)

```
#contents {
  position: absolute;
  top: 0;
  left: 0;
}
```

The second criterion is harder to achieve across all browsers, but here's a magic formula that works in many cases:

File: **footer.css** (excerpt)

```
html, body, #contents {
  min-height: 100%;
  width: 100%;
  height: 100%;
}
html>body, html>body #contents {
  height: auto;
}
```

This technique works well in IE5 and up, and in Mozilla-based browsers. It fails in Konqueror and Safari—in those browsers, the footer behaves as it does in Figure 8.36, falling just below the content. However, in browsers in which this technique fails, it represents no more than an aesthetic issue—it doesn't render the page unusable in any way.

The technique we've applied here is detailed among others on the css-discuss Wiki.[2] It's worth checking this resource periodically for new techniques to get around this and many other problems.

How do I display a thumbnail gallery without using a table?

If you need to display a collection of images—perhaps for a photo album—a table may seem like the easiest way to go. However, the layout shown in Figure 8.38 can also be achieved using CSS, and this brings with it some additional benefits that the tabled version lacks.

---

[2] http://css-discuss.incutio.com/?page=FooterInfo

Figure 8.38. The image gallery of thumbnails is built using CSS.

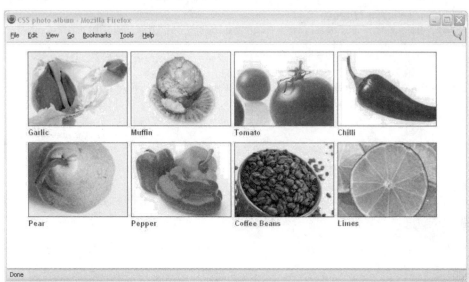

Solution

This solution uses a list for the album images and positions them using CSS.

File: **gallery.html**

```
<!DOCTYPE html PUBLIC "-//W3C//DTD XHTML 1.0 Transitional//EN"
    "http://www.w3.org/TR/xhtml1/DTD/xhtml1-transitional.dtd">
<html xmlns="http://www.w3.org/1999/xhtml">
<head>
<title>CSS photo album</title>
<meta http-equiv="content-type"
    content="text/html; charset=iso-8859-1" />
<link href="gallery.css" rel="stylesheet" type="text/css" />
</head>
<body>
<ul id="albumlist">
  <li><img src="thumb1.jpg" alt="Garlic" width="180" height="130"
        />Garlic</li>
  <li><img src="thumb2.jpg" alt="Muffin" width="180" height="130"
        />Muffin</li>
  <li><img src="thumb3.jpg" alt="tomato" width="180" height="130"
        />Tomato</li>
  <li><img src="thumb4.jpg" alt="chilli" width="180" height="130"
```

```
        />Chilli</li>
  <li><img src="thumb5.jpg" alt="pear" width="180" height="130"
      />Pear</li>
  <li><img src="thumb6.jpg" alt="pepper" width="180" height="130"
      />Pepper</li>
  <li><img src="thumb7.jpg" alt="coffee beans" width="180"
      height="130" />Coffee Beans</li>
  <li><img src="thumb8.jpg" alt="lime" width="180" height="130"
      />Limes</li>
</ul>
</body>
</html>
```

File: **gallery.css**

```
body {
  background-color: #FFFFFF;
  color: #000000;
  margin: 0;
  padding: 0;
}
#albumlist {
  list-style-type: none;
}
#albumlist li {
  float: left;
  margin-right: 6px;
  margin-bottom: 10px;
  font: bold 0.8em Arial, Helvetica, sans-serif;
  color: #333333;
}
#albumlist img {
  display: block;
  border: 1px solid #333300;
}
```

Discussion

The starting point for this layout is to create an unordered list and to store each image in a list item. I've also added a caption for each image, within the <li> tag. Without the application of CSS, this list with display as shown in Figure 8.39.

File: **gallery.html (excerpt)**

```
<ul id="albumlist">
  <li><img src="thumb1.jpg" alt="Garlic" width="180" height="130"
      />Garlic</li>
```

```
<li><img src="thumb2.jpg" alt="Muffin" width="180" height="130"
       />Muffin</li>
<li><img src="thumb3.jpg" alt="tomato" width="180" height="130"
       />Tomato</li>
<li><img src="thumb4.jpg" alt="chilli" width="180" height="130"
       />Chilli</li>
<li><img src="thumb5.jpg" alt="pear" width="180" height="130"
       />Pear</li>
<li><img src="thumb6.jpg" alt="pepper" width="180" height="130"
       />Pepper</li>
<li><img src="thumb7.jpg" alt="coffee beans" width="180"
       height="130" />Coffee Beans</li>
<li><img src="thumb8.jpg" alt="lime" width="180" height="130"
       />Limes</li>
</ul>
```

Figure 8.39. The list of images is unstyled.

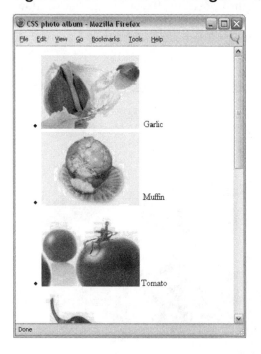

To create the grid-style layout of the thumbnails, we're simply going to use `float` to position the images. We'll achieve this by floating the `<li>` tag that contains them.

Add the following to your style sheet:

```
#albumlist {
  list-style-type: none;
}
#albumlist li {
  float: left;
}
#albumlist img {
  display: block;
}
```

`albumlist` is the ID that should be applied to the list that contains the photos. All we're aiming to achieve with these rules is to remove the bullet points from the list and float the images left, as shown in Figure 8.40. Also, by setting the images to display as blocks, we force their captions to display below them.

Your pictures should now have moved into position. If you resize the window, you'll see that they wrap to fill the available width. If the window becomes too narrow to contain a given number of images side by side—the last image simply drops down to start the next line.

Figure 8.40. The page displays after the images are floated left.

We have our basic layout and can now add to this to make it look more attractive. For example, we could add some rules to create space between the images in the list, along with a nice font for the captions:

File: **gallery.css** (excerpt)

```
#albumlist li {
  float: left;
  margin-right: 6px;
  margin-bottom: 10px;
  font: bold 0.8em Arial, Helvetica, sans-serif;
  color: #333333;
}
```

We could also add a border to the images:

File: **gallery.css** (excerpt)

```
#albumlist img {
  border: 1px solid #333300;
}
```

The flexibility of this layout method makes it particularly handy when you're pulling your images from a database—you don't have to calculate the number of images, for example, so that you can build table cells on the fly as you create your page.

All the same, you might not always want to allow this wrapping effect. You can stop unwanted wrapping by setting the width of the list tag, <ul>.

```
#albumlist {
  list-style-type: none;
  width: 500px;
}
```

This forcibly sets the width to which the images will wrap, as shown in Figure 8.41.

Figure 8.41. The images cease to wrap after we set the width of the containing <ul> tag.

Summary

I hope this chapter has given you some starting points and ideas for your own layouts. By combining other solutions in this book, such as the innovative use of navigation and images, with your own creativity, you should be able to come up with many designs based upon the layouts we've explored here. As with tables, most CSS layouts are really just variations on a theme.

Once you have a grasp of the basics, and you've learned the rules, you'll find that you are really only limited by your imagination. For inspiration, and to see what other designers are doing with CSS layouts, have a look at the CSS Zen Garden.[3]

[3] http://www.csszengarden.com/

Experimentation, Browser Specific CSS, and Future Techniques

The solutions we've discussed in previous chapters should work well across modern browsers from IE 5 onward, without any show-stopping problems or causing those browsers to crash.

In this chapter, we're going to look at some techniques that, for a variety of reasons, are problematic in certain browsers. Some are just difficult to get working—they may involve a large number of CSS hacks, for example—others make use of nonstandard features supported only by certain browsers. So, if you're planning to use any of these techniques, careful cross-browser checking is essential. Be sure to read the Discussion part of each solution, as this is where I'll highlight the problems that might occur.

In what circumstances might you want to experiment with techniques that are not functional across browsers, or are very difficult to implement? The obvious situation would be one in which your environment and audience are limited—perhaps you're that lucky person developing an intranet for a company that uses Mozilla exclusively (if you are that person, and you ever want to quit, there will be a line of CSS developers just ready to jump into your seat). Or, perhaps you have a significant number of visitors who use a browser that supports the technique, and you are able to add it in a way that makes it an extra nicety for those users without causing a problem for everyone else.

How do I build those colored scrollbars?

If you use Internet Explorer you may have seen sites that use colored scroll-bars—either changing the main browser scrollbar, or just the internal scrollbars that appear on elements such as <iframe>s or <textarea>s, as shown in Figure 9.1.

Figure 9.1. Change the scrollbar colors on the document and a text area.

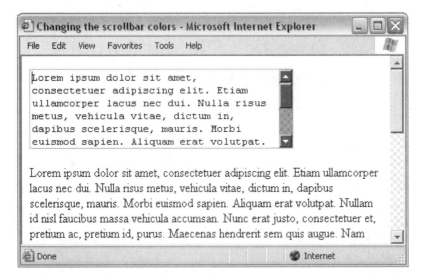

Solution

This solution will work in Internet Explorer 5.5 or later only. It does not cause problems in other browsers, but will prevent your CSS from validating.

File: **scrollbars.html**

```
<!DOCTYPE html PUBLIC "-//W3C//DTD XHTML 1.0 Transitional//EN"
    "http://www.w3.org/TR/xhtml1/DTD/xhtml1-transitional.dtd">
<html xmlns="http://www.w3.org/1999/xhtml">
<head>
<title>Changing the scrollbar colors</title>
<meta http-equiv="content-type"
    content="text/html; charset=iso-8859-1" />
<style type="text/css">
```

```
.largetext {
  scrollbar-3dlight-color: #B0C4DE;
  scrollbar-arrow-color: #FFFFFF;
  scrollbar-base-color: #8BA9CF;
  scrollbar-darkshadow-color: #436DA3;
  scrollbar-face-color: #34547E;
  scrollbar-highlight-color: #E6ECF4;
  scrollbar-shadow-color: #000000;
}
html {
  scrollbar-3dlight-color: #B0C4DE;
  scrollbar-arrow-color: #34547E;
  scrollbar-base-color: #8BA9CF;
  scrollbar-darkshadow-color: #436DA3;
  scrollbar-face-color: #E6ECf4;
  scrollbar-highlight-color: #FFFFFF;
  scrollbar-shadow-color: #34547E;
}
</style>
</head>
<body>
<textarea name="mytext" id="mytext" rows="6" cols="40"
    class="largetext">
Lorem ipsum dolor sit amet, consectetuer …</textarea>
<p>Lorem ipsum dolor sit amet, consectetuer adipiscing elit. …</p>
</body>
</html>
```

Discussion

As I've already noted, this effect uses Microsoft extensions to CSS and, therefore, will only work on Internet Explorer. If you do decide to use it, you should be aware that changing the scrollbars—particularly those of the browser window itself—can be confusing for visitors who expect the scrollbars to look as the defaults do.

There is a fun test page at the Microsoft Website[1] on which you can try out different scrollbar color combinations.

---

[1] http://msdn.microsoft.com/workshop/samples/author/dhtml/refs/scrollbarColor.htm

How do I create a menu that stays fixed while the page scrolls below it?

If you have a lot of very long documents on your site, allowing users to click on the menu no matter how far they've scrolled down a page can make it easier for them to navigate. You might think you'd have to resort to frames to achieve this effect, but you don't!

Solution

Newer, CSS supporting browsers such as Mozilla allow you to achieve the fixed navigation effect shown in Figure 9.2 easily. However, the following solution fails in Internet Explorer—the menu will simply scroll up with the content.

Figure 9.2. The menu stays static while the page scrolls.

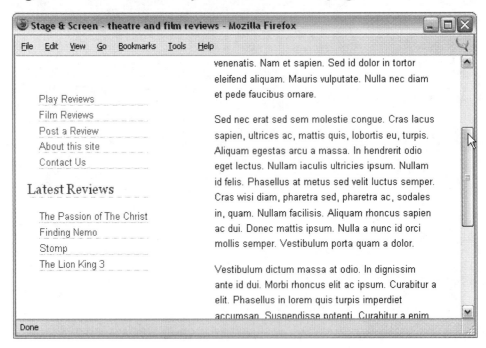

File: **fixedmenu.html**

```
<!DOCTYPE html PUBLIC "-//W3C//DTD XHTML 1.0 Transitional//EN"
    "http://www.w3.org/TR/xhtml1/DTD/xhtml1-transitional.dtd">
<html xmlns="http://www.w3.org/1999/xhtml">
<head>
<title>Stage &amp; Screen - theatre and film reviews</title>
<meta http-equiv="content-type"
    content="text/html; charset=iso-8859-1" />
<link rel="stylesheet" type="text/css" href="fixedmenu.css" />
</head>
<body>
<div id="content">
  <h1>Welcome to Stage &amp; Screen</h1>
  <p>Lorem ipsum dolor sit amet, consectetuer adipiscing …</p>
</div>
<div id="nav">
  <ul>
    <li><a href="#">Play Reviews</a></li>
    <li><a href="#">Film Reviews</a></li>
    <li><a href="#">Post a Review</a></li>
    <li><a href="#">About this site</a></li>
    <li><a href="#">Contact Us</a></li>
  </ul>
  <h2>Latest Reviews</h2>
  <ul>
    <li><a href="#">The Passion of The Christ</a></li>
    <li><a href="#">Finding Nemo</a></li>
    <li><a href="#">Stomp</a></li>
    <li><a href="#">The Lion King 3</a></li>
  </ul>
</div>
</body>
</html>
```

File: **fixedmenu.css**

```
body {
  margin: 0;
  padding: 0;
  background-color: #FFFFFF;
  color: #000000;
  font-family: Arial, Helvetica, sans-serif;
}
#nav {
  position: absolute;
  top: 2em;
  left: 1em;
```

```
    width: 14em;
}
body > #nav {
    position: fixed;
}
#nav ul {
    list-style: none;
    margin-left: 1em;
    padding-left: 0;
}
#nav li {
    font-size: 80%;
    border-bottom: 1px dotted #B2BCC6;
    margin-bottom: 0.3em;
}
#nav a:link, #nav a:visited {
    text-decoration: none;
    color: #2A4F6F;
    background-color: transparent;
}
#nav a:hover {
    color: #778899;
}
#nav h2 {
    font: 110% Georgia, "Times New Roman", Times, serif;
    color: #2A4F6F;
    background-color: transparent;
    border-bottom: 1px dotted #cccccc;
}
#content {
    margin: 2em 2em 0 16em;
}
h1 {
    font: 150% Georgia, "Times New Roman", Times, serif;
}
#content p {
    font-size: 80%;
    line-height: 1.6em;
    padding-left: 1.2em;
}
```

Discussion

Mozilla-based, and other up-to-date browsers support `fixed` as a value of the `position` property, as prescribed by the CSS2 specification:

```
position: fixed;
```

For the effect to work in these browsers, the only change you need to implement is to alter the rules for #nav. Take the code you would normally use to place the menu with absolute positioning:

File: **fixedmenu.css** (excerpt)

```
#nav {
  position: absolute;
  top: 2em;
  left: 1em;
  width: 14em;
}
```

...and change the position property:

```
#nav {
  position: fixed;
  top: 2em;
  left: 1em;
  width: 14em;
}
```

Unfortunately, implementing this change will cause Internet Explorer to make a mess of the layout. IE doesn't understand position: fixed at all, and displays the menu beneath the content, as shown in Figure 9.3.

Figure 9.3. Internet Explorer doesn't understand position:fixed.

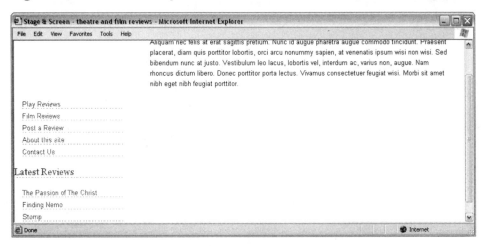

However, there's an easy way to overcome this problem. Leave the rules for **#nav** as they are (i.e., set to `position: absolute`) so that Internet Explorer doesn't break the layout. Now, add the following rule to the style sheet:

File: **fixedmenu.css (excerpt)**

```
body>#nav {
  position: fixed;
}
```

Internet Explorer 5 and 6 do not understand the > child selector, either. Conversely, the browsers that support `position: fixed` also support the child selector. By sticking the `position: fixed` property declaration in this rule, you can hide it from Internet Explorer, which will simply use the `position: absolute` declaration in the rule for **#nav**.

The end result of this approach is that you achieve the scrolling effect in supporting browsers, but, in Internet Explorer, the page behaves as it did before—the menu scrolls up with the text. The next solution looks at a fix that gets this working in Internet Explorer.

Figure 9.4. A static menu can be placed on a scrolling page in Internet Explorer.

How do I get a fixed menu to work in Internet Explorer?

In the last example, we created a great fixed menu effect without using frames. But, is it possible to get this effect to work in Internet Explorer? Figure 9.4 shows what we hope to achieve.

Solution

It is possible to make this effect work, although it's frustratingly complex when you consider that, for supporting browsers, all we need is one line of CSS!

File: **fixedmenu2.html**

```
<!--force IE into Quirks Mode-->
<!DOCTYPE html PUBLIC "-//W3C//DTD XHTML 1.0 Transitional//EN"
    "http://www.w3.org/TR/xhtml1/DTD/xhtml1-transitional.dtd">
<html xmlns="http://www.w3.org/1999/xhtml">
<head>
<title>Stage &amp; Screen - theatre and film reviews</title>
<meta http-equiv="content-type"
    content="text/html; charset=iso-8859-1" />
<link rel="stylesheet" type="text/css" href="fixedmenu2.css" />
<!--[if IE]>
<style type="text/css" media="screen">
body
{
  overflow-y: hidden;
}
div#content
{
  height: 100%;
  overflow: auto;
}
</style>
<![endif]-->
</head>
<body>
<div id="content">
 <h1>Welcome to Stage &amp; Screen</h1>
 <p>Lorem ipsum dolor sit amet, consectetuer adipiscing …</p>
 <p>…</p>
</div>
```

```
<div id="nav">
 <ul>
  <li><a href="#">Play Reviews</a></li>
  <li><a href="#">Film Reviews</a></li>
  <li><a href="#">Post a Review</a></li>
  <li><a href="#">About this site</a></li>
  <li><a href="#">Contact Us</a></li>
 </ul>
 <h2>Latest Reviews</h2>
 <ul>
  <li><a href="#">The Passion of The Christ</a></li>
  <li><a href="#">Finding Nemo</a></li>
  <li><a href="#">Stomp</a></li>
  <li><a href="#">The Lion King 3</a></li>
 </ul>
</div>
</body>
</html>
```

File: **fixedmenu2.css**

```
body {
  margin: 0;
  padding: 0;
  background-color: #FFFFFF;
  color: #000000;
  font-family: Arial, Helvetica, sans-serif;
}
#nav {
  position: absolute;
  top: 2em;
  left: 1em;
  width: 14em;
}
body > #nav {
  position: fixed;
}
#nav ul {
  list-style: none;
  margin-left: 1em;
  padding-left: 0;
}
#nav li {
  font-size: 80%;
  border-bottom: 1px dotted #B2BCC6;
  margin-bottom: 0.3em;
}
```

```
#nav a:link, #nav a:visited {
  text-decoration: none;
  color: #2A4F6F;
  background-color: transparent;
}
#nav a:hover {
  color: #778899;
}
#nav h2 {
  font: 110% Georgia, "Times New Roman", Times, serif;
  color: #2A4F6F;
  background-color: transparent;
  border-bottom: 1px dotted #cccccc;
}
#content {
  padding: 2em 2em 0 16em;
}
h1 {
  font: 150% Georgia, "Times New Roman", Times, serif;
}
#content p {
  font-size: 80%;
  line-height: 1.6em;
  padding-left: 1.2em;
}
```

Discussion

As I have already mentioned, implementing this effect successfully in IE is tricky and, in fact, we don't really end up with the effect working at all! Instead, we create something that *looks* as if it is working, while leaving the correct version in place for use by browsers that support it.

The Style Sheet

The interpretation of `position: fixed` in other browsers allows the entire page to scroll as normal, leaving the fixed element in position. As we have seen, though, this doesn't work in Internet Explorer. The workaround that we'll use will fake the effect by scrolling the actual content area. To be able to do this, we need to make sure that our content area actually bumps up against the edges of the viewport. In the previous example, space around the content area was created using a margin. However, if that approach were used in this solution, it would cause the scrollbar to appear at the edge of the content, with a space between it and the edge of the browser window. To be able to create the effect in IE, we must change the rules for the content div, and use padding to create this space:

```
#content {
  padding: 2em 2em 0 16em;
}
```

The Document

The first thing we have to do is to force Internet Explorer into Quirks Mode by adding a comment above the DOCTYPE. For an XHTML document, we have to utilize the fact that Internet Explorer goes into Quirks Mode if anything appears above the DOCTYPE:

File: **fixedmenu2.html** (excerpt)

```
<!--force IE into Quirks Mode-->
<!DOCTYPE html PUBLIC "-//W3C//DTD XHTML 1.0 Transitional//EN"
    "http://www.w3.org/TR/xhtml1/DTD/xhtml1-transitional.dtd">
```

Below the imported style sheet, we now add an IE-only conditional block, containing two additional style rules. You could add these to an external style sheet, too—just remember that it needs to come after the main style sheet, and be applied only to Internet Explorer browsers.

File: **fixedmenu2.html** (excerpt)

```
<!--[if IE]>
<style type="text/css" media="screen">
body
{
  overflow-y: hidden;
}
div#content
{
  height: 100%;
  overflow: auto;
}
</style>
<![endif]-->
```

What we've actually done for Internet Explorer, is to set up the main content area as a `<div>` that will scroll when the content is too long. As such, the scrollbar at the right hand side of the page isn't the browser window's scrollbar, as it is in Mozilla and other compliant browsers. It is, in fact, the scrollbar on the right hand side of the content `<div>`.

This technique works in IE 5 or later; however, you do need to put IE 6 into Quirks Mode to get the solution to work, and this may cause other inconsistencies between the appearance of your layout in IE and in other browsers. That said, if it's used carefully, I believe this is a better and more accessible solution that the alternative of using a frameset just to keep the menu static on the page.

Can I create a page footer that remains fixed in position, like a frame, using CSS?

In Chapter 8, we discussed the creation of a footer that sticks to the bottom of the screen, or the bottom of the content, if that is longer than the viewable area. But, what about a footer that always remains visible at the bottom of the viewport, as shown in Figure 9.5—like a frame would?

Figure 9.5. The fixed footer is achievable in CSS.

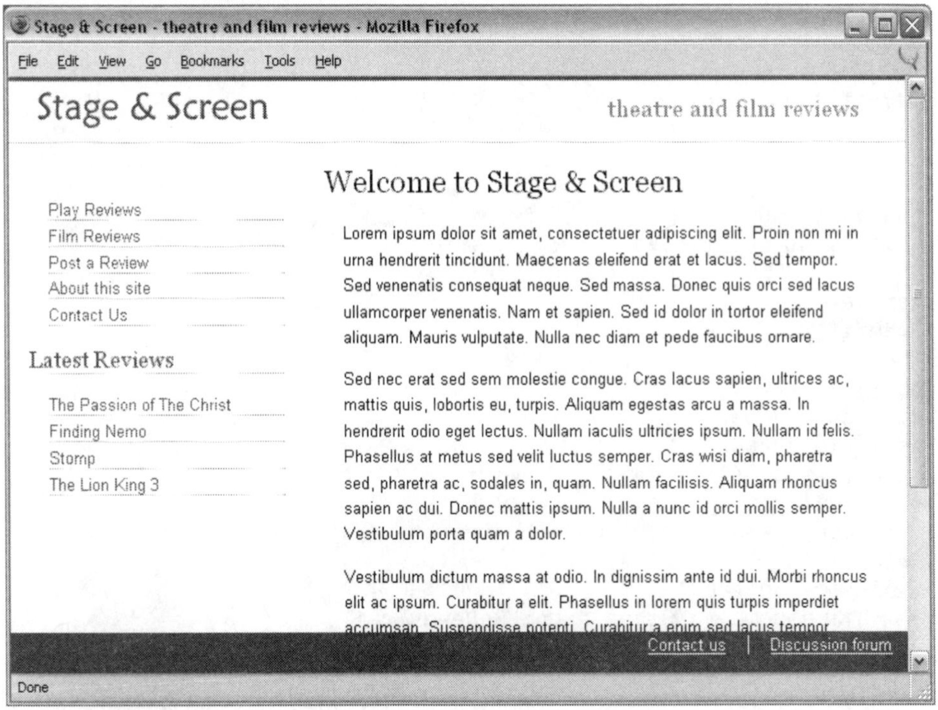

Solution

Using a technique that's similar to the one we saw in the last solution, we can get this effect working across recent browsers. Once again, it would be a matter of adding a simple line of code, but for Internet Explorer's lack of support for `position: fixed`.

File: **footerframe.html**

```
<!--force IE into Quirks Mode-->
<!DOCTYPE html PUBLIC "-//W3C//DTD XHTML 1.0 Transitional//EN"
    "http://www.w3.org/TR/xhtml1/DTD/xhtml1-transitional.dtd">
<html xmlns="http://www.w3.org/1999/xhtml">
<head>
<title>Stage &amp; Screen - theatre and film reviews</title>
<meta http-equiv="content-type"
    content="text/html; charset=iso-8859-1" />
<link rel="stylesheet" type="text/css" href="footerframe.css" />
<!--[if IE]>
<style type="text/css">
body
{
  overflow-y: hidden;
}
div#wrapper
{
  height: 100%;
  overflow: auto;
}
</style>
<![endif]-->
</head>
<body>
<div id="wrapper">
  <div id="header">
    <img src="stage-logo.gif" width="187" height="29"
        alt="Stage &amp; Screen" class="logo" />
    <span class="strapline">theatre and film reviews</span>
  </div>
  <div id="content">
    <h1>Welcome to Stage &amp; Screen</h1>
    <p>Lorem ipsum dolor sit amet, consectetuer adipiscing …</p>
    <p>…</p>
  </div>
  <div id="nav">
    <ul>
```

```
    <li><a href="#">Play Reviews</a></li>
    <li><a href="#">Film Reviews</a></li>
    <li><a href="#">Post a Review</a></li>
    <li><a href="#">About this site</a></li>
    <li><a href="#">Contact Us</a></li>
  </ul>
  <h2>Latest Reviews</h2>
  <ul>
    <li><a href="#">The Passion of The Christ</a></li>
    <li><a href="#">Finding Nemo</a></li>
    <li><a href="#">Stomp</a></li>
    <li><a href="#">The Lion King 3</a></li>
  </ul>
  </div>
</div>
<div id="footer">
  <a href="#">Contact us</a> | <a href="#">Discussion forum</a>
</div>
</body>
</html>
```

File: **footerframe.css**

```
body {
  margin: 0;
  padding-bottom: 2em;
  background-color: #FFFFFF;
  color: #000000;
  font-family: Arial, Helvetica, sans-serif;
  border-top: 2px solid #2A4F6F;
}
#header {
  border-top: 1px solid #778899;
  border-bottom: 1px dotted #B2BCC6;
  height: 3em;
}
#header .strapline {
  font: 120% Georgia, "Times New Roman", Times, serif;
  color: #778899;
  background-color: transparent;
  float: right;
  margin-right: 2em;
  margin-top: 0.5em;
}
#header .logo {
  float: left;
  margin-left: 1.5em;
```

```
  margin-top: 0.5em;
}
#footer {
  position: absolute;
  bottom: 0;
  left: 0;
  width: 100%;
  height: 2em;
  background-color: #2A4F6F;
  color: #FFFFFF;
  border-top: #778899;
  text-align: right;
}
html > body #footer {
  position: fixed;
}
#footer a:link, #footer a:visited {
  padding: 0.5em 1em 0.5em 1em;
  color: #FFFFFF;
  background-color: transparent;
  font-size: 80%;
}
#footer a:hover {
  text-decoration: none;
}
#nav {
  position: absolute;
  top: 5em;
  left: 1em;
  width: 13em;
}
#nav ul {
  list-style: none;
  margin-left: 1em;
  padding-left: 0;
}
#nav li {
  font-size: 80%;
  border-bottom: 1px dotted #B2BCC6;
  margin-bottom: 0.3em;
}
#nav li a:link, #nav li a:visited {
  text-decoration: none;
  color: #2A4F6F;
  background-color: transparent;
}
```

```
#nav li a:hover {
  color: #778899;
}
#nav h2 {
  font: 110% Georgia, "Times New Roman", Times, serif;
  color: #2A4F6F;
  background-color: transparent;
  border-bottom: 1px dotted #cccccc;
}
#content {
  margin-left: 16em;
  margin-right: 2em;
}
h1 {
  font: 150% Georgia, "Times New Roman", Times, serif;
}
#content p {
  font-size: 80%;
  line-height: 1.6em;
  padding-left: 1.2em;
}
```

Discussion

As with the previous solution, getting this effect to work in standards-compliant browsers such as Mozilla, Safari, and Konqueror, requires that we add the footer <div> to the document, then style it with CSS using position: fixed.

The footer is the last element in the document:

File: **footerframe.html** (excerpt)

```
<div id="footer">
  <a href="#">Contact us</a> | <a href="#">Discussion forum</a>
</div>
```

In the style sheet, we position and style the footer, using the child selector, as in the previous solution, to ensure the footer uses absolute positioning in IE 5 and 6:

File: **footerframe.css** (excerpt)

```
#footer {
  position: absolute;
  bottom: 0;
  left: 0;
```

```
  width: 100%;
  height: 2em;
  background-color: #2A4F6F;
  color: #FFFFFF;
  border-top: #778899;
  text-align: right;
}
html > body #footer {
  position: fixed;
}
```

Since the footer will have a height of 2 ems, we need to add that same amount of padding to the document body, so that the last of the content is visible above the footer when the user scrolls all the way to the bottom:

```
body {
  margin: 0;
  padding-bottom: 2em;

  ...
}
```

This code will now display in compliant browsers, as shown in Figure 9.5, with a static menu always at the bottom of the viewport, and the text appearing to scroll beneath it.

If we leave the code like this, the page will load without error in Internet Explorer, but, when the user scrolls, the page footer will stay in the same place across the content, scrolling up with it, as seen in Figure 9.6.

As in the last solution, we need to force Internet Explorer into Quirks Mode to get the scrolling effect. We can do this by adding a comment above the XHTML DOCTYPE:

File: **footerframe.html** (excerpt)

```
<!--force IE into Quirks Mode-->
<!DOCTYPE html PUBLIC "-//W3C//DTD XHTML 1.0 Transitional//EN"
    "http://www.w3.org/TR/xhtml1/DTD/xhtml1-transitional.dtd">
```

We then add the IE-specific code to the <head> of the document, beneath the linked style sheet:

File: **footerframe.html** (excerpt)

```
<!--[if IE]>
<style type="text/css">
body
```

```
{
  overflow-y: hidden;
}
div#wrapper
{
  height: 100%;
  overflow: auto;
}
</style>
<![endif]-->
```

Figure 9.6. The footer scrolls up with the page.

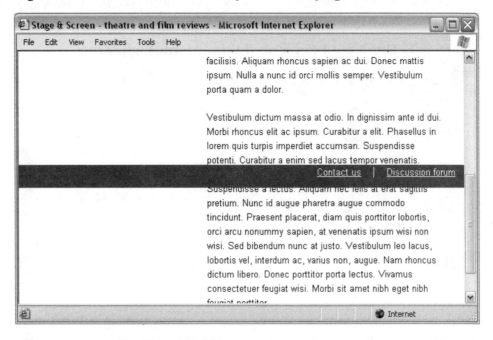

We also need to wrap the page content, excluding the footer, in a <div> with ID wrapper, which we reference in the IE-specific CSS. Open this <div> just after the opening <body> tag:

File: **footerframe.html (excerpt)**

```
<body>
<div id="wrapper">
```

And close it just before the footer:

File: **footerframe.html (excerpt)**
```
</div>
<div id="footer">
  <a href="#">Contact us</a> | <a href="#">Discussion forum</a>
</div>
```

If you compare the layout in Figure 9.7 with that in Figure 9.5, you'll see that there are a couple of obvious differences between the two implementations. In Firefox (and other browsers that support position: fixed), the scrollbar is the browser scrollbar, and it goes all the way down the page—as you'd expect. However, because we've faked the scrolling effect in Internet Explorer, the scrollbar only extends the length of the content area—almost as if the bottom area were a separate frame.

Figure 9.7. The layout is successful in Internet Explorer.

If you have particularly good eyes, you may also have noticed that, in IE, the blue line at the very top of the document, which is CSS applied to the <body> tag, actually runs across the top of the scrollbar. It remains at the top of the page when you scroll, whereas, in other browsers, it will disappear. What this shows is that it is the content <div> that you are scrolling, not the entire page itself, as in the compliant browsers. So, to use this technique, you will have to plan your layout carefully to accommodate it. Using a wrapper to contain everything other than the footer—as seen in this example—should work reasonably well for most layouts.

Can I create pure CSS drop-down menus?

In Chapter 4, we saw how to create image- and JavaScript-free rollovers. Can the same be achieved for drop-down menus?

Solution

The answer is yes... but they don't work in Internet Explorer! Nevertheless, Figure 9.8 illustrates this interesting technique that will, I hope, be more useful in the future.

Figure 9.8. Create a CSS-only drop-down menu.

File: **menus.html**

```
<!DOCTYPE html PUBLIC "-//W3C//DTD XHTML 1.0 Transitional//EN"
    "http://www.w3.org/TR/xhtml1/DTD/xhtml1-transitional.dtd">
<html xmlns="http://www.w3.org/1999/xhtml">
<head>
<title>CSS Flyout menus</title>
<meta http-equiv="content-type"
    content="text/html; charset=iso-8859-1" />
<link rel="stylesheet" type="text/css" href="menus.css" />
</head>
```

```
<body>
<ul id="nav">
  <li><a href="#">Starters</a>
    <ul>
      <li><a href="">Fish</a></li>
      <li><a href="">Fruit</a></li>
      <li><a href="">Soups</a></li>
    </ul>
  </li>
  <li><a href="#">Main courses</a>
    <ul>
      <li><a href="">Meat</a></li>
      <li><a href="">Fish</a></li>
      <li><a href="">Vegetarian</a></li>
    </ul>
  </li>
  <li><a href="#">Desserts</a>
    <ul>
      <li><a href="">Fruit</a></li>
      <li><a href="">Puddings</a></li>
      <li><a href="">Ice Creams</a></li>
    </ul>
  </li>
</ul>
</body>
</html>
```

File: **menus.css**

```
#nav, #nav ul {
  padding: 0;
  margin: 0;
  list-style: none;
}
#nav li {
  float: left;
  position: relative;
  width: 10em;
  border: 1px solid #B0C4DE;
  background-color: #E7EDF5;
  color: #2D486C;
  font: 80% Verdana, Geneva, Arial, Helvetica, sans-serif;
  margin-right: 1em;
}
#nav a:link, #nav a:visited {
  display: block;
  text-decoration: none;
```

```
    padding-left: 1em;
    color: #2D486C;
}
#nav ul {
    display: none;
    position: absolute;
    top: 1.3em;
    left: 0;
    padding-top: 0.5em;
}
#nav ul li {
    float: none;
    border: 0 none transparent;
    border-bottom: 1px solid #E7EDF5;
    background-color: #F1F5F9;
    font-size: 100%;
    margin: 0;
    margin-bottom: 0.5em;
    padding: 0;
}
#nav li > ul {
    top: auto;
    left: auto;
}
#nav li:hover ul {
    display: block;
}
```

Discussion

This attractive and easy effect will not work in Internet Explorer, but it is supported by several other, newer browsers. This solution allows you to create a drop-down menu without using any JavaScript at all. The technique is based on the Suckerfish menus detailed on A List Apart.[2]

The menus themselves are based on simple unordered lists. The top-level menu items constitute one main list; the items that fall under each main item are contained in nested lists.

File: **menus.html (excerpt)**

```
<ul id="nav">
  <li><a href="#">Starters</a>
    <ul>
```

[2] http://www.alistapart.com/articles/dropdowns

```
      <li><a href="">Fish</a></li>
      <li><a href="">Fruit</a></li>
      <li><a href="">Soups</a></li>
    </ul>
  </li>
  ...
```

As shown in Figure 9.9, without CSS applied to the menu, browsers display it as a logically structured, ordered list with subsections that are easy to spot.

Figure 9.9. Lists display logically in browsers that don't support CSS.

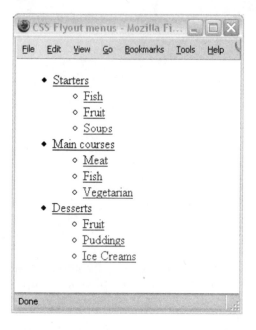

To begin with, we style the top-level menu, removing its list style and floating the list items to the left so that they stack horizontally. The list items are given a `position` value of `relative` so that we can position our fly-out menus within them later on.

File: **menus.css (excerpt)**

```
#nav, #nav ul {
  ...
  list-style: none;
}
```

```
#nav li {
  float: left;
  position: relative;
  width: 10em;
  ...
  margin-right: 1em;
}
```

We coerce the links in the menu to display as blocks, so they fill the rectangular areas defined by the menu items:

File: **menus.css** (excerpt)

```
#nav a:link, #nav a:visited {
  display: block;
  ...
}
```

Next, we set the nested lists that make up our fly-out menus to not be displayed by default (`display: none`). We do, however, specify that absolute positioning is to be used when they *are* displayed, so that they do not affect the flow of the rest of the document:

File: **menus.css** (excerpt)

```
#nav ul {
 display: none;
 position: absolute;
  ...
}
```

To prevent our fly-out menu list items from being floated horizontally the way the main menu items are, we need to set their `float` property back to `none`:

File: **menus.css** (excerpt)

```
#nav ul li {
  float: none;
  ...
}
```

Finally, we use the `:hover` pseudo-class to display the fly-out menu within any main menu item when the mouse is over it:

File: **menus.css** (excerpt)

```
#nav li:hover ul {
  display: block;
}
```

With these basic CSS rules in place, the menus display as shown in Figure 9.10.

Figure 9.10. The menu display alters with the addition of basic CSS.

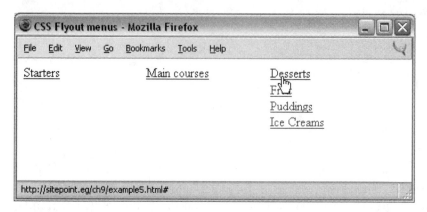

This code initially sets the nested lists to `display: none`. When the user hovers over a main menu list item, the property of the nested list within that list item is set to `display: block`—and the menu appears. This approach doesn't work in Internet Explorer, however, as the `:hover` pseudo-class works on links only—not on any other element.

The rest of the CSS simply applies visual styles to make the menus look good.

Falling Between the Cracks

When a fly-out menu opens, the user must then move the mouse down to the fly-out menu items to select one. If in this motion the mouse moves outside of the list item that opened the fly-out menu, the menu will close immediately, as the `:hover` pseudo-class will no longer be in effect.

Looking back at the CSS code for this page, you can see that the nested list uses absolute positioning to display over top of the rest of the page content without disturbing it. By simply adding a little padding to the top of the list, we can leave a little space between the top-level menu item and the fly-out menu.

```
#nav ul {
    display: none;
    position: absolute;
    padding-top: 0.5em;
}
```

Since this space is padding, and therefore technically inside the nested list, which itself is inside the top-level menu item, the :hover pseudo-class remains in effect as the mouse moves over this area, and the fly-out menu stays open.

Accessibility Concerns

IMPORTANT

When using any drop-down menu—with or without JavaScript—make sure that users who don't see the full effect of the menus are still able to move around your site.

In this example, users who don't have CSS support will see the expanded nested lists, and will be able to navigate through the site. Anyone who uses a browser (such as Internet Explorer) that doesn't support the display of the submenus will be able to navigate so long as the pages linked-to by the top-level menu items contain the same links as the corresponding fly-out menu in a format that Internet Explorer can display.

Any menu system that prevents users whose browsers don't support it from navigating the site is bad news.

Can you create rounded corners on CSS borders?

CSS designs can seem to be a case of "too many little boxes." Is there a simple way to make rounded corners on those borders?

Solution

If this solution doesn't have you forcibly converting all your friends to Mozilla, nothing will! This solution, illustrated in Figure 9.11, works only in Mozilla-based browsers, and currently uses a Mozilla extension to CSS.

Figure 9.11. Curved borders are achieved using CSS.

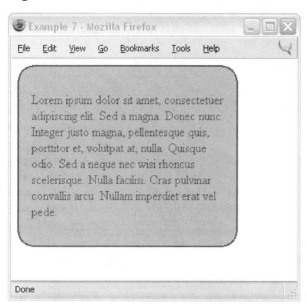

File: **corners1.html**

```
<!DOCTYPE html PUBLIC "-//W3C//DTD XHTML 1.0 Transitional//EN"
    "http://www.w3.org/TR/xhtml1/DTD/xhtml1-transitional.dtd">
<html xmlns="http://www.w3.org/1999/xhtml">
<head>
<title>Rounded Corners</title>
<meta http-equiv="content-type"
    content="text/html; charset=iso-8859-1" />
<link rel="stylesheet" type="text/css" href="corners1.css" />
</head>
<body>
<div class="curvebox">
  <p>Lorem ipsum dolor sit amet, consectetuer adipiscing …</p>
</div>
</body>
</html>
```

File: **corners1.css**

```
.curvebox {
  width: 250px;
  padding: 1em;
  background-color: #B0C4DE;
```

```
    border: 2px solid #33527B;
    color: #33527B;
    -moz-border-radius: 25px;
}
```

Discussion

This examples does not make use of a single image! The CSS property that creates those nicely rounded corners on the box borders is:

File: **corners1.css** (excerpt)

```
-moz-border-radius: 25px;
```

Remove this line from the CSS, and the box displays (as it does in browsers other than those that are Mozilla-based) with the usual square corners shown in Figure 9.12.

Figure 9.12. Remove `-moz-border-radius: 25px;` and the box displays as normal.

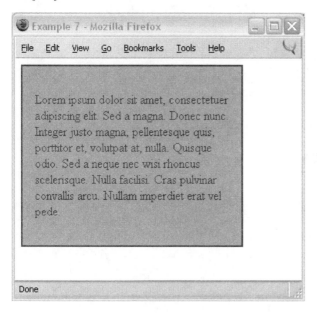

The Mozilla-only `-moz-border-radius` property corresponds to the `border-radius` property that will be part of the CSS3 recommendation[3] when it is finalized. A further example of this technique used to great effect can be seen in Figure 9.13. This image shows the drop-down menus discussed in the previous example with rounded corners.

Figure 9.13. The drop-down menu displays buttons with curved corners.

 Not Just for Blocks

Rounded corners may be applied to other elements, such as form fields. Have some fun experimenting!

How do I create cross-browser, rounded corners using CSS?

Using a Mozilla extension is all very well, but, if 98 per cent of your viewers use a version of Internet Explorer, it isn't a realistic design option. It's possible to create curved corners using images, but is there a cross-browser, CSS-only way to create this effect?

---

[3] http://www.w3.org/TR/css3-border/#the-border-radius

Solution

It is possible to create the effect of rounded corners using a number of stacked, mostly 1-pixel-high <div>s. The result is shown in Figure 9.14.

Figure 9.14. Yes, you *can* build cross-browser, curved corners using pure CSS.

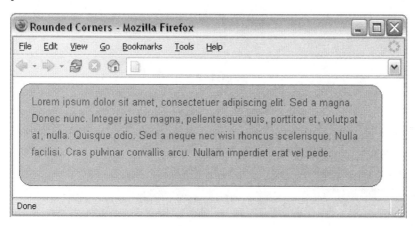

File: **corners2.html**

```
<!DOCTYPE html PUBLIC "-//W3C//DTD XHTML 1.0 Transitional//EN"
    "http://www.w3.org/TR/xhtml1/DTD/xhtml1-transitional.dtd">
<html xmlns="http://www.w3.org/1999/xhtml">
<head>
<title>Rounded Corners</title>
<meta http-equiv="content-type"
    content="text/html; charset=iso-8859-1" />
<link rel="stylesheet" type="text/css" href="corners2.css" />
</head>
<body>
<div id="box">
  <div class="roundborder c1"></div>
  <div class="roundborder c2"></div>
  <div class="roundborder c3"></div>
  <div class="roundborder c4"></div>
  <div class="roundborder c5"></div>
  <div class="roundborder c6"></div>
  <div class="roundborder c7"></div>
  <div class="roundborder c8"></div>
  <div class="roundborder c9"></div>
```

```
<div class="roundborder content">
  Lorem ipsum dolor sit amet, consectetuer adipiscing elit. …
</div>
<div class="roundborder c9"></div>
<div class="roundborder c8"></div>
<div class="roundborder c7"></div>
<div class="roundborder c6"></div>
<div class="roundborder c5"></div>
<div class="roundborder c4"></div>
<div class="roundborder c3"></div>
<div class="roundborder c2"></div>
<div class="roundborder c1"></div>
</div>
</body>
</html>
```

File: **corners2.css**

```
#box {
  font: 80%/1.6 Arial, Helvetica, sans-serif;
  color: #2D486C;
  background-color: transparent;
  margin: 0 20px 10px 0;
}
.roundborder {
  height: 1px;
  overflow: hidden;
  background-color: #B0C4DE;
  border-right: 1px solid #33527B;
  border-left: 1px solid #33527B;
}
.c1 {
  margin: 0 12px 0 12px;
  border: none;
  background-color: #33527B;
}
.c2 {
  margin: 0 9px;
  border-width: 0 3px;
}
.c3 {
  margin: 0 7px;
  border-width: 0 2px;
}
.c4 {
  margin: 0 6px 0 6px;
}
```

```
.c5 {
  margin: 0 5px 0 5px;
}
.c6 {
  margin: 0 4px 0 4px;
}
.c7 {
  margin: 0 3px 0 3px;
}
.c8 {
  margin: 0 2px 0 2px;
  height: 2px;
}
.c9 {
  margin: 0 1px 0 1px;
  height: 3px;
}
.content {
  height: auto;
  padding: 0 15px;
}
```

Discussion

The technique works by stacking mostly 1-pixel-high <div>s atop one another. The first <div> has left and right margins and a background color that allow it to masquerade as the horizontal top edge of the box. The second <div> has slightly smaller left and right margins, and three-pixel-wide left and right borders that match the first <div>'s background color. The third <div> again has smaller margins but this time only has two-pixel-wide left and right borders.

This pattern continues, with the borders of nine <div>s in all lining up in just the right way to create curving lines for the top left and right corners of the containing <div>.

File: **corners2.html** (excerpt)

```
<div id="box">
  <div class="roundborder c1"></div>
  <div class="roundborder c2"></div>
  <div class="roundborder c3"></div>
  <div class="roundborder c4"></div>
  <div class="roundborder c5"></div>
  <div class="roundborder c6"></div>
  <div class="roundborder c7"></div>
```

```
<div class="roundborder c8"></div>
<div class="roundborder c9"></div>
```

File: **corners2.css** (excerpt)

```css
.roundborder {
  height: 1px;
  overflow: hidden;
  background-color: #B0C4DE;
  border-right: 1px solid #33527B;
  border-left: 1px solid #33527B;
}
.c1 {
  margin: 0 12px 0 12px;
  border: none;
  background-color: #33527B;
}
.c2 {
  margin: 0 9px;
  border-width: 0 3px;
}
.c3 {
  margin: 0 7px;
  border-width: 0 2px;
}
.c4 {
  margin: 0 6px;
}
.c5 {
  margin: 0 5px;
}
.c6 {
  margin: 0 4px;
}
.c7 {
  margin: 0 3px;
}
.c8 {
  margin: 0 2px;
  height: 2px;
}
.c9 {
  margin: 0 1px;
  height: 3px;
}
```

Double Shorthand

When shorthand properties like `margin` and `border-width` are given only two values (e.g. `margin: 0 4px`), the first value affects the top and bottom margin/border and the second value affects the left and right margin/border.

The actual text content comes in yet another `<div>` with single-pixel left and right borders, and the padding necessary for the content to appear "balanced" within the rounded corners.

File: **corners2.html (excerpt)**

```
<div class="roundborder content">
  Lorem ipsum dolor sit amet, ...
</div>
```

File: **corners2.css (excerpt)**

```
.content {
  height: auto;
  padding: 0 15px;
}
```

The effect that created the top rounded corners is then reversed in another series of sliver-thin `<div>`s to create the rounded bottom corners of the box.

This is probably not an effect that you'd use for many small boxes, as it involves a considerable amount of extra markup. However, it might be workable for one featured block.

If you need to create a rounded corner effect, and don't want the markup overhead of a pile of stacked `<div>`s, you'll need to use a technique that creates this effect using small images.

Rounded Corners Using Images

First, create the corner images using a graphics program. You'll need a small image for each corner of the box. The easiest way to create these is to quarter a circle so that you end up with a set, as shown in Figure 9.15.

Figure 9.15. Slice up a circle to create the curved corner images.

The markup for this example is as follows. The top- and bottom-left images are included in the document itself, within top and bottom <div>s:

File: **corners3.html**

```
<!DOCTYPE html PUBLIC "-//W3C//DTD XHTML 1.0 Transitional//EN"
    "http://www.w3.org/TR/xhtml1/DTD/xhtml1-transitional.dtd">
<html xmlns="http://www.w3.org/1999/xhtml">
<head>
<title>Rounded corners</title>
<meta http-equiv="Content-Type"
    content="text/html; charset=iso-8859-1" />
<link rel="stylesheet" type="text/css" href="corners3.css" />
</head>
<body>
<div class="rndbox">
  <div class="rndtop"><img src="topleft.gif" alt="" width="30"
      height="30" /></div>
  <p>Lorem ipsum dolor sit amet, consectetuer adipiscing ...</p>
  <div class="rndbottom"><img src="bottomleft.gif" alt=""
      width="30" height="30" /></div>
</div>
</body>
</html>
```

The top- and bottom-right images are included as background images in the CSS for the <div>s rndtop and rndbottom:

File: **corners3.css (excerpt)**

```
.rndbox {
  background: #C6D9EA;
  width: 300px;
  font: 11px Verdana, Arial, Helvetica, sans-serif;
  color: #000033;
}
.rndtop {
  background: url(topright.gif) no-repeat right top;
}
```

```
.rndbottom {
  background: url(bottomright.gif) no-repeat right top;
}
.rndbox p {
  margin: 0 8px;
}
```

This creates a curved box like that shown in Figure 9.16:

Figure 9.16. The curved corner images are added to the display.

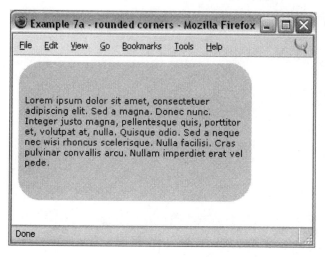

How do I make elements translucent both in Mozilla-based browsers, and in Internet Explorer?

The well-supported `visibility` property lets you control whether objects are opaque or transparent, but various browsers support a number of different ways to create translucency effects. When an element is **translucent**, it only partially obscures the element(s) behind it, as shown in Figure 9.17.

Figure 9.17. The overlaid box is translucent.

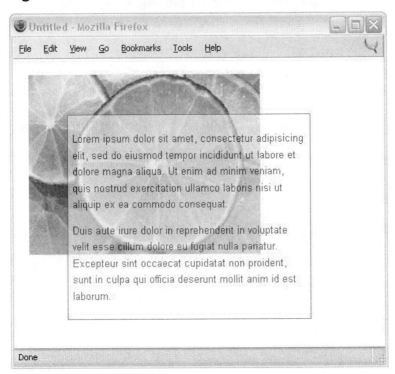

Is it possible to use CSS to create translucency effects that work in most browsers?

Solution

We can achieve this effect using a combination of unfinished standards supported by Mozilla and Internet Explorer extensions to CSS.

File: **translucent.html**

```
<!DOCTYPE html PUBLIC "-//W3C//DTD XHTML 1.0 Transitional//EN"
    "http://www.w3.org/TR/xhtml1/DTD/xhtml1-transitional.dtd">
<html xmlns="http://www.w3.org/1999/xhtml">
<head>
<title>Translucency</title>
<meta http-equiv="content-type"
    content="text/html; charset=iso-8859-1" />
<link rel="stylesheet" type="text/css" href="translucent.css" />
</head>
```

```
<body>
<div id="container">
  <div class="textblock">
    <p>Lorem ipsum dolor sit amet, consectetur adipisicing …</p>
  </div>
</div>
</body>
</html>
```

File: **translucent.css**

```
#container {
  position: absolute;
  top: 20px;
  left: 20px;
  width: 400px;
  height: 300px;
  background: url(limes.jpg) no-repeat;
}
#container .textblock {
  filter: alpha(opacity=60);
  opacity: 0.6;
  margin-top: 50px;
  margin-left: 50px;
  width: 300px;
  background: #ffffff;
  border: 1px solid #007101;
  padding: 0.5em;
  font: 80%/1.6 Arial, Helvetica, sans-serif;
}
```

Discussion

The current draft of CSS3[4] describes a property named `opacity` that is supported by current Mozilla browsers. This property lets you assign a level of translucency to any HTML element. In this example, we used it to make the `<div>` of class `textblock` 60 per cent opaque:

File: **translucent.css (excerpt)**

```
opacity: 0.6;
```

For Internet Explorer on Windows, we can apply an alpha filter to achieve the same effect:

[4] http://www.w3.org/TR/css3-color/#transparency

365

File: **translucent.css** (excerpt)

```
filter: alpha(opacity=60);
```

Since no browser supports both of these methods, we can simply apply both of them to the same element to achieve the widest possible support.

Because of the lack of support for these features, this technique will only work for Mozilla-based browsers and Internet Explorer browsers operating on Windows. IE5 on Mac will not render the translucency, nor will browsers such as Safari and Konqueror. You may yet feel that the feature availability is sufficient to use this technique and, as long as you're careful, it need not hinder the readability of your site for those using other browsers. As an example, Figure 9.18 shows the same document rendered by Konqueror 3.2, which does not show the opacity.

Figure 9.18. The effect as displayed by a browser that does not support these opacity techniques.

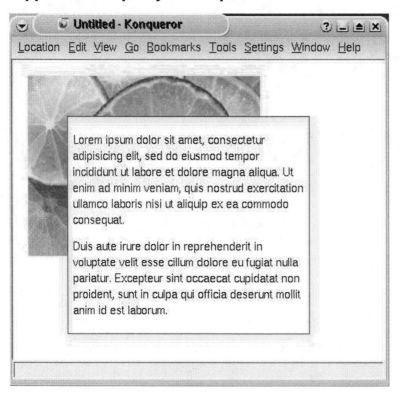

How do I use CSS to indicate to visitors which links are external?

Is it possible to differentiate between internal and external links, as shown in Figure 9.19, using CSS?

Figure 9.19. These internal and external links are styled using CSS3 selectors.

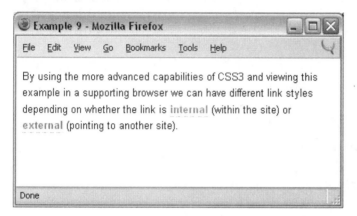

Solution

Using CSS3 selectors, you can create different rules for links that go to different locations. This solution will work only in supporting browsers, such as those that are based on recent versions of Mozilla.

File: **external.html**

```
<!DOCTYPE html PUBLIC "-//W3C//DTD XHTML 1.0 Transitional//EN"
    "http://www.w3.org/TR/xhtml1/DTD/xhtml1-transitional.dtd">
<html xmlns="http://www.w3.org/1999/xhtml">
<head>
<title>External Links</title>
<meta http-equiv="Content-Type"
    content="text/html; charset=iso-8859-1" />
<link rel="stylesheet" type="text/css" href="external.css" />
<body>
<p>By using the more advanced capabilities of CSS3 and viewing
  this example in a supporting browser we can have different link
```

```
styles depending on whether the link is
<a href="foo.html">internal</a> (within the site) or
<a href="http://www.google.com/">external</a> (pointing to
another site).</p>
</body>
</html>
```

File: **external.css**

```
body {
  background-color: #FFFFFF;
  color: #000000;
}
p {
  font: 80%/1.6 Arial, Helvetica, sans-serif;
}
a:link, a:visited {
  color: #CD853F;
  background-color: transparent;
  font-weight: bold;
  text-decoration: none;
  padding-bottom: 1px;
  border-bottom: 1px dotted #EBCEB1;
}
a:hover {
  background-color: #FAF3EC;
}
a[href^="http:"]:link, a[href^="http:"]:visited {
  color: #7B68EE;
  background-color: transparent;
  font-weight: bold;
  text-decoration: none;
  padding-bottom: 1px;
  border-bottom: 1px dotted #B0C4DE;
}
a[href^="http:"]:hover {
  background-color: #DEE6F1;
}
```

Discussion

Among the new attribute-based CSS3 selectors[5] is the "attribute begins with" selector. In this example, we can use it to isolate <a> tags that have an href attribute beginning with http:, and thus leading off-site.

---

[5] http://www.w3.org/TR/css3-selectors/

File: **external.css** (excerpt)

```
a[href^="http:"]:link, a[href^="http:"]:visited {
  ...
}
a[href^="http:"]:hover {
  ...
}
```

These CSS3 selectors enable you to create sets of CSS rules that style links depending on where they take the user. One style might be applied to links leading offsite; another style is applied to internal links. You could even set a different style for `mailto:` links:

```
a[href^="mailto:"]:link, a[href^="mailto:"]:visited {
  ...
}
```

Unfortunately, this technique will not work in Internet Explorer, nor in other browsers that do not support CSS3 selectors.

Can I use CSS to insert text into my document?

If you have a small piece of text that needs to be added to every instance of an element on your site, you can get the job done with CSS.

Solution

Once again, this useful trick does not work in Internet Explorer. The "last updated" date in the footer shown in Figure 9.20 was inserted using CSS.

The markup for the footer is as follows:

File: **generatedcontent.html** (excerpt)

```
<div id="footer">
  <a href="#">Contact us</a> | <a href="#">Discussion forum</a>
</div>
```

Figure 9.20. The "Last updated" text is inserted using CSS.

The CSS that inserts the text is:

File: **generatedcontent.css (excerpt)**

```
#footer:after {
  content: "Last Updated 23rd March, 2004";
}
```

Discussion

To insert text using CSS, use the `content` property in conjunction with the `:before` and `:after` pseudo-elements, as shown in the code above. Text added in this way is called **generated content**. In browsers that support it, you should be able to use this technique to add fixed text to the start or end of any HTML element.

How do I style the first line or first letter of a block?

Using lots of `<span>` tags to get precise control over text styling can leave you with code as cluttered as in the old days, when it would have been riddled with `<font>` tags. Can we use CSS to select portions of text that we want to display differently, as shown in Figure 9.21?

Figure 9.21. Use pseudo-elements to gain precise control over first lines, first letters, and first child elements.

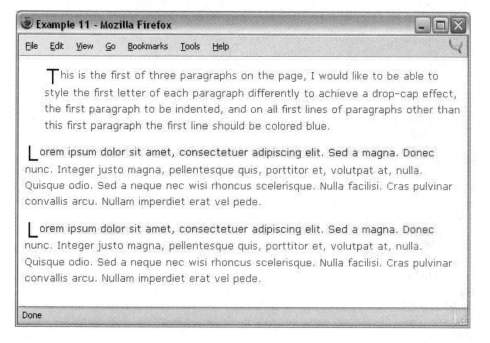

Solution

CSS pseudo-elements can help us achieve this. Again, support for this solution is patchy across browsers, so be sure to test your code thoroughly.

File: **first.html**

```
<!DOCTYPE html PUBLIC "-//W3C//DTD XHTML 1.0 Transitional//EN"
    "http://www.w3.org/TR/xhtml1/DTD/xhtml1-transitional.dtd">
<html xmlns="http://www.w3.org/1999/xhtml">
<head>
<title>Pseudo-Elements</title>
<meta http-equiv="content-type"
    content="text/html; charset=iso-8859-1" />
<link rel="stylesheet" type="text/css" href="first.css" />
</head>
<body>
<div id="content">
  <p>This is the first of three paragraphs on the page, ...</p>
  <p>Lorem ipsum dolor sit amet, consectetuer adipiscing ...</p>
  <p>Lorem ipsum dolor sit amet, consectetuer adipiscing ...</p>
</div>
</body>
</html>
```

File: **first.css**

```
body {
  background-color: #FFFFFF;
  color: #595959;
}
#content p {
  font: 80%/1.6 Verdana, Geneva, Arial, Helvetica, sans-serif;
}
#content p:first-letter {
  font-size: 2em;
  padding: 0.1em;
  color: #000000;
  vertical-align: middle;
}
#content p:first-line {
  color: #191970;
}
#content p:first-child {
  margin-left: 2em;
}
#content p:first-child:first-line {
  color: inherit;
}
```

Discussion

As you can see from the markup, this solution does not necessitate the addition of <span>s or classes to the content. We can avoid these kinds of additions because the pseudo-elements allow us to target useful fragments of our document without tags.

The first two that we've used in this example are `:first-letter` and `:first-line`, which allow you to target the first line and first letter of an element, respectively.

File: **first.css (excerpt)**

```css
#content p:first-letter {
  font-size: 2em;
  padding: 0.1em;
  color: #000000;
  vertical-align: middle;
}
#content p:first-line {
  color: #191970;
}
```

The good news is that these two pseudo-elements work flawlessly in Internet Explorer, as well as other modern browsers. A third pseudo-element, `:first-child`, however, is not supported by Internet Explorer.

File: **first.css (excerpt)**

```css
#content p:first-child {
  margin-left: 2em;
}
```

`:first-child` works a little differently from the other pseudo-elements. Whereas `:first-letter` and `:first-line` target the first letter or line *of* the specified element, `:first-child` targets elements which *are* the first child of their parent element. So in this case, the rule targets any <p> tag within the content element which is the first tag within its parent element. You can see this in the margin added to the first paragraph in Figure 9.21.

Like pseudo-classes, pseudo-elements can be combined to be even more specific. The last CSS rule in this example, for instance, targets the first line of any first-child paragraphs within the content element.

File: **first.css (excerpt)**

```
#content p:first-child:first-line {
  color: inherit;
}
```

This rule prevents the first line of the first paragraph from being highlighted in blue, as has been done for the other paragraphs in the document.

In Figure 9.22, you can see this example displayed in Internet Explorer, which ignores the rules that use the `:first-child` pseudo-element.

Figure 9.22. The example is displayed in Internet Explorer.

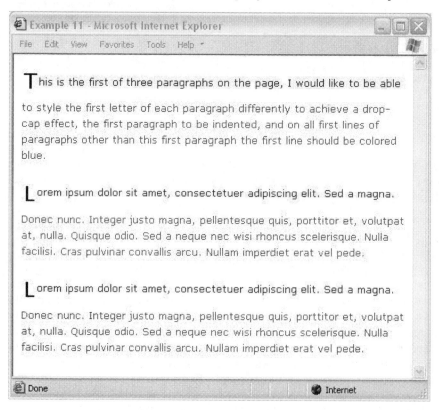

Two Colons are Better than One

The CSS3 standard prescribes that pseudo-element selectors should use two colons (`::`) instead of one, to differentiate them from pseudo-classes (`:link`, `:visited`, `:hover` et al.).

```
#content p::first-line {
    color: #191970;
}
```

For now, one-colon notation is still standard and will continue to be supported for existing pseudo-elements in the foreseeable future. Two-colon notation is supported in current Mozilla browsers, however, if you want your code to be particularly forward-looking.

Is it a bad thing to use effects that don't work in some browsers?

Using CSS that might only work in a small proportion of browsers is a waste of time, surely? And, isn't it "bad design" to make choices that affect only a small number of browsers?

Solution

Unfortunately, CSS is developing more quickly than are the browser manufacturers! Open source projects, such as Mozilla and Konqueror, make frequent "dot" releases of their browsers, which is why the newer CSS is finding its way into these browsers, while Internet Explorer seems to be frozen in time. However, most of the techniques we've seen, which do not work at all in Internet Explorer, will not actually cause problems in that browser. Users might see square corners instead of rounded ones. They may not see different colored links identifying internal and external destinations. But, they won't know that Mozilla users are *ooh*-ing and *ahh*-ing at your rounded corners, either, and, most importantly, they'll be able to use the site just as well as their Mozilla-wielding counterparts.

The term **progressive enhancement** refers to the practice of making the most of newer browsers' enhanced capabilities, while ensuring that users of browsers that don't support advanced CSS also have a fulfilling experience on your site. As we found in Chapter 7, it is possible to go so far as to hide sections of the CSS from Internet Explorer to enable the use of newer techniques without causing problems for IE users.

Summary

The solutions provided in this chapter have differed from those in the rest of the book. Many of these techniques constitute workarounds that can be successful, but are tricky to get up and running. Most require a great deal of testing to ensure that they don't make your site unusable for some visitors.

We have also looked at browser-specific CSS, either because it comprises part of the extensions designed by particular browser manufacturers, or because it's new CSS: part of the CSS3 specification that's not yet implemented by all new browsers. You might, like me, be frustrated by the fact that there are so many tasks that could be so much simpler if only the browser support was there. However, it's heartening to look to the future of CSS. The language is evolving, and keeping up with the latest CSS will give you the ability to implement new developments to benefit visitors using newer browsers.

This is the last chapter of this book. I hope the examples and solutions provided here have been useful, and have answered your questions. Even more so, I hope that, by using these examples as starting points, you will be able to develop your own ideas, and have fun being creative with CSS.

Index

Symbols

\# ID prefix, 9

:: pseudo-element selector prefix, 375

\> child selector symbol, 334, 343

^ attribute begins selector, CSS3, 368

A

\<a> tags (*see* links)

absolute keyword font sizes, 16

absolute positioning, 272–277
  advantages, 288
  alternative to, for content, 285
  fixed positions in IE using, 334
  footer positioning problem, 318–319
  three-column liquid layouts, 301
  two-column liquid layouts, 284
  within other elements, 275
  within relatively-positioned elements, 297

access keys, 169

accessibility
  (*see also* screen readers; text-only devices)
  absolute positioning and, 288
  access keys, 170
  \<blockquote> tags and, 40
  designing in, 116
  drop-down menus and, 353
  image text and, 68
  non-CSS browsers and, 197
  pixels sizing and, 13
  tabular data, 113
  testing in text-only browsers, 192

accesskey attribute, 170

accounts data spreadsheet, 112

:active pseudo-class, 24–25
  image shift for rollovers, 108

:after pseudo-element, 370

align attribute alternatives, 259

alignment
  in two-column liquid layouts, 279, 287
  of footers, 314
  of form fields, 158, 161–162
  of logo and strapline in headers, 267–272
  of tabular data, 124
  of text, 36–37, 40

alistapart.com site, 244, 349

alpha filters, 365

alternate style sheets, 237–241
  avoiding code duplication, 245–250
  style sheet switchers, 20, 241

alternating row color effects, 125, 173
  dynamic tables, 128

anchor tags (*see* links)

attribute-based selectors (CSS3), 368

author's sites (*see* edgeofmyseat.com site; rachelandrew.co.uk site)

auto setting, margin properties, 278–279

B

background colors
  (*see also* highlighting)
  changing, on mouseover, 128
  changing, on receiving focus, 181
  empty \<div>s and full-height backgrounds, 312
  headings, 29
  link styling and, 27
  navigation menu example, 76
  Netscape 4 unexpected behavior, 201

background images
  movement, rollover effects, 108

justified text, 36

K

Kaufman, Joshua, 98
KDE Darwin project, 188
keyboard shortcuts (*see* access keys)
keywords
    font sizing using, 16
    image positioning using, 60
KHTML-based browsers, 184, 187
Knoppix, 186
Konqueror browser
    footer positioning problem, 320
    Mac OS X and, 187–188
    translucency not supported, 366

L

<label> tags, 155, 157
    use with float property, 163
large text style sheets, 238, 240
last update information, 369
layouts, 251–326
    absolute positioning, 272
    allowing for margins and padding, 258
    grid layouts, 323
    positioning footers, 313
    positioning items on the page, 272
    redesign with unchanged markup, 288
    relative positioning, 290
    three-column liquid layouts, 300–313
    two-column centered layouts, 288–300
    two-column liquid layouts, 279–288
leading (*see* line-height property)
<legend> tags, 163–168
    styling, 168
    unstyled display, 167
    use with access keys, 171

<li> tags
    (*see also* list items)
    display property, 49, 89
    nesting sub-lists, 86
    styling, in navigation menu, 81
line-height property, 35–36
<link> tags, 4
    high pass filter and, 209
    media attribute, 226, 234
    Netscape 4 and, 196, 198
    rel attribute, 238
links
    applying background images, 65
    differentiating internal and external, 367
    distinguishing, among <a> tags, 8
    distinguishing, using pseudo-classes, 8
    forcing block-level display, 82, 255, 351
    mouseover color change, 24
    multiple styles for, 7, 27
    pseudo-class formatting, 6
    removing underlining from, 21, 77
    styling, in navigation menu, 81
Linux, browser testing, 186, 188
liquid layouts
    image placement and, 61
    positioning using percentages and, 61
    text resizing and units, 286
    three-column, 300–313
    two-column, 279–288
list items
    displaying horizontally, 49, 89
    events as, calendar example, 139
    left indenting adjustment, 48
    left indenting removal, 47
    per-item bullets, 47
    styling bullets, 43, 46
lists
    basis of navigation menu, 78

fixed, scrolling content IE solution, 335

horizontal menus, 89

lists, as the basis of menus, 78

printing difficulties and, 232, 234

problems with image-based, 72

retrofitting to existing sites, 74, 77

rollover effects, 82, 105

sub-navigation, 83–88

tabbed navigation, 95–103

two-column centered layouts, 296–297

two-column liquid layouts, 279, 283–284, 287

negative margins

closing up paragraphs, 32

placing text on borders, 311

nested elements

absolute positioning and, 275

multiple background image effect, 68

nested <div> tags, 275

sub-navigation with nested lists, 84–85

table cell font sizing problems, 18

Netscape 4 browser

alternate style sheet for, 198

hiding style sheets from, 195

media types and, 228

unexpected text display, 198

O

one-pixel high <div>s, 357

onfocus and onblur attributes, <input> tag, 182

opacity property (CSS3), 365

Opera browser

Opera 5 parsing bug, 209

spacing idiosyncracies, 51

operating systems

effect on browser choice, 184

running additional systems, 184

overlining, 23

overriding style definitions, 7, 201

P

<p> tag styling, 12

padding

IE 5.x interpretation of, 258

in horizontal navigation lists, 92

margins distinguished from, 255, 258

padding properties, 256–258

padding property

adding background color, 30

'editable table' form, 179

Opera browser and, 51

scrolling content in IE, 338

two-column centered layout using, 295

underlining and, 31

padding-bottom property for fixed footers, 344

padding-left property, 38, 47

padding-top property, 163, 352

paragraphs (*see* <p> tags; text)

Peekaboo Bug, IE 6, 223

percentages

font sizing and, 16

image placement and, 61

periods, preceding class names, 7

phantom boxes browser bug, 191

photo album application, 320

pica font sizing, 13

pixel font sizing, 13

placement (*see* positioning)

point font sizing, 13, 235

position property

(*see also* absolute positioning; relative positioning)

absolute positioning, 274

fixed value, 332, 340, 343

Books for Web Developers
from SitePoint

Visit http://www.sitepoint.com/books/
for sample chapters or to order!

Build Your Own

Database Driven Website

Using PHP & MySQL

By Kevin Yank

A Practical Step-by-Step Guide

The PHP Anthology

Object Oriented PHP Solutions

Volume I

By Harry Fuecks

Practical Solutions to Common Problems

The PHP Anthology

Object Oriented PHP Solutions

Volume II

By Harry Fuecks

Practical Solutions to Common Problems

Build Your Own

ASP.NET Website

Using C# & VB.NET

By Zak Ruvalcaba

A Practical Step-by-Step Guide

HTML Utopia:

Designing Without Tables

Using CSS

A Practical Step-by-Step Guide

By Dan Shafer

The CSS Anthology

101 Essential Tips, Tricks & Hacks

By Rachel Andrew

Practical Solutions to Common Problems

DHTML Utopia:

Modern Web Design
Using JavaScript & DOM

By Stuart Langridge

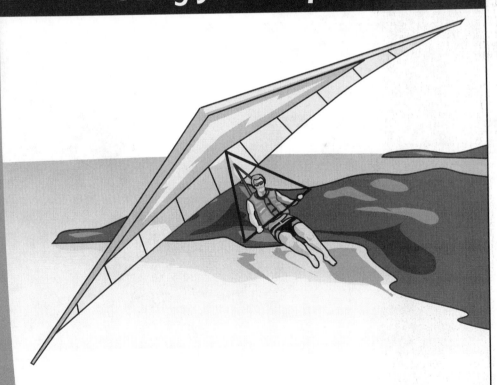

A Practical Step-by-Step Guide

Flash
MX 2004

 sitepoint

The Flash Anthology

Cool Effects &
Practical ActionScript

By Steven Grosvenor

Practical Solutions to Common Problems

Kits for Web Professionals
from SitePoint

Available exclusively from
http://www.sitepoint.com/